To Ruth

With my very best wishes and thanks

from

Diana Kleyn.

_____

28th September 1991.

Richard
of England

D. M. KLEYN

THE
KENSAL
PRESS

British Library Cataloguing in Publication Data

Kleyn, Diana
    Richard of England
    1. England, 1483–1485
    I. Title
    364.1523092

ISBN 0–946041–63–6

Published by The Kensal Press
Riverview, Headington Hill, Oxford

Printed in Great Britain

To My Father

The Late Thomas Harding-Newman, M.C.,

who first told me what I am convinced is the truth about

King Richard III

Contents

List of Illustrations

Introduction

To those prosaic people who, hearing of my labours, pose the questions 'Why bother?' and 'Does it really matter after five hundred years?', I cannot do better than to take the words from the lips of a dear friend, herself a lecturer in history, who replied 'If certain things are evidently — or even just possibly — not true, then it is time we stopped recording them as history'.

Distortion of the truth was of course a necessity for a dynasty such as that of the Tudors, who had surprisingly triumphed over the reigning House of Plantagenet without the benefit of a legitimate claim to the throne, and we can hardly blame them for wishing to survive — or their Yorkist opponents, reduced to a handful by the first two Tudors, for fleeing the country if they could and accepting the situation until the Tudor dynasty ended in 1603. But there is no necessity for us to continue to swallow what was in any case a propaganda pill.

For the past twenty or thirty years it seems to have been fashionable for biographers to treat their subjects with harsh and even sometimes libellous belittlement — men and women who we have hitherto looked upon as great. Now there seems to be a pleasing and no doubt just trend away from this denigrating approach; a determination to get at and present the real truth about some of these victims of the propaganda of hatred. One of the best examples of this is the story of the mutiny on the *Bounty*, which in the days of black and white films starred Charles Laughton as the dreaded, cruel and barbaric Captain Bligh who flogged and starved his wretched crew until, under their heroic leader Fletcher Christian, they mutinied and put their tormentor overboard with the worst of his lieutenants, in an open boat with little food and water. Now, in Gavin Kennedy's splendidly researched book 'Bligh', as in the new film version of it starring Anthony Hopkins in the leading rôle, Bligh is revealed as the hard-done-by victim of Christian's treacherous seduction of the crew into mutiny against a first class seaman and a brilliant navigator who steered his faithful men to land, and who ended by having his reputation cleared and his sword returned to him with honour by the Board of Admiralty. The lesson is surely for us who care about the truth to refuse to accept the harsh disparagement of history, and to find out for ourselves what the victims of hostile propaganda did, or did not do, to merit their fate.

The subject of imposture is, of course, a prickly one, and can probably never be resolved. One cannot prove or disprove paternity, except to say that there is a possibility that a person could be related to someone of a similar blood group or conversely, could not possibly be related because of a differing blood group. But about someone who lived five hundred years ago, there is obviously not even that remote possibility. No one who has ever written anything about 'Perkin Warbeck' has ever regarded him as other than an impostor. Those who took his side mainly used him as a pawn to further their own designs, and those who opposed him were activated by political necessity or ambition.

The suggestion that 'Perkin Warbeck' could have been who he claimed to be, the younger of the Princes escaped from the Tower, is a speculative one; but then the idea that the Princes were murdered in the Tower is not only speculative, but is founded on hearsay evidence. Examination of contemporary evidence, what little of it there is, reveals not only the Tudor bias but, surprisingly, a young man of refinement, a powerful personality and a 'princely bearing'. His perfect English, robustly English handwriting, ability to inspire men to follow him; his tall, handsome appearance, fair hair and features very similar to those of Edward IV, hardly suggests the 'humble Dutchman' which King Henry tried so desperately to make him out to be. His case surely merits careful research, which I have endeavoured to carry out, but I realise there is much, much more still to be unearthed. I very much hope that I have influenced some disbelievers, at least, to revise their opinions about this fascinating young man.

I have been reproved for using 'discredited historians' in some of my sources, but it has been hard to avoid where real evidence is so scarce. Gainsford quotes the old chroniclers Hall, Grafton and Vergil, embellishing them all in his own flowery style, but unfortunately he does not specify which source he is using, while Madden's letter, reproduced in *Archaeologia*, scrupulously documents each point he makes. After the

Tudor dynasty came to an end in 1603, we have the Yorkist case presented by Sir George Buck (in a splendid edition rescued from defacement by George Buck, his great nephew, and from subsequent fire, by the scholarship of Dr.A.N.Kincaid); Caroline Halsted, and in our own time, Audrey Williamson's award-winning book 'The Mystery of the Princes: An Investigation into a Supposed Murder', which started me on my own investigations.

D.M.K. Frimley, 1990.

Acknowledgments

I would like to express my profound gratitude to all those dear friends who have helped me so kindly in the preparation of this book: especially to dear Isolde Wigram for her good advice, criticism, much-needed encouragement and invaluable support; to the Croydon Branch of the Richard III Society, who with great generosity donated their hard-earned funds to help in the setting up of this book; to the late Audrey Williamson whose kind support and encouragement was an unexpected bonus, because she had had the same idea of writing a book on 'Perkin Warbeck' but abandoned it when she heard of my efforts; to Peter and Carolyn Hammond, Research Officer and Librarian of the Richard III Society, especially to Peter for his permission to quote from his article 'The Sons of Edward IV: a re-examination of the evidence on their deaths and on the Bones in Westminster Abbey', and to his co-author W.J. White; to J.A. Speares, O.B.E., for his permission to quote from his lecture to the Richard III Society at a Seminar at Leicester University in 1976, and to my friend Ken White for kindly undertaking to index the book.

Next, my most grateful thanks are due to Dr. J.A. Varela, Minister for Cultural Affairs at the Spanish Embassy in London, whose great kindness in translating my letter into Spanish for the Director of General Archives in Simancas, Spain was an act of outstanding courtesy, undimmed by the fact that the Simancan authorities refused to allow the required document to be photo-statted; to Father P. Boyle of the Salesian College, Farnborough and Mr. Martin Baillie of Farnborough Abbey for their elegant translations of fifteenth century Latin excerpts to Mr. Kitching and the Assistants in the Round Room at the Public Record Office for their help and advice, and to the Public Record Office for photocopying the Introduction to the Calendar of Spanish State Papers 1485–1509 in lieu of the one I had hoped to receive from Simancas; to Dr. Arthur

Noel Kincaid for his permission to quote from his incredible work of scholarship in editing the MS of Sir George Buck's 'History of King Richard the Third', and from Dr. Kincaid's 'Notes and Queries'? Vol.28, No.2, April 1981; to the late Alan Smithies for permission to quote from his lecture to the Richard III Society at a Seminar at Leicester University in 1976, with my acknowledgment that his views on 'Perkin Warbeck' do not coincide with mine; to Geoff Cox and Stephen Curry of the Surrey Heath Public Library in Camberley, for their help in obtaining books for me, especially in having *Archaeologia XXVII* photocopied for me.

I would also like to thank Dr. Peter Spufford, Fellow and Keeper of Pictures at Queen's College, Cambridge, for so kindly sending me gratis the reproduction of the portrait of Elizabeth Woodville; to the Librarian at the Royal Military Academy, Sandhurst, who obtained some long-sought French mediæval history books for me; to the National Portrait Gallery for their permission to include portraits of Richard III, Henry VII, Elizabeth of York and Lady Margaret Beaufort; to Dr. Georg Kugler of the Kunsthistorisches Museum in Vienna for his permission to reproduce de Predis' portrait of the Emperor Maximilian I; to the Scottish Portrait Gallery for their permission to reproduce the portrait of King James IV of Scotland; to the Scottish Record Office for their advice and help; to the Society of Antiquaries in London for their permission to reproduce the portraits of Edward IV and Margaret of York and to quote from 'Archaeologia' XXVII; to M. G. Preud'homme of the State Archives in Tournai for his help and advice, and to M. Jacques Debilde of Leuze for his photocopies of the 'Notes sur la famille de l'aventurier Perkin Werbecque' (all that is left of the Tournaisian Archives on the subject, due to German bombing in the last war), and the article '*Un tournaisien prétendant au trône d'Angleterre*', written c.1910 by Dr. Desmons and published in the *Revue tournaisienne*.

Lastly, my long overdue thanks and apologies go to my family and friends who have endured my time-consuming commitment to my own interests over the last few years, and especially do I thank my son Peter whose herculean efforts on behalf of my book ensured that I should finish my task.

D.M. Kleyn.
Frimley, 1990.

Genealogical tree of the York Family

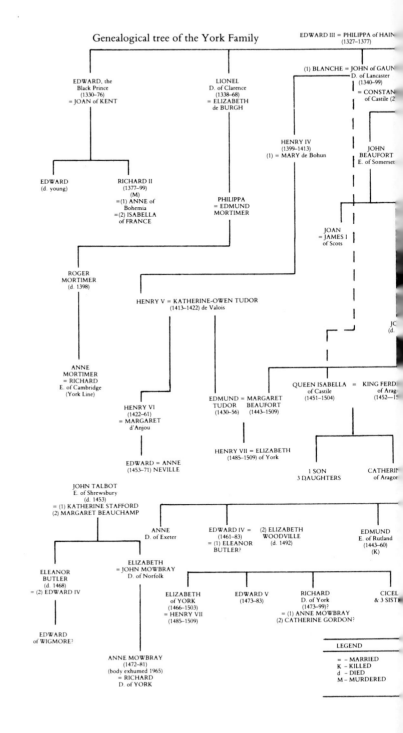

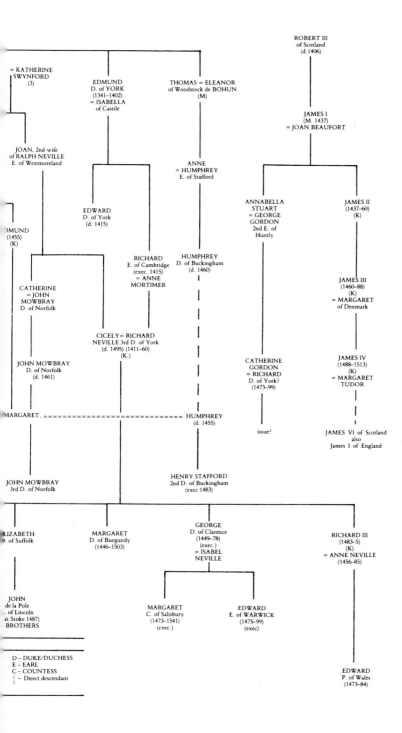

ROBERT III
of Scotland
(d. 1406)

= KATHERINE
SWYNFORD
(3)

EDMUND
D. of YORK
(1341–1402)
= ISABELLA
of Castile

THOMAS = ELEANOR
of Woodstock de BOHUN
(M)

JAMES I
(M. 1437)
= JOAN BEAUFORT

JOAN, 2nd wife
of RALPH NEVILLE
E. of Westmoreland

ANNE
= HUMPHREY
E. of Stafford

EDWARD
D. of York
(d. 1415)

ANNABELLA
STUART
= GEORGE
GORDON
2nd E. of
Huntly

JAMES II
(1437–60)
(K)

)MUND
(1455)
(K)

RICHARD
E. of Cambridge
(exec. 1415)
= ANNE
MORTIMER

HUMPHREY
D. of Buckingham
(d. 1460)

JAMES III
(1460–88)
(K)
= MARGARET
of Denmark

CATHERINE
= JOHN
MOWBRAY
D. of Norfolk

CICELY = RICHARD
NEVILLE 3rd D. of York
(d. 1495) (1411–60)
(K.)

CATHERINE
GORDON
= RICHARD
D. of York?
(1473–99)

JAMES IV
(1488–1513)
(K)
= MARGARET
TUDOR

JOHN MOWBRAY
D. of Norfolk
(d. 1461)

MARGARET , = HUMPHREY
(d. 1455)

issue?

JAMES VI of Scotland
also
James I of England

JOHN MOWBRAY
3rd D. of Norfolk

HENRY STAFFORD
2nd D. of Buckingham
(exec 1483)

LIZABETH
. of Suffolk

MARGARET
D. of Burgundy
(1446–1503)

GEORGE
D. of Clarence
(1449–78)
(exec.)
= ISABEL
NEVILLE

RICHARD III
(1483–5)
(K)
= ANNE NEVILLE
(1456–85)

JOHN
de la Pole
.. of Lincoln
at Stoke 1487)
BROTHERS

MARGARET
C. of Salisbury
(1473–1541)
(exec.)

EDWARD
E. of WARWICK
(1475–99)
(exec)

D – DUKE/DUCHESS
E – EARL
C – COUNTESS
| – Direct descendant

EDWARD
P. of Wales
(1473–84)

'J'ay veu filz d'Angleterre
Richard d'Yorc nommé
Que l'on disoit en terre
Estainct et consommé,
Endurer grant souffrance;
Et, par nobles exploitz,
Vivre en bonne espérance
D'estre roy des Angloys'

From a poem made by Jean Molinet on the subject of 'Richard of York'
based on 'Récollection des merveilles advenues en nostre temps' begun
by Georges Chastellain.

(1435–1507)

Background to Lancaster and York

'It was one of the longest playes of that kind that hath been in memorie' wrote Francis Bacon of the dramatic career of 'Perkin Warbeck'. It was indeed an amazing drama, involving many European rulers and much devious politicking, and it was a contest to the death between the first Tudor, Henry VII, and the young man who claimed to be his brother-in-law. To set the characters in the drama in their context however, it may be helpful to give a brief resumé of the origins of the Wars of the Roses from the purely dynastic standpoint, and for this it is necessary to go back to the days of Edward III and his Queen, Philippa of Hainault.

In an age when child mortality was so high that, in order to ensure the succession it was necessary to have at least four sons in the hope that one might survive, to have produced five healthy, gifted and ambitious sons as Edward III did, was to bring its own disasters. As early as the second generation the first cousins began their internecine strife, resulting in the murder of the rightful but childless King, Richard II, by his cousin Henry of Bolingbroke, who had already usurped the throne, and thus became Henry IV.

Henry IV's was the Lancastrian faction, since he was the legitimate son of John of Gaunt, Duke of Lancaster, the third son of Edward III. John of Gaunt had taken a beautiful mistress, Katherine Swynford, and had had by her four illegitimate children, who were given the surname Beaufort after the castle in France where they were born. After the death of his second wife he married his mistress Katherine, and his nephew King Richard II made the kindly gesture to his uncle of revoking the illegitimacy of the Beaufort children. Richard's cousin, the usurper Henry IV confirmed their legitimacy, but specifically forbade their succession to the throne, though this is denied by some historians.

After the death of Henry of Bolingbroke's son, Henry V, at the age of thirty-five, his French widow Katherine de Valois was denied any part in the upbringing of her infant son Henry VI. She turned for comfort to an ardent young Welshman, Owen Tudor, who was a Clerk of the Wardrobe in her Household. Whether any marriage took place between them or not is a somewhat academic question (the College of Arms has no record of any such marriage), for in 1427–8 Parliament passed an Act making it illegal for any man to espouse the widow of a King of England: permission could only be granted by the new King when he himself reached the age of discretion. At all events, three sons and a daughter were born to Owen and Queen Katherine, of whom the youngest son, Owen, and the daughter chose the religious life, and the two elder sons, Edmund and Jasper, became the father and uncle respectively of Henry Tudor, later King Henry VII. Queen Katherine died in 1437, and only after her death did her 'marriage' with Owen Tudor come to light.

In the meantime the young Beauforts went from strength to strength, as did eventually the young Tudors. The feeble-minded King Henry VI created his half-brothers Jasper, Earl of Pembroke, and Edmund, Earl of Richmond. The Beauforts were also received at court: the eldest, John, had been created Earl of Somerset; his sister Joan married the immensely powerful Ralph Neville, Earl of Westmorland, and their daughter Cecily was to marry Richard Duke of York, father of the Yorkist Kings Edward IV and Richard III. John Beaufort's second son John, eventually Duke of Somerset, had an only daughter, Margaret Beaufort, a studious and pious girl who at thirteen married her illegitimate cousin Edmund, now Earl of Richmond, and at not quite fourteen became the mother of a posthumous son, Henry Tudor.

It will be seen from the accompanying genealogical table that, while the Lancastrians had usurped the throne of the line of Edward III's eldest son, the Yorkist claim was the legitimate one (though disputed by the Beauforts) since it devolved both through the second son, Lionel Duke of Clarence, and the fourth son, Edmund of Langley, Earl of Cambridge and Duke of York. As Henry VI's reign continued, the periods of insanity inherited from his French grandfather, from which he suffered, resulted in the country being ruled by his wife, the formidable Margaret of Anjou and her favourites. The anarchy which prevailed, exacerbated by the excesses of the Queen, inevitably led to war, which rumbled on from 1455 to 1460. Eventually the Duke of York, the rightful heir, was proclaimed as successor to Henry VI in place of Henry's son who, some thought, was the son of Queen Margaret by one of her favourites, probably the Duke of Somerset. However, the Duke of York was caught at a disadvantage and killed, and his head, crowned with a paper crown, displayed on Micklegate Bar in York. Meanwhile his nineteen-year-old son, known as 'The Rose of Rouen' for his good looks, was chosen as King without waiting for the death of Henry VI, and thus became King Edward IV.

The man who had done most to make him King was his cousin, the powerful Richard Neville, Earl of Warwick, the 'Kingmaker', who gradually found that he was losing control over Edward. His fury at Edward's secret marriage to a Lancastrian widow with two sons, Elizabeth Woodville, daughter of Earl Rivers and widow of Sir John Grey, turned to open rebellion when Edward arranged a marriage for his sister Margaret of York with the heir of the Duke of Burgundy while Warwick was promoting a French marriage. Edward was driven into exile in Flanders, while Warwick restored Henry VI as King, and Queen Elizabeth Woodville, who had fled to sanctuary, at last gave birth to a male heir, the future Edward V. The situation was complicated by the defection of Edward's next brother, George, Duke of Clarence, to Warwick and the Lancastrian party, but when Edward returned in six months with a small army supplied by his brother-in-law the Duke of Burgundy, Clarence returned his allegiance to Edward, and by his abandonment of Warwick (whose elder daughter he had married) helped Edward to win his kingdom back again in two battles. At this time there existed in England the intriguing if confusing situation of two anointed kings, two queens, and two Princes of Wales, both named Edward. This confusion was speedily resolved with the death of Prince Edward of Lancaster at the battle of Tewkesbury, and the very convenient discovery of King Henry dead in the Tower of London shortly afterwards, though his death warrant was probably signed as the result of a damaging raid on London by one of his party. Thus ended the legitimate line of Lancaster, leaving only Henry Tudor as a remote claimant. The 'Kingmaker' too had been killed in battle.

Meanwhile Edward IV's youngest brother Richard Duke of Gloucester had remained steadfastly loyal to him, had accompanied him into exile and at eighteen distinguished himself in battle. He now applied to marry Warwick's younger daughter Anne, whom he had known in childhood, though her father had married her to the Lancastrian Prince of Wales. Clarence violently opposed sharing any of the Warwick inheritance with his brother, as he had hoped to get it all in right of his own wife, and the quarrel was only settled with difficulty after Richard had married Anne Neville. Eventually Clarence became so outspoken about Edward's unpopular marriage, and the greed of the Queen and her numerous family that a charge of treason was trumped up against him and he was condemned to death. The story was soon current on the Continent that he had been drowned in a butt of malmsey wine, but nothing certain is known about the method of his execution. He left a son Edward, Earl of Warwick, and a daughter.

Finally Edward IV, whose early military prowess and good intentions had given way to self-indulgence and sloth, died suddenly shortly before his forty-first birthday, leaving his twelve-year-old son with a legacy of bitter feuds at court between the Queen and her relations and the older nobility. Besides two sons by her first husband, the Queen had five daughters by Edward and a second son, Richard Duke of York, whose later career it is the object of the following pages to trace.

CHAPTER ONE

The Early Years

Richard of York was born, the sixth child and second son of King Edward IV and Queen Elizabeth Woodville, probably on 17th August 1473, at Shrewsbury. Though the exact date is uncertain, news of the birth was conveyed to the Duke of Burgundy, Edward's brother-in-law, by Chester Herald, on 3rd September 1473[1].

Nothing is known of the earliest years of this young Prince, but he was presumably brought up in the royal household with his five sisters, in contrast to his elder brother Edward who, in accordance with royal custom, had early been established with his own little court at Ludlow Castle, under the tutelage of his maternal uncle Anthony, Lord Rivers.

The next mention of Richard, Duke of York, is in January 1477/8, when at the age of four and a half he was married to the five-year-old Anne Mowbray, heiress of the Duke of Norfolk. Child marriages were regarded by wealthy property owners as insurance against seizure by some powerful and greedy neighbour; as a measure for family aggrandisement, or as useful for buying money and estates. Love had nothing to do with marriage, and in many cases parents did not care what happened to their children after marriage, so long as they themselves pocketed the money. The case of the little Anne Mowbray was an example, not of cupidity of parents, but of a seemingly happy solution of a potentially distressing situation.

The young Duke and Duchess of Norfolk, whose marriage was childless, had made a pilgrimage to the shrine of Our Lady of Walsingham in 1471, hoping for a resultant miracle. Their prayers were answered, for on 5th June 1472 Squire Paston wrote: 'Tidings here are that my Lady of Norfolk is with child . . .', but when the child duly arrived on 10th December 1472, both parents must have been bitterly disappointed that it was a girl. Ill fortune followed, for the Duchess did not produce the longed-for boy, and when the little girl was only three years old her father, still only in his late twenties, suddenly died. The war ship of the little heiress passed to the King, and the situation was fraught with anxiety for the young Duchess, for who knew how the King might decide to bestow her hand in marriage, and with it all her lands? After many months, the Duchess must have been overwhelmed with relief when the King decided to take the little girl into his own family and bestow her hand, title and lands on his second son, Richard.

There is a charming description of the marriage of the two small children in 'Illustrations of Ancient State and Chivalry' by W.H.Black, writing for the College of Arms. On 15th January 1478, the little Anne Mowbray, described as 'this High Princess', was brought to St. Stephen's Chapel and was there received by the Royal family, of whom only the Prince of Wales appears to have been absent, and there she was married to Richard, the little Duke of York, by the Bishop of Norwich. The rejoicings continued for a week, concluding with a tournament at which the small bride, styled 'The Princess of the Feast', distributed jewelled prizes to those who had performed best in the jousting[2].

The Parliament held the next day ratified the agreement made between her mother and the King, whereby the Duchess of Norfolk agreed to forgo a great part of her jointure in favour of her daughter and the Duke of York[3]. This Act also settled the Norfolk lands and titles on Duke Richard and his heirs should Anne Mowbray predecease her husband leaving no heirs.

It is probable that the small bride was brought up in her mother-in-law's Household at Court, where she would learn the accomplishments expected of the wife of a Prince second in line to the throne.

But to such auspicious beginnings great ill-fortune was to follow. On 19th November 1481, just three weeks before her ninth birthday, the little girl died suddenly at Greenwich Palace, the favourite residence of her mother-in-law, Elizabeth Woodville. No details of the cause of death survive.

The King sent three barges to Greenwich to escort Anne's body to Westminster Abbey, where she lay in state in the Jerusalem chamber. She was buried, at a cost of £215.16.10d. in the Chapel of St. Erasmus which formed part of the Lady Chapel of the Abbey, and which had been founded by her mother-in-law.

Four hundred and eighty-three years later, workmen excavating a site in Stepney, London, where the Convent of the Minoresses of St. Clare had formerly stood, found in a sealed vault a lead coffin bearing the inscription in Latin: 'Here lies Anne, Duchess of York, daughter and heiress of John, late Duke of Norfolk, Earl Marshal, Earl of Nottingham and Warenne, Marshal of England, Lord of Mowbray, Segrave and Gower. Late wife of Richard Duke of York, second son of the most illustrious Prince Edward the Fourth, King of England and France, and Lord of Ireland, who died at Greenwich on the 19th day of November in the Year of Our Lord 1481 and the 21st year of the said Lord King'. When the Chapel of St. Erasmus was destroyed to make way for Henry VII's Chapel, the coffins in it were temporarily transferred to the convent of the Minoresses, but Anne's coffin was not returned with the others to the Abbey. This was rectified on 31st May 1965 when Anne Mowbray, Duchess of York, was reburied in the Henry VII Chapel in Westminster Abbey.

Her husband, the little Duke of York, aged eight at the time of his wife's death, was to experience a most bizarre and extraordinary fate, and it is arguable which of the two children was the more unfortunate.

CHAPTER TWO.

Tumultuous Events.

When King Edward IV died at his Palace of Westminster on 9th April 1483, the uneasy calm over which he had ruled for nearly twenty-two years with one short interval, was suddenly broken into a three-way struggle for power. Fearing that this would happen, the dying King had named as Lord Protector of the Realm and thus of his five daughters and two young sons Edward and Richard, his own youngest brother Richard, Duke of Gloucester.

At the head of one faction was King Edward's widow, Elizabeth Woodville, whose greedy and ambitious family occupied positions of power and privilege and who sought to consolidate that power by the seizure and manipulation for their own purposes of the young twelve-year-old King Edward V; while the Lancastrian party, who had been in virtual eclipse since the death of their King Henry VI and his heir, now sensed that their chance lay in the very great and unexpected turmoil into which the country had been thrown. At their head in England were, the Lady Margaret Beaufort, the mother of Henry Tudor, and John Morton, the Bishop of Ely, who had overcome his Lancastrian sympathies for the prize of high office under the Yorkist King Edward, but whose eyes now turned towards the last possible Lancastrian claimant Henry Tudor, then a refugee at the court of Duke Francis of Brittany. In the centre of the maelstrom was of necessity Richard Duke of Gloucester, virtual governor of the North, whose power centre was Middleham Castle and the City of York.

Warned of the potential explosiveness of the situation in London by the late King's friend William, Lord Hastings, and urged by Henry, Duke of Buckingham, his cousin, Richard of Gloucester came South to escort his nephew the new King to London, with six hundred gentlemen dressed in mourning. A man of action rather than words, Gloucester with his general's eye summed up the situation: his nephew the young King was being brought to London by his Woodville uncle Anthony, Earl Rivers, under armed escort which amounted to a small army, in order to get him crowned in haste, and thus prevent Gloucester becoming Protector, as designated by his brother. Gloucester therefore arrested Rivers, the King's half-brother Lord Richard Grey, and two others involved, and sent them to different castles in his power base of Yorkshire. Meanwhile he and the Duke of Buckingham escorted the King to London and, welcomed by the Mayor, Aldermen, Sheriffs and 500 citizens of London, lodged him in the Bishop of London's Palace at St. Paul's, leading the lords in swearing fealty to him.

But news of this bloodless coup panicked the widowed Queen Mother, Elizabeth Woodville, and she rushed into sanctuary at Westminster, taking with her her five daughters and her younger son, Richard Duke of York, and as much furniture and valuables as she could lay her hands on. Her brother Sir Edward Woodville had already put to sea with a small fleet and half the treasure of England, and her son by her first marriage, the Marquis of Dorset, divided the rest of the treasure between himself and his mother.

Richard of York was now nine years and eight months old. His life up to that point had been that of a pampered young Prince in a pleasure-loving family, able to have their own way in everything. Whereas the sons of wealthy and aristocratic families were almost invariably sent to the households of other great families to learn the military and courtly skills expected of sons of the nobility, the young Richard appears to have been kept at his mother's side. According to the French chronicler Jean Molinet, he was 'joyous and witty, nimble and ever ready for dances and games',[1] but to have deprived him of the knowledge and skill at handling weapons and the toughening of his young body and mind was to imperil his very ability to survive in a cruel and militaristic world.

The Coronation of the new King was set for 22nd June: plans went ahead, clothes were ordered and invitations sent out.

But into this temporarily restored calm a bombshell was thrown by the Bishop of Bath and Wells, Robert Stillington, who revealed that the late King had been secretly married by 'troth-plight', the binding engagement recognized as lawful marriage by the Church, to the Lady Eleanor Butler, before his secret and unpopular marriage to Elizabeth Woodville. This meant that the King's marriage to Elizabeth Woodville was bigamous and the seven children of that union, including the new young King Edward V and his brother Richard Duke of York, were illegitimate.

Questioned before the Three Estates, Bishop Stillington further stated that he had been present at the 'troth-plight' between King Edward and Lady Eleanor Butler, and had been sworn to silence by the late King. It was known that he had for a short time actually been imprisoned for 'uttering words prejudicial to the King and his state' and had only been released on giving his solemn promise not to repeat the offence. It is worthy of note here that Edward's brother the Duke of Clarence had been charged with a similar offence; possibly the Bishop had 'leaked' the dangerous secret, hence the hostility between Clarence and the Woodvilles, who were universally blamed for his death. It is thus possible, as hinted by the contemporary Italian monk Mancini, that it was fear of revenge for Clarence's death which caused the Woodvilles to plot against Richard as Protector.

Such were the natural reactions of the thwarted Woodville faction that the Duke of Gloucester, Lord Protector, had to send to the City of York asking for reinforcements 'ayanst the Quiene, hir blode adherentts and affinitie, which have entended and daly doith intend, to murder and utterly distroy us and our cousyn, the duc of Bukkyngham, [now both potential heirs to the crown] and the old royall blode of this realme . . .'[2].

Moreover, at a Council meeting at the Tower of London on Friday, 13th June, Gloucester's chief opponents were revealed as having joined forces to kill him; John Morton, Bishop of Ely; Lord Stanley, who was now married to the mother of Henry Tudor, Lady Margaret Beaufort; the Archbishop of York and Lord Chancellor, Thomas Rotherham, along with the King's old friend and drinking companion, that same William Lord Hastings who had warned Gloucester of the Woodville plot. Hastings' motives were probably mixed, but it seems more than likely that the late King's mistress Jane, or to give her her correct name Elizabeth Shore, played a leading part in luring him to his destruction. Hastings was the only conspirator to lose his head; the others were merely put under temporary arrest, from which they were soon released to begin plotting anew. Lord Stanley's wife, in particular, was writing to her son in Brittany, Henry Tudor, telling him of this new turn of events which must surely favour his claim to be the Lancastrian heir to the throne.

On 16th June the Archbishop of Canterbury was sent to Elizabeth Woodville in her sanctuary at Westminster, to ask that she allow her second son Richard of York to join his brother in the Royal apartments at the Tower of London, where Kings of England had traditionally awaited their Coronation. Apart from the welcome diversion it would give to the twelve-year-old Edward, it was a wise move to ensure that the Woodville conspiracy could not send him out of the country.

Events now moved rapidly to a conclusion. The Three Estates having accepted Bishop Stillington's statement about King Edward having 'married' Elizabeth Woodville while still being troth-plight to the Lady Eleanor Butler, a deputation headed by the Duke of Buckingham waited on the Duke of Gloucester where he was staying with his mother at Baynard's Castle, and offered him the crown, making it clear that if he refused, then 'must they needs seek, and should not fail to find, some other nobleman that would'.[3] In the light of what was to come, this dark hint probably referred to Henry Tudor, in waiting in Brittany, or to Buckingham himself, whose claim was certainly stronger than Henry Tudor's, descended as he was from the fifth son of Edward III.

Richard of Gloucester accepted, and history has vilified him ever since. But the lesson of the civil war, erroneously known as the Wars of the Roses, had surely been to avoid the perils of having a boy as King, through whom unscrupulous relatives could manipulate events to their own satisfaction. This was what Richard alleged against Rivers, Vaughan and Grey, who were at this point summarily tried and executed in Yorkshire.

Gloucester had proved himself in war and in the peace that followed, a brave and brilliant general in war, and a just and honourable viceroy in the North, whose people loved him and trusted his equitable judgments. Whether he wanted it or no, he was arguably the best man for the job.

The Coronation took place on 6th July 1483, and all parties appeared to have buried their differences for the moment, to make it the most brilliant occasion attended by almost all the great nobles of either side.

But evidently the very happiness of the occasion lulled the new King Richard III into a false sense of security for, instead of consolidating his power in the South, where he was comparatively unknown, he set out with his Queen, the delicate Anne Neville, on a Royal Progress in the West and Midlands, on the way to his beloved Yorkshire.

Elizabeth Woodville, now styled by the name of her first marriage, Dame Elizabeth Grey, was still in sanctuary at Westminster with her five daughters, and her two sons were in their apartments at the Tower. There they were observed 'shotyng and playng in the garden of the Tower by sundry times'.[4] This report must clearly refer to the year of 1483, since the Great Chronicle claims that it was during the mayoralty of Sir Edmund Shaa, whose term ran from October 1482 to October 1483; the Mayor for the year 1483–4 was Sir Robert Billesdon.

Of the other conspirators, Lord Stanley had been allowed to return to his wife, the Lady Margaret Beaufort, whose correspondence with her son amounted to treason; Rotherham was soon released; and John Morton, Bishop of Ely was confined, with every comfort and luxury, in the Duke of Buckingham's castle at Brecknock in Wales.

The people everywhere showed their joy and delight in their new King and Queen, showering them with presents wherever they went. Thomas Langton, Bishop of St. David's, summed up the people's feelings in a private letter to the Prior of Christ Church. 'The Kyng . . . contents the people wher he goys best that ever did prince; for many a poor man that hath suffred wrong many days have be relevyd and helpyd by hym and his commands in his progresse. And in many grete citeis and townis wer grete summis of mony gif hym which he hath refusyd. On my trouth I lykyd never the condicions of ony prince so wel as his; God hathe sent hym to us for the wele of us al . . .'[5].

But the joy was to be short-lived.

John Morton, Bishop of Ely, and Henry Tudor's mother Lady Margaret had not been idle. It is uncertain how far they co-ordinated an organised rising of Lancastrian sympathisers with a simultaneous rising of disaffected Yorkists resentful of Richard's 'planting' of his Northern supporters in key positions in the South. What is certain is that Morton himself, the chief instigator of the rebellion, set about suborning his captor, the shallow, ambitious and conceited Duke of Buckingham in his castle at Brecknock. Morton possibly pointed out to Buckingham that, while he had a better claim to the throne than Henry Tudor, it was the latter who had the better chance of success since he was free to marry the Lady Elizabeth of York, by which means the Houses of York and Lancaster would be united and all rivalry between them would be at an end. If Buckingham privately believed he could turn things to his own advantage when the time came, he badly underestimated both Morton and Henry. However, the existence of the Princes remained a problem. The Yorkist elements of the rebellion aimed at releasing them from the Tower. There was only one solution. To quote the Croyland Chronicle: 'At last it was determined by the people in the vicinity of London . . . as well as some others of the southern counties of the kingdom, to avenge their grievances before stated [i.e. to rescue Edward IV's sons from captivity] upon which public proclamation was made that Henry Duke of Buckingham . . . had repented of his former conduct and would be the chief mover in this attempt, *while a rumour was spread* [my italics] "Vulgatum est, regis Edwardi pueros concessisse in fata, sed quo genere interitus ignoratur" [It was commonly known that the sons of King Edward had been destroyed, but by what kind of violence is unknown]. Accordingly, all who had set on foot this insurrection, seeing that if they could find no-one to take the lead in their designs, the ruin of all would speedily ensue, turned their thoughts to Henry Earl of Richmond . . . To him a message was accordingly sent by the Duke of Buckingham, by the advice of the Lord Bishop of Ely who was then his prisoner at Brecknock, requesting him to hasten to England as soon as he possibly could for the purpose of marrying Elizabeth, the eldest daughter of the late King, and at the same time, together with her, taking possession of the throne.' If Henry was to claim the throne through marriage with Elizabeth of York, the Princes' eldest sister, it must be known that they were out of the way: ideally, dead. The rumour certainly gave pause to some of the rebels, who did not realise that they were being used for a revival of Lancastrian fortunes. Polydore Vergil, later Henry VII's historian, recorded that at this point Henry's mother, Lady Margaret Stanley, 'began to hope well of hir soones [son's] fortune, supposing that that dede wold withowt dowt proove for the profyt of the commonwelth'.[6] She therefore lost no time in sending a messenger to Elizabeth Woodville, still in sanctuary, condoling with her on the reported death of her sons, and proposing a marriage between Elizabeth's daughter, Elizabeth of York, and Lady Margaret's son Henry Tudor, Earl of Richmond.

When Richard's progress reached Lincoln therefore, Richard received the news that the Duke of Buckingham, who only three months before had helped to put him on the throne, had risen in rebellion against him. In the meantime the wily Morton, having accomplished his purpose, escaped from captivity and betook himself to his diocese of Ely in the Fen country, whence he soon fled to Flanders.

It was not, however, to be Henry's year. Appalling rainstorms swept the West country, turning the roads into quagmires and the River Severn into a raging torrent, which with Buckingham's own incompetence, turned the rebellion into a rout even before Richard's hastily gathered army could get to grips with the rebels. Buckingham himself was captured and brought before Sir James Tyrell, the Master of the King's Horse and Master of the Henchmen, at Salisbury, where Buckingham was beheaded.

Henry Tudor had set sail from Paimpol in the independent duchy of Brittany on October 31st with a fleet of fifteen ships and some 5,000 Breton soldiers with which Duke Francis of Brittany had provided him. Most of Henry's fleet was scattered by the storm, but Henry with two remaining ships found himself off Poole in Dorset, and was invited ashore. But years of fleeing from danger had taught Henry to be wary of seemingly friendly overtures; he sailed away, back to Brittany, and on arrival was given a loan of 10,000 crowns by Duke Francis to maintain himself and his friends.

A little later the French Chancellor in a speech to the States-General, reported that it had been put about that the Princes were dead — by the orders of the man who had usurped his nephew's throne — their uncle Richard, calling himself King.

CHAPTER THREE

The Key Figures

We have seen from the report of the Great Chronicle of London, that the Princes were seen playing in the garden of the Tower during the mayoralty of Sir Edmund Shaa, which ran from October 1482-October 1483. We also know that the little Duke of York did not join his brother Edward in the Garden Tower until June 16th 1483, so that we can establish the sighting of them at play there as between that date and October 1483.

Yet after the unmasking of the Woodville-Hastings-Morton plot at the Council meeting on June 13th, the Lord Protector, Richard of Gloucester, must surely have realised that no plot in which Morton and the Stanleys, husband and wife, were concerned, would have as its motive the affirmation of Edward V's right to the throne. But until the outbreak of the second, far more dangerous Stanley-Morton-Buckingham plot in the middle or end of September, he does not seem to have fully appreciated the imminent danger to their lives from any conspiracy which aimed to put Henry Tudor on the throne. He certainly did what he could to put his defences in order; he sent Edward Brampton in command of a fleet to seek out and capture Sir Edward Woodville's fleet with the royal treasure aboard, with the offer of pardon for all who would declare for King Richard. All but two of Sir Edward Woodville's fleet surrendered; he himself, with part of the treasure, fled with the remaining ships to join Henry Tudor in Brittany. Richard attempted to renew a treaty of friendship and mutual help with Duke Francis of Brittany, hoping of course if he were successful that he might also negotiate the handing over of Henry Tudor to him, though Henry's name was not mentioned. But the Duke was playing his old game of using Henry as a pawn between France and England; he returned a haughty answer to Richard, demanding military aid against King Louis XI of France.

But by September 1483 France itself was in turmoil. King Louis died at the end of August, leaving a boy King, Charles VIII, on the throne under the regency of his sister, Anne of Beaujeu. The Houses of Orleans and Bourbon were trying to unseat the boy-King; they were only united in their hatred of England. Richard proposed to the Regency that a truce be arranged to settle past injuries and claims, and at the same time he managed to conclude a truce with Brittany, with a secret clause promising to aid Duke Francis with 1,000 archers against France. In return the Duke promised to return Henry Tudor to safe custody. Unfortunately Duke Francis' bouts of insanity prevented the implementation of this clause, with the result that Henry and his followers escaped to the Kingdom of France. In spite of this setback, Richard extended the truce with Brittany to 1492.

In dealing with the rebels who had joined Buckingham and Morton, Richard executed only ten men and later pardoned many who were attainted. Even Bishop John Morton, the Marquess of Dorset and another of Elizabeth Woodville's brothers were offered clemency, and Henry's mother, the very centre of the conspiracy, was stripped of her titles, but handed over to her husband Lord Stanley, and the punishment of attainder was remitted. Lord Stanley was rewarded with some of the late Duke of Buckingham's estates in Wales and made Constable of England, and his brother Sir William Stanley was also given estates in Wales and made Chief Justice of Wales, and later Constable of Caernarvon Castle. All this was an acknowledgment of his dependence on the Stanley brothers' immensely powerful position.

Richard had assumed responsibility for his orphaned niece and nephew, the son and daughter of his dead brother the Duke of Clarence (who were barred from the succession because their father had been attainted), and sent them to Sheriff Hutton Castle in Yorkshire with their cousin John, Earl of Lincoln, in charge of them. After Buckingham's rebellion, it is possible that he saw the necessity of his nephews the Princes being moved from the Tower, where they might be at the mercy not only of Henry Tudor's friends, but of Woodville schemes to remove them to become the focus of future plots. The possibility of their having been moved from house to house in the country and of their mother Elizabeth Woodville being with them, is given support by Thomas More himself, writing in his 'History of King Richard III' of the attempt to persuade Elizabeth Woodville to allow her second son to join his brother in the Tower. According to More, the Duke of Buckingham said: 'And we all, I think, be content that both be with her, if she come thence and bide in such place where they may with their honour be'.[1] One of Henry Tudor's own agents, Bernard de Vignolles, referred in later years to a home of the Tyrells, possibly Gipping Hall in Suffolk, which he says had often been the scene of King Edward IV having made 'good cheer' there, and the then owner, Thomas Tyrell, expressed the hope that 'by God's Will, King Edward's son would make like cheer there.'

The Tyrell family had been at one time Lancastrians and had fought against Edward IV as late as in the Battle of Barnet in early 1471 under the banner of the Earl of Oxford, yet a few weeks later James Tyrell fought for Edward at Tewkesbury, and was there knighted by the victorious King after the battle. From then on Sir James advanced steadily in honours; he became a Commissioner of Array in Suffolk in 1475–6, and through his wife Anne, a Cornish heiress, he became an M.P. for Cornwall in 1478. But he seems to have become an especial companion of Richard, Duke of Gloucester, whose service he joined as early as 1473, when he escorted the widowed Countess of Warwick (Richard's mother-in-law) from her sanctuary at Beaulieu to one of Richard's Northern castles. Thereafter Tyrell accompanied King Edward to France on Edward's abortive invasion of that country, for Tyrell made his Will in May of that year. He accompanied the Duke of Gloucester on his invasion of Scotland in the summer of 1482, and was made Banneret there on 24th July. After Edward's death he rose higher in Richard's honours; it was into his keeping that Richard handed Archbishop Rotherham after the Council meeting of 13th June 1483; and his name heads the list of Knights who attended Richard's and Anne's Coronation on 6th July. Tyrell was made Knight of the Body to the King and Master of the Henchmen (pages). He took charge of, and sat in judgment on, the rebel Duke of Buckingham at Salisbury and was probably present at his execution there on 2nd November 1483. A few days later he was made Commissioner of Array together with William Herbert, Earl of Huntingdon, husband of Richard's illegitimate daughter, Katherine, for the resistance of the rebels in Wales, and the next day was made Sheriff of Cornwall. He had evidently been with the King and Queen on their Progress to the West, the Midlands and Yorkshire after the Coronation, for he was in attendance as Master of the Horse and of the Henchmen when the King and Queen and their ten-year-old son Prince Edward visited York.

In effect, Sir James Tyrell was to become what we might now call Richard's Chief of Intelligence; the man he most trusted in all aspects of defence and secrecy.

In addition, Richard was to rely on the services of one of the most colourful and dashing figures of his day, Edward Brampton. This exotic Commando-type man, born in Portugal as Duarte Brandao about the year 1440 of Jewish parents, his father having been a blacksmith, made a boast of having been born out of wedlock; he claimed that his natural father was one Rui Barba, a scion of a well-known family of Leiria. But since he was a boastful swashbuckler, this may have been just part of his attempt to claim noble blood. Dark, but probably equally false, stories circulated of a homicide in which he had been involved: at any rate he left his native country at the age of about twenty-four and came to England. Being almost penniless he applied to the Domus Conversorum, or Home for converted Jews in London but found that, in order to qualify for its benefits he would have to be baptized. Edward IV became in the conventional fashion his godfather, and he thus adopted the English version of his name and that of his godfather, Edward. He seems to have lived in the Home for the next four years on a pittance of 1½d. a day. But the fact that he was the King's godson, combined with his flamboyant style of self-glorification, soon gave him an entrée to Edward's court.

In June 1472 he and others were appointed to the command of an armed force which the King sent to sea to 'resist his enemies and rebels', and he figured in comparable deeds of daring from now on. He must have distinguished himself as a fighting man, and it is reasonable to assume that in this respect he appealed to the young King who had proved himself so outstandingly in the field; for later in 1472 Brampton received an independent command, the first of many.

The next year he was sent in charge of a squadron of four ships to 'do all feasible hurt and annoyance to the Earl of Oxford', the Lancastrian leader who had shut himself up in St. Michael's Mount. Oxford's capture was inevitable, since he was blockaded by sea and land, and he surrendered on 15th February 1474.

Brampton, as he now called himself, received many honours; he accompanied the King's army to France in 1475, and boasted afterwards that he often distinguished himself in the tourney in single combat, defeating a German champion in the presence of the King and his court: when the English King and his army were 'bought off' by the French

King, Brampton boasted that he had sat at the royal table. Whether there was in fact any substance in all this bragging or not, he did undoubtedly meet at this time Charles, Duke of Burgundy, Edward's brother-in-law, and he soon afterwards set up an establishment in Bruges, one of the most prosperous towns of Northern Europe; and here he began to improve his fortunes by trading all over the countries of Europe. As a newly rich man, he returned to Portugal and assisted the dethroned King Alphonso by lending him money, and when the King was restored, Brampton went to live in Portugal for some time. He seems to have had dual nationality, was given arms in England and married an English wife, for he came to London on his wife's death in 1479, and was confirmed by Letters Patent issued in London in the possessions of Isabelle Peche 'his late wife'. He was now making a great deal of money in trade, and acted as royal agent for the payment of large sums of money to various Spanish merchants, and shipped vast amounts of duty free wool through the Straits of Gibraltar. In 1482 he was appointed to the office of Captain, Keeper and Governor of Guernsey and its appurtenances: the death of King Edward the next year making no difference to his progress, for the boy King Edward V, under the guidance of Richard of Gloucester, put him in command of the fleet sent to chase the ships of Sir Edward Woodville, with some success.

When Richard became King, he gave Brampton various grants and appointments[2] and in 1484 Brampton was given the outstanding honour of Knighthood for services unspecified. He was in fact the first Jew to be Knighted — and for a Portuguese Jewish adventurer it was an incredible honour — and, typically, he afterwards boasted that he was a Knight of the Garter. A few months later he received, amongst other properties, a manor in Folkestone and an annuity of £100 for the next twenty years. He travelled extensively, and after Richard's Queen died he was sent as Ambassador to Portugal in March 1485, to ask for the hand of the Princess Joanna of Portugal for King Richard.[3] This important mission kept Brampton out of England for some months, because he was not present at the Battle of Bosworth in August 1485. He certainly returned to Portugal from the Low Countries in 1486 or 1487, embarking at Middelburgh for his native country, accompanied by his wife, Lady Brampton and a young man attendant on her whom Henry Tudor was to call 'Perkin Warbeck'.

This connection may throw light on an earlier association, for it is known that there were many Jews in Tournai[4], a town which is described by Philippe de Commynes in his 'Mémoires' as a free city, that is, one to which access could be had without the normal safe-conducts, and it is not stretching the imagination unduly to believe that the de Werbecques, (though they seem to have dropped the 'de' later) are described in the 'Notes sûr la famille de Werbecque' by Comte du Chastel de la Howarderie, knew Brampton since Jehan Werbecque's wife Nicaise de Faro was of Portuguese extraction. Moreover, they were not the humble family which Henry Tudor later tried to make out; Nicaise Werbecque was of a well-to-do bourgeois family well-known and respected in Tournai, with a comfortable home on the banks of the Scheldt in the parish of St. John des Cauffours, and her husband Jehan was doyen of the boatmen of Tournai.

CHAPTER FOUR

Reasonable Possibility

Since history is 'essentially a speculative and critical science', as an eminent historian said recently in a television series, it is surely not unreasonable to explore the possibilities of what happened to the Princes in the light of what slender evidence we have, and to make sensible deductions both from what we know, and from the actions of those most closely involved, particularly since those who believe that the Princes were killed have only hearsay to support their case.

Any doubts about King Richard's loyalty to his dead brother and to the illegitimised children of that brother are surely dispersed by the tribute paid to him in the Continuation of Sir Thomas More's 'History of King Richard III' by Richard Grafton, who reports that the Duke of Buckingham said of Richard: 'He promised me, on his fidelity, laying his hand on mine at Baynard's Castle, that the two young princes should live, and that he would so provide for them and so maintain them in honourable estate that I and all the realm ought and should be content.' — an oath which is duplicated almost exactly by the words of the assurances Richard was to give to Elizabeth Woodville that he would maintain and provide fitting husbands for his nieces, her daughters, when they came out of sanctuary in March 1484.

When King Richard and Queen Anne returned to London after Buckingham's rebellion, the city of London and the South generally, were buzzing with speculation and rumour. French spies abounded — Philippe de Commynes says in his 'Mémoires' that he himself was one of the French King's intelligence agents, and that he knows of at least 400 agents sent abroad, mostly by himself. His patron was Angelo Cato, Archbishop of Vienne, a Neapolitan who became Louis XI's physician-astrologer, and at whose request de Commynes undertook the writing of his 'Mémoires', and who was probably the organiser in chief of an immense spy ring for Louis. Dominic Mancini, the Italian priest who came to England in 1482 to report on English affairs and who left hurriedly soon after Richard's Coronation in early July 1483, was also probably one of Louis' agents, though he disclaimed any particular knowledge of the people and events he was reporting on, and it is doubtful if he even understood much English.

It is also reasonable to assume that neither of the young Princes would be feeling at all friendly towards their uncle Richard. They might be ignorant of the real reason the elder had been set aside, and they would attribute their own position to their uncle's greed for power. After young Edward's brief taste of the trappings of sovereignty, the loss of it must have been indeed bitter for him. It is doubtful if the younger boy at ten would have been considered old enough to be told the real position, nor the potential dangers of their situation. It would thus hardly occur to them that a threat to their uncle's life was equally a threat to their own, nor that the real danger to them would come from a revival of the Lancastrian cause.

In fact, Dominic Mancini wrote (whether from hearsay, imagination or fact, we cannot know) that the Princes' physician, Dr. Argentine (who later became doctor to Henry VII's son Arthur) reported that the elder Prince 'sought daily remission of his sins by confession and penance, because he believed that death was facing him'. Whether the death he feared was by violence or natural causes Dr. Argentine and Mancini naturally do not specify.

What would have happened to them if Richard had won the Battle of Bosworth is obviously of academic interest only; nevertheless it deserves to be taken into account because we judge from hindsight, whereas Richard must have believed he had the situation in hand and would easily defeat whatever invasion the Tudor could mount. Richard had an unrivalled reputation as a soldier and a general, and his actions would all be in line with the belief that he would be triumphant. He would believe that time was on his side, and any disclosures he had to make could wait until he had defeated Tudor. He was not to know that for him that time would never arrive.

What Richard did was to send his other nephews and nieces north to his castle of Sheriff Hutton[1] under the care of his nephew and later heir, the Earl of Lincoln. But for the Princes in the Tower, whose lives had already been in dire peril from the Buckingham rebellion, Richard would have had to make especially secure and secret arrangements. What more natural than that he should call upon the two men whom he trusted most, Sir James Tyrell and that dashing Commando, Edward Brampton, with his shipping contacts in the Low Countries?

There is however the possibility that his own intention to send the boys overseas had been pre-empted. Sir George Buck, whose great-grandfather fought for Richard at Bosworth and was beheaded by the Tudor after the battle, has no doubt of what happened. In his 'History of King Richard the Third', edited by Dr. A.N. Kincaid, he says that 'some write that they were both secretly taken out of the Tower and both set afloat in a ship and conveyed together over the seas.' However, he goes on to say that the elder died of a natural sickness, pointing out that none of Edward IV's children lived to old age. He suggests the instigator of their journey was 'that worthy and faithful knight, Sir Robert Brakenbury . . .' and goes on to be more specific: '. . . it hath been made plain enough that the younger son of King Edward was conveyed into a foreign land by sea, and that foreign country was Flanders, as all the stories testify . . . And he was still, and a long time, kept close. And there may the more credit be given to that report of these matters because it agreeth well with that which was made thereof by Duke Richard, or Perkin Warbeck himself (for so he was now called or nicknamed)'. Buck continues by saying that the Prince was later, after Henry Tudor's triumph, put into the care of the Duchess of Burgundy who provided him with 'all princely and virtuous education in Tournay, in Antwerp, and after in the court of the Duke of Burgundy [Buck must here be referring to the Burgundian court at Malines, rather than to the Duke, who had died in 1477] . . . because he was not yet of years and of strength and knowledge ripe enough to undertake the enterprise for the recovery or gaining of a kingdom . . .'[2]

Polydore Vergil, Henry VII's historian, records: 'It was generally reported and believed that the sons of Edward IV were still alive, having been conveyed secretly away and obscurely concealed in some distant region.'[3] Francis Bacon, writing much later, says: 'Neither wanted there even at that time [on Henry's accession] secret rumours and whisperings, which afterwards gathered strength and turned to great troubles, that the young sons of King Edward the Fourth, or one of them, which were said to be destroyed in the Tower, were not indeed murdered but conveyed secretly away, and were yet living.'[4]

Referring to the rumour of the Princes' deaths, 'spread' at the time of the Buckingham rebellion in 1483, Caroline Halsted, writing in her life of Richard III in 1844, argues for the belief that the Princes were sent abroad, by virtue of the fact that plots were formed for sending the Princesses abroad, indicating that the princes may have already been sent out of the country. She goes on to say that this is why their violent deaths were rumoured and why no contradiction was given by King Richard who, with the South in open rebellion, would scarcely have proclaimed the escape of his nephews and 'thus feed the very opposition to his newly-enjoyed dignity.' She goes on: 'The greater probability however, is this: that the Duke of Buckingham, aware of their disappearance from the Tower, but not made acquainted with the place of their exile, spread the report with a view of irritating the populace against the new monarch, and thus advancing more effectually his own selfish and ambitious views; and that King Richard unwilling, and indeed unable, to produce his nephews, was driven to sanction the report as his only defence against their friends, and the surest method of keeping secret from his enemies their actual place of concealment.'[5]

However, more than one writer has connected Buckingham with the murder of the Princes: the Dutch Divisie Chronicle ('Some others will say that the Duke of Buckingham killed these children hoping to become king himself')[6], and de Commynes both suggest it, though elsewhere they repeat the traditional accusation against Richard III. Of more weight perhaps are the 'Historical Notes of a London Citizen, 1483–1488', published by Richard Firth Green in No. 380 of the *English Historical Review*. In this it is stated that the sons of Edward IV 'wer put to deyth in the Towur of London be the vise of the duke of Buckingham'. This is believed to be the earliest suggestion of Buckingham's involvement in the crime, though it seems to contradict the report of the Princes 'shooting and playing' in the garden of the Tower 'by sundry times', and does no more than report common gossip. Perhaps in fact the truth lay between the two rumours. As Buck reports elsewhere 'some others . . . say that these young princes were embarked in a ship at Tower wharf, and that they were conveyed from hence into the seas, and so cast into the deeps and drowned. But some others say that they were not drowned, but were set safe on shore beyond the seas.'[7]*

---

*Audrey Williamson says in her book 'The Mystery of the Princes' (p. 105) that Richard III granted leave to Catherine Woodville, widow of the Duke of Buckingham, for herself, her children and her servants, to join her sister the Queen, in sanctuary. What secrets did Catherine have to tell her sister Elizabeth about the possible fate of her sons?

It is indeed difficult to believe that they could have been removed from the Tower without Richard's knowledge, but it is not impossible that a 'mole', acting for Buckingham, may have made an attempt to drown them and only succeeded in the case of young Edward. This view is given some credibility by the bitter words King Richard used in his letter to his Chancellor, John Russell, Bishop of Lincoln, when he referred to Buckingham as 'hym that hadde best cawse to be trewe' and 'the most untrewe creature lyvyng'[8]. Drowning, whether accidental or intentional, does seem to offer an explanation for the total lack of any information on the fate of the elder boy, and perhaps another reason for Richard's silence, occasioned as much by shame and embarrassment at having lost one of his nephews confided to his care by his brother King Edward as by the necessity for concealing the whereabouts of the surviving boy.

There are some tantalising pointers at any rate to King Richard's interest in Flanders contained in Harleian MSS 433, the register of grants which passed the signet in Edward V's short reign (under his uncle's guidance), and later under Richard III. The first is dated the 13th day of January year two (1485) and runs: '. . . Where as we of late sent oure righte trusty knighte for oure body and Counsailloure Sir James Tyrelle over the See into the parties of Flaundres for diverse maters concernyng gretely oure wele. Whoo in his Retornyng ayen unto us landed in oure poort of Dovor the charges whereof amounting to the somme of iiij markes as we certainly knowe were borne by the maire and othre inhabitauntes of oure said Towne of Dovor . . .'[9]

The second grant is to Sir Philip Goguet 'Chapelyn to the duchesse of Burgoyne and for iij persones with him Yevene [given] at Notingham the xxiij day of Aprile Anno etc. primo' (1484)[10], but far the most intriguing is that for 'Clement Goguet hath a like lettre to passe & repasse to my lady Burgoyn with a servant with him/ & ij horses without any Serche etc. Yevene at Westminstre the vj day of Decembre Anno ij^{do}'* (1484)[11]. What exactly was Clement Goguet, a relation probably of the Duchess of Burgundy's chaplain, carrying that was to pass without search? More significant perhaps, what was the object of Sir James Tyrell's journey to Flanders and back; what did he do in Flanders that was so greatly to the King's weal (benefit)? Was it to visit the surviving Prince (if one of them had died) in his hiding-place in Flanders, possibly recommended by Edward Brampton as a result of his trading contacts, and bearing in mind that Tournai was a free city that anyone could enter without safe-conducts? The very nature of such a mission, then as now, would ensure that the instructions could never be written down; equally true then that Richard would maintain complete silence about their fate and the whereabouts of the surviving Prince, so that agents of Henry Tudor would not know whether to continue to search for them or not.

The most significant and undeniable benefit to Richard's good name was that Elizabeth Woodville, for so long incarcerated in her self-inflicted sanctuary at Westminster, was finally persuaded to come out and to release her five daughters into Richard's care; he received them at court and took an oath on March 1st 1484 to treat them honourably and to provide suitable husbands for them. 'Dame Elizabeth Grey', the former Queen-Mother, went further: she not only accepted from Richard a pension for herself, but she wrote to her elder son by her first marriage, the Marquess of Dorset (who had fled to France to join Henry Tudor), advising him to come home, and assuring him that Richard would treat him well. He evidently preferred Richard's word to the more doubtful promises of Henry, for he attempted to escape to England, but was intercepted by Henry's furious emissaries, who 'persuaded' him to return to Henry's little court. There can surely be only one conclusion to all this: that Elizabeth Woodville had received the news she most wished to hear — that her sons, or one of them, were alive and in hiding abroad. Henry certainly never forgot that she had trusted Richard with her daughters; he was later to make it the excuse for sending her to a nunnery and confiscating all her goods. Greedy and ambitious she certainly was, but to pretend that she could come to terms, and so soon, with the man she believed had murdered her two sons, is surely straining credulity beyond even the most partisan limits, knowing what people would say about it.

Moreover Elizabeth could well have recalled that Henry's mother, Lady Margaret, had sought her daughter's hand for Henry at the same time as condoling with her on the death of her sons, which may have been the first that Elizabeth had heard of it. As Lady Margaret had 'begun to hope well of her son's fortune' as a result of the Princes' deaths, 'supposing that that deed would without doubt prove for the profit of the commonwealth', Richard would have been able to open Elizabeth's eyes as to where the real danger lay.

*In case of confusion about the figures given in the register of grants in Harleian MSS 433, the explanation is that the whole register of grants and warrants given under the Royal Seal, have been translated from the original Latin, and therefore Roman numerals were used for the figures in the dates.

Examples: ij = 2; vj = 6; xxiij = 23, and so on. The first year of King Richard III's reign was dated from his Coronation on 6th July 1483. Therefore year One was from 6th July 1483 to 6th July 1484 (Anno Primo); Year Two was dated from 6th July 1484 to 6th July 1485 (Anno Secundo).

CHAPTER FIVE

The Lancastrian Claimant

To try to understand the actions and reactions of Henry VII towards the man he called 'Perkin Warbeck', it is necessary to investigate first, his tenuous claim to the throne and second, the precarious, often humiliating upbringing which had helped to form him into the man who stood, at the age of twenty-eight, as victor on the field of Bosworth.

As to his claim, he came from a doubly flawed line. On his father's side he was descended from the love affair of Henry V's widow Katherine with the Clerk of her Wardrobe, Owen Tudor; on his mother's side from the love affair of John of Gaunt, third son of Edward III, and the beautiful Katherine Swynford (whom John of Gaunt, Duke of Lancaster, afterwards married). This marriage produced the Beaufort family, at the time the offspring of a double adultery.

Relinquished by his mother when she married Sir Henry Stafford soon after Henry's birth, he was brought up by his uncle Jasper and spent most of his early life as a penniless fugitive from the various battlefields of the Wars of the Roses. But even in his unhappy youth, it was possible to discern the stirrings of lucky chances which were to lead on to great good fortune. Captured in Pembroke Castle by Lord Herbert, Henry had been brought up for a time as the Herberts' son, destined to marry their daughter Maud. But he was saved from anonymity by the death of Lord Herbert in 1469, and two years later the Lancastrian armies suffered their final and apparently decisive defeat with the loss of both Henry VI's heir and a little later, Henry VI himself.

Jasper Tudor fled once more with his nephew for France but, owing to adverse winds they landed in the independent Duchy of Brittany whose Duke, Francis, was an enemy of France.

From now on, Henry became a pawn in Anglo-French-Breton politics; both France and England tried by every means to get hold of Duke Francis' 'guest', but by a sixth sense, no doubt sharpened by adversity,

Henry managed to avoid being handed over. When Edward IV died at the age of not quite forty-one, Henry's star was suddenly in the ascendant. The new King, Edward V, was a boy of twelve, and memories of the last unhappy minority rule of Henry VI arose in many minds, and many Lancastrians who had had to make their peace with the Yorkist King Edward IV, now made their way to Brittany to join Henry Tudor. Among Henry's staunchest friends was John Morton, Bishop of Ely, who joined in the plots against the Lord Protector, Richard Duke of Gloucester, and kept Henry advised of the situation in England. The Earl of Oxford, a stalwart Lancastrian commander in the field, who had had to surrender to Edward IV from St. Michael's Mount, escaped from captivity and fled to join Henry at the Breton court. Henry's mother the Lady Margaret, wrote to Henry telling him of Elizabeth Woodville's consent to her daughter Elizabeth's marriage to him. With the Duke of Buckingham's treachery at Bishop Morton's instigation, plans were brought forward for invasion soon after the Duke of Gloucester became King: Henry Tudor was supplied with a fleet by Duke Francis, and Buckingham was to raise an army to march eastwards to link up with the men of the South.

But Henry's star was not yet at its zenith; as we have seen, the great rainstorms broke up Henry's fleet and brought Buckingham to the block. Morton fled to Flanders and, with his mother prompting him, Henry swore an oath in Rennes Cathedral on Christmas morning 1483, to marry Elizabeth of York. His followers knelt round him as though he were already King.

Once more the English King attempted to persuade the Bretons to hand over Henry Tudor: once more, warned by Morton, Henry avoided capture by a sudden dash across the border into France. He was now to receive massive aid from the French King: a fleet of fifteen ships; an army of about 2,000 men, mainly of men let out of prison for the enterprise; and an advance of 40,000 livres. He also received the welcome news from his mother that the Stanleys (her husband Thomas, Lord Stanley and his brother, Sir William) would support him on his arrival with men and arms. With their newly acquired lands in Wales granted to them by King Richard from the estates of the traitor Buckingham, this was the deciding factor in the choice of where to land.

As the wizard Merlin had foretold many centuries earlier, the true heir of King Arthur and the ancient Celtic Kings would come from Wales to rescue England from the tyrant.

On 1st August 1485, Henry set sail from Harfleur with his fleet, and had the good fortune to avoid the ships sent out by King Richard to intercept them.

Henry landed with his army at Milford Haven on Sunday, 7th August and began to march inland, calling on all Welshmen to join him, when he would reward them with honours and estates. But he found most of them reluctant to declare themselves, just as King Richard found that those who had sworn to defend him now kept silent, waiting on events.

Henry's temperament was not that of a soldier; there had been too many enforced flights and gory battles for him to wish to play the part of heroic loser. His mind was that of a clerk; he kept an account book of expenses, every page of which he signed: this was something he could understand and enjoy. He reached Stafford before he met his step-uncle, Sir William Stanley, with promises of help; but of Lord Stanley, there was no word. The thought of the coming battle, with its uncertain outcome oppressed him so much that, on the evening of 19th August, when his army left for Tamworth, he remained behind with a small bodyguard. He was missing all night, and found shelter in a small hut: the Earl of Oxford, his principal commander and his uncle Jasper, were deeply shaken, but when they found him in the morning, he declared he had only withdrawn from the camp to receive good news from certain friends.

Henry's participation in the Battle of Bosworth was restricted to observation, surrounded by a posse of faithful knights including the gigantic Sir John Cheyney and Sir William Brandon, who bore in consummate defiance of his true Sovereign the Royal Standard. King Richard's call for volunteers to ride with him down Ambien Hill to attack Tudor himself and thus avoid vast numbers of casualties, was answered by nearly a hundred knights and squires; the Stanley brothers and their armies were poised on either side of the opposing main forces, ready to throw their weight on whichever side it became safest to support.[1] Northumberland, slightly to Richard's rear, returned an equivocal answer to Richard's request for support, and he and his army remained inactive. The gallant band of heroes led by their Sovereign thundered down the hill and clashed with Tudor's posse. Down went the huge

Cheyney, unhorsed by the small, slight King. Down went Brandon, the Royal Standard soaked in his blood. It was a horrifying moment for Henry: local legend says he wheeled his horse about in the breathing space Richard's attack on Brandon had given him, and rode off to the South-east towards Stoke Golding. But fate had decreed that he should be King; three thousand men under Sir William Stanley to the right of Richard, rode to Tudor's rescue and crashed into Richard's small band, literally hacking them to pieces, together with their King.[2] Hideously mutilated, stark naked and with a felon's halter round his neck, the King's body was flung across the back of a pack-horse, which one of Richard's heralds was forced to ride into Leicester to the house of the Grey Friars, where the body was put on public view for two days and then given burial by the friars, without either stone or epitaph. Henry later relented and paid for a tomb of sorts for Richard's grave.[3] King Richard's golden circlet, which he had worn upon his helmet, was retrieved from a bush where it had fallen in the conflict, probably by Lord Stanley, who then rode after Henry and, kneeling, proferred it to him.[4] There is to this day a spot marked on Ordnance Survey maps 'Crown Hill'. It is some three miles from the centre of the battlefield, near Stoke Golding.

Having perhaps unexpectedly gained the victory at Bosworth, Henry now had to tackle the thousand and one problems of kingship, for which his first twenty-eight years had hardly fitted him. He had never been of sufficient importance to attract much attention, except as a pawn to be bargained with; he had had no resources and very little clothing of his own: no experience of administration or government. But if all the frustrations and dangers of his life had constrained and seared him, they had also forged within him a steely determination to survive; a shrewd, if not cynical assessment of the men with whom he had to deal, and a detachment which allowed him to bide his time to achieve his ends. He was cautious, suspicious, ruthless and without scruples: probably just the man England needed at this time to force her to forget the thirty years of destructive civil war, and to set her on the road to becoming a European power whose friendship would be valuable to all the kings and princes of the West.

The first weeks were spent in rewarding his followers for their treachery to Richard; appointing suitable men to administrative posts and making preparations for his Coronation and for his first Parliament. One of his first acts was a typical one: he decreed that his reign was to be dated from the day before Bosworth, so that he could indict King Richard and most of his followers of treasonable rebellion against their lawful Sovereign, thus neatly bringing a vast number of estates and honours into the Royal exchequer by attainder. 'Oh God!' recorded the Croyland Chronicler, 'What security shall our kings have henceforth, that in the day of battle they may not be deserted by their subjects?' The obstinacy of the English in resisting tyranny succeeded in this instance; when it came to Henry's turn to face insurrection, he had to alter his own law in this respect. But it was not in his nature to seek popularity; security was the first consideration, and with this in mind he set up a personal bodyguard of some two hundred 'yeomen of the guard', probably in imitation of the French pattern, but he was the first English King to feel the need of protection against his own subjects.

He was presented with an awkward dilemma regarding the Princess Elizabeth whom he had sworn, in Rennes Cathedral, to marry and who, with her brothers, had been declared illegitimate by the Titulus Regius Act. Henry had no intention of appearing to establish his claim to the throne through her, so he ordered the destruction of Titulus Regius without being read. But this at once created a further problem: while it restored Elizabeth to legitimacy, it did the same for her brothers who, if alive, would become very dangerous rivals. In his son's, Henry VIII's reign, the Ambassador of the Emperor Charles V was to write to him (referring to the unpopularity of Henry VIII because of his desire to marry Anne Boleyn) '. . .the people would willingly have helped you [the Emperor] to dethrone him [Henry VIII]. . .they refer to the case of Warwick, who chased away King Edward. . .and they say you have a better title than the present king, who only claims by his mother, who was declared by sentence of the Bishop of Bath a bastard, because Edward had espoused another wife before he married the mother of Elizabeth of York'.[5] The Emperor's 'right' or 'title' to the throne derived only from the Pretender's 'gift', as we shall see.

It was therefore imperative for Henry to find out what had become of the Princes. The French Chronicler, Jean Molinet, has an almost incredible story that, after his victory at Bosworth, Henry '. . .taking the oath of allegiance in some towns in the neighbourhood of London, proclaimed everywhere before his Coronation that if there were anyone of the line of King Edward who had a right to the throne, that he should show himself, and he himself would help to crown him'.[6] This story is so staggering that it can only be explained as a clumsy attempt to draw one or both Princes, if they were alive, into the open, where they could be summarily dealt with. In any case, one of those who had a strong claim to the throne was the little Edward, Earl of Warwick, son of King Edward's dead brother Clarence, whom Richard had taken to Sheriff Hutton Castle for safety, and whom Henry now imprisoned in the Tower, precisely because he was a possible heir to the throne. Fourteen years later Henry executed him, allegedly for trying to escape. Richard's appointed heir was his nephew, John de la Pole, Earl of Lincoln, the eldest of the seven sons of Elizabeth and John de la Pole, sister and brother-in-law of King Edward, of the Yorkist line, all of whom had a better title to the throne than did Henry. Sir Clements Markham, a vigorous defender of King Richard, says he is convinced that the Act of Parliament declaring the children of Edward IV illegitimate must have had a solid foundation: 'In no other way can Henry's cruel treatment of the young Earl of Warwick be accounted for. If his (Henry's) wife was the legitimate heiress of York, there could be no danger from Warwick. . .a harmless young Prince far removed from the succession. But if Elizabeth and her sisters were not legitimate, the case was very different'.[7] In fact, there was an attempt in London to rescue Warwick from the Tower and set him on the throne instead of Henry.

In the absence of positive proof that the two young Princes were dead, Henry had to use what weapons he could to destroy the reputation of King Richard and the popularity in which he was still held in the North. An Act of Attainder was drawn up, accusing Richard of almost every crime imaginable, including tyranny and 'the shedding of infants' blood', but no specific charge was made that he had murdered his nephews; a somewhat odd omission in view of the fact that the French Chancellor had made that very charge while Henry was still at the Breton court.

There were to be several uprisings against his harsh rule; the North particularly which had known the justness of Richard's government, rose in rebellion. That same year (1486) a young man was put forward by a priest named Simonds, to pretend to be the Earl of Warwick: Henry's answer was to produce the real Warwick and parade him through the streets. The false Warwick then appeared in Ireland, where the Irish received him joyfully, and crowned him in Dublin Cathedral as 'Edward VI'. Henry learned to his chagrin that among the supporters of the false boy were Richard's nephew and heir, the Earl of Lincoln, whom Henry had appointed to his Council; Richard's friend Lord Lovell; Richard's sister Margaret, Duchess of Burgundy and, apparently, his own mother-in-law, Elizabeth Woodville. Lincoln had visited the Duchess Margaret in Malines; there was evidently agreement between them. The putting up of an impostor was the first slight indication that the real boy was in the background, too young as yet to be risked on the battlefield. But it is Elizabeth Woodville's role in this which is so baffling; she was the mother of the Queen and grandmother of the heir to the throne, Prince Arthur. She risked her whole position, perhaps her life as well, for what was bound to be a most hazardous undertaking. Did she, too, know or suspect, that one of her sons was in the background, waiting for the outcome of this trial of strength, to come forward and seize the throne? It seems highly unlikely, though Henry's swift riposte, suddenly stripping her of all her possessions and banishing her to the Abbey of Bermondsey, where she remained until her death in 1492, on a charge of having released her daughters into Richard's care, certainly sounds equally far-fetched.

The Earl of Lincoln, at the head of a small force of 2,000 German mercenaries, armed and equipped by the Duchess Margaret, and led by a noted and well-tried fighter, Martin Swart, and enthusiastically supported by swarms of wild-looking partly-armed Irish, crossed over from Ireland on 4th June 1487, apparently with the object of setting the false Warwick on the throne. Lincoln made his stand south of Newark near Stoke: Henry's army of 4,000 was joined by 5,000 men provided by Lord Stanley. The Earl of Oxford was in command, supported by Jasper Tudor, now Earl of Bedford.

Lincoln and his men fought with fanatical bravery, and at one point seemed to have victory within their grasp, but they were overwhelmed by numbers and arms: half the Irish were not armed at all, and were killed like cattle. Lincoln, Swart and Sir Thomas Broughton perished where they stood. The boy 'king' was found to be one Lambert Simnel, an Oxford tradesman's son. He and the priest were captured; the priest was condemned to life imprisonment and Simnel was sent to the royal kitchens to be a scullion, later to be promoted to a falconer.

If it was a disaster for the Duchess Margaret and her hopes for a Yorkist revival, it was also the start of a long nightmare for Henry, whose reign was to be troubled throughout by rebellion, treachery and the most serious claimant of all, 'Perkin Warbeck'. His actions henceforward would belie his words; he could afford to be lenient to Simnel the obvious impostor, by showing his contempt for him, since ridicule is often the most potent weapon of all, but Francis Bacon, an admirer of Henry, was to write in his 'The Reign of Henry VII' that Simnel was left 'as a continual spectacle before peoples' eyes of how they had been fooled, and as a kind of remedy against the like enchantments of people in time to come.' In other words, a tacit admission that the real Prince might still be expected.

Henry's own pronouncement on the battle of Stoke was as incautious as it is enlightening; he said that he regretted the death of the Earl of Lincoln as he had hoped to learn from him 'the bottom of his danger'.[8]

CHAPTER SIX

The Bones

King Henry VII had failed to find the bodies of the Princes in the Tower, yet close by the resting place of the little Duchess of York in Westminster Abbey is an urn containing the bones of two children, alleged to be those of King Edward V and his brother Richard, Duke of York.

Many people must know the story of how in 1674 workmen, digging down stone stairs leading from the King's Lodgings, or Royal Apartments, in the Tower of London to the chapel in the White Tower, found a wooden chest containing the bones of two children. One of the skulls and many of the other bones were broken.

John Knight, Principal Surgeon to King Charles II, and John Gibbon, Bluemantle Herald, were both called in to see the pathetic remains. Both apparently decided without question that these bones must be those of the two Princes in the Tower, missing for one hundred and ninety-one years. Bluemantle recorded the find, somewhat in the manner of a daily paper reporter who believes he has made a scoop: 'July 17 Anno 1674 in diggin some foundacons in ye Tower, were discovered ye bodies of Edw 5 and his brother murdered 1483. I my selfe handled ye Bones Especially ye Kings Skull. Ye other wch was lesser was broken in ye digging. Johan Gybbon, Blewmantle.'

John Knight, King Charles' Principal Surgeon, gave at least two somewhat fuller accounts of the find:-

'Ao 1674. In digging down a pair of stone staires leading from the Kings Lodgings to the chappel in the white tower there were found bones of two striplings in (as it seemed) a wooden chest which upon the presumptions that they were the bones of this king and his brother Rich: D. of York, were by the command of King Charles the 2nd put into a marble urn and deposited amongst the R: Family in H: 7th Chappel in Westminster at my importunity. Jo.Knight.'

Secondly:- (Knight given as the authority) '. . . in order to the rebuilding of the several Offices in the Tower, and to clear the White Tower from all contiguous buildings, digging down the stairs which led from the King's Lodgings, to the Chappel in the said Tower, about ten foot in the ground were found the Bones of two striplings in (as it seemed) a wooden Chest, which upon the survey were found proportionable to the ages of those two Brothers viz. about thirteen and eleven years. The skul of the one being entire, the other broken, as were indeed many of the other Bones, also the Chest, by the violence of the labourers, who . . . cast the rubbish and them away together, wherefore they were caused to sift the rubbish, and by that means preserved all the bones. The circumstances . . . being . . . often discoursed with . . . Sir Thomas Chichley, Master of the Ordinance, by whose industry the new Buildings were then in carrying on, and by whom this matter was reported to the King' (1674).

In an anonymous and undated account, differing from the above, is the following statement:- 'This day I, standing by the opening, saw working men dig out of a stairway in the White Tower, the bones of those two Princes who were foully murdered by Richard III, . . . they were small bones, of lads in their teens and there were pieces of rag and velvet about them. . . . Being fully recognised to be the bones of those two Princes, they were carefully put aside in a stone coffin or coffer.'

Sir Christopher Wren himself, who was Surveyor-General to King Charles II, gave his own account (undated):- '[states that the bones were found] . . . about ten feet deep in the ground . . . as the workmen were taking away the stairs, which led from the royal Lodgings into the Chapel of the White-tower.'

A still later account, published in 1719, states:- '. . . when . . . great heaps of records and bills and answers lying in the Six Clerkes Office were removed thence to be reposited in the White Tower and a new pair of stairs were making into the Chappel there, for the easier conveyance of them thither, the labourers in digging at the foot of the old stairs came to the bones of consumed Corps, cover'd with an heap of stones.'

Almost seven months after the find, Sir Christopher Wren received a Warrant, signed by the Earl of Arlington, one of the King's Ministers, commissioning him to design 'A Marble Coffin for two princes': 'These are to signifie his Majesties pleasure that you provide a white Marble Coffin for the supposed bodies of ye two Princes lately found in ye Tower of London and that you cause the same to be interred in Henry ye 7th Chappell in such convenient place as the Deane of Westminster shall appoynt. And this shalbe yor warrant. Given under my hand this 18th day of February 1675. ARLINGTON.' [1].

Three things become clear from the above accounts. First, that the bones were at first thrown out with other rubbish by the workmen, who were then ordered to replace them when their find became known, and especially the significance of the place where they had been found. It is therefore possible that, while the bones were lying among other rubbish, some of them may have been lost or stolen, or even mixed with other bones which may have belonged to other skeletons or, once their possible importance was realised, some bones may even have been sold as relics, for certain finger bones were missing, and some chicken bones and three rusty nails were amongst them when they were examined in 1933.

Second: the bones were then handed over to the custody of Sir Thomas Chichley, Master of the Ordinance, under whose direction the workmen were clearing the steps with a view to rebuilding several offices in the Tower. Chichley kept them, it is not stated where, until Sir Christopher Wren had designed a suitable White Marble Coffin for the bones. But it was about four years before they were actually deposited, in their urn, in the Henry VII Chapel in Westminster Abbey.

Thirdly: it will be realised that there were two reasons why King Charles' advisers persuaded the King that these were in fact the bones of the two Princes: one, that some rags of velvet were found with them (signifying a noble family), and two, that Sir Thomas More had written in his unfinished 'History of King Richard III': . . . 'caused those murderers to bury them at the stayre-foote, metely depe in the grounde under a great heape of stones.' Evidently the King's advisers had not troubled to read the next paragraph but one in More's 'History', where he twice refutes his own story: first, by adding that a priest was sent to dig them up and rebury them elsewhere 'secretly' but that, as the priest died almost immediately with his secret undisclosed, no-one knew where they were; and second, that 'some remain yet in doubt whether they were in his [Richard III's] days destroyed or no'.[2]. In other words, that nobody had been able to find the bodies of the two boys. Sir Thomas More goes even further in destroying his own evidence by saying that, when Sir James Tyrell was held in the Tower for 'treason against the most famous Prince, King Henry the Seventh, both Dighton [one of the murderers named by More] and he were examined, and confessed the murder in manner above

written, but whither the bodies were removed they could nothing tell'.[3].
In fact, Sir James Tyrell was not accused of the murder of the Princes and
no confession has ever been seen.

The strangest part of the whole story of the bones, surely, is that
although it was of extreme importance to Henry when he came to the
throne, to find either the whereabouts or the remains of the two boys, and
if he had done so, he would hardly have kept quiet about the discovery;
but as Sir George Buck says: 'For this is clearly true, that there was much
and diligent search made for their bodies in the Tower. And all these
places were opened and digged where it was said or supposed their
bodies were laid. But they could never be found by any search.'[4].
How is it, then, that no bones or bodies were found during Henry
VII's reign, but that two children's skeletons were found one hundred
and ninety-one years later more or less where More first said they were
located, but from whence he said they were removed? Could it be that
the reason is that they were the bones of completely different children?
— for, if we are asked to believe that a priest dug them up and reburied
them somewhere else, it follows that the bones found in that particular
spot cannot be those of the Princes.

As if this were not confusing enough, there are other stories of
children's bones being discovered in the Tower (many human bones
were found in the moat when it was drained in 1830), and one set was
believed to be those of the Princes.

There is a reference in a note on the flyleaf of a 17th Century edition
of Sir Thomas More's 'Historie of the Pitifull life and Unfortunate death
of Edward Fifth', which states:- 'August 17th, 1647, When ye Lord Grey
of Wilton and Sir Walter Ralegh were prisoners in ye Tower, the wall
of ye passage to ye Kings Lodgings then sounding hollow, was taken
down and at ye place marked A was found a little roome about 7 or 8ft
square, wherein there stood a Table and upon it ye bones of Two children
supposed of 6 or 8 yeares of age, which by ye aforesayd nobles and all
present were credibly beleeved to bee ye carcasses of Edward ye 5th and
his brother the then Duke of York. This gent was also an eye witness at ye
opening of it with Mr. Palmer and Mr. Henry Cogan, officers of ye mint
and others, with whom having since discoursed hereof they affirmed ye
same to me and yt they saw the skeletons'[5]. The 'gent' referred to was
a Mr. Johnson, son of Sir Robert Johnson, and a Counsellor. There is a
plan appended, showing the place where the remains were found, marked

with an A. The note is signed 'J. Webb.' and is in the handwriting of the period. The date of the find can be established by the mention of Lord Grey and Sir Walter Ralegh who were imprisoned together in the Tower from 1603 to 1613. The 'Webb', writer of this note on the flyleaf, is not further identified, but the information appears over the signature 'Evan Daniel' in 'Notes and Queries', Dec.21.1889; a gentleman who says the book is in his possession, or was at that time.

This story of an earlier find of children's bones in the Tower appears to receive confirmation from an MS which is a translation from Sir Aubrey de Maurier's 'History of the Prince Maurice, Prince of Orange'. The relevant passage is:- 'The same Prince Maurice likewise told my Father that in Queen Elizabeth's time, the Tower of London being full of Prisoners of State, on account of the frequent conspiracies against her person, as they were troubled to find room for them all, they bethought themselves of opening a door of a Chamber that had been walled up for a long time; and they found in this Chamber upon a bed the skeletons of King Edward V and the Duke of York, his brother, whom their Uncle Richard the Cruel had strangled to get the Crown to himself, which Henry VII, Grandfather to Queen Elizabeth, deprived him of, together with his life. But the prudent Princess, not willing to revive the memory of such an action, ordered the door to be walled up as before. Nevertheless, I am informed that this same door having been opened some time since, and the skeletons being found in the same place, the King of England, out of compassion that these two princes were deprived of burial, or from other reasons that I am ignorant of, has resolved to erect a Mausoleum to their memory, and have them buried in Westminster Abbey among the Kings'.

The whole story, however, appears to be a muddle of dates and facts, since Queen Elizabeth died in 1603 and, unless the discovery was made in the last months of her life, the monarch on the throne would then be James I; but the story goes on to say that the King had them buried in Westminster Abbey among the Kings; which brings the whole event into confusion with the bones in the urn now in Westminster Abbey: yet it is hardly likely that the bones discovered in a Chamber in the Tower in 1603 would have been reburied in a wooden chest beneath the stone stairs, to be re-discovered by workmen in 1674!

If the account on the flyleaf of Sir Thomas More's book were not so detailed and circumstantial, and apparently well attested, one would take

FIGURE 1

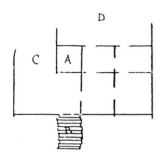

A   The "Little roome".
B   The Stayres leading out of Cole Harbour to ye King's Lodgings.
C   Passage to ye Kings Lodgings.
D   Ye Guard Chamber.

1   St. Thomas' Tower
2   Bloody (or Garden) Tower
3   Cole (Cold) Harbour Tower and Gate
4   "Forebuilding" demolished 1674 (where bones found 1603-13?)
5   Steps to White Tower (where bones found 1674)
6   Spiral stair leading to Chapel of St. John
7   King's Lodgings (demolished 1674-1900)

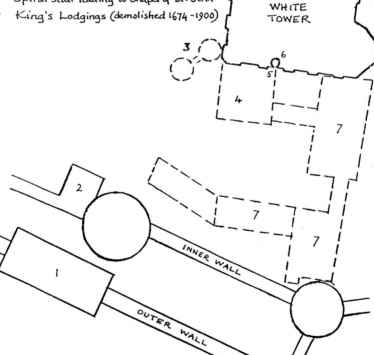

Diagram of the White Tower

the date 17th July 1647 to be a confusion with the finding of the later skeletons on 17th August 1674. Though the earlier find must have been between 1603 and 1613, the coincidence of the *report* of this find with the date of the second find is striking. If this does in fact refer to two separate finds reported on confusingly similar dates, why should not the finding of bones of two children of approximately the same ages as the Princes, in the second excavation, also be a coincidence?

Sir George Buck in his 'History of King Richard the Third' written in 1619, reports another finding of bones said to be those of the Princes, which were found in a 'high and desolate turret in the Tower', but this was only one skeleton, and was eventually concluded to be the carcase of an ape (the Tower at that time housing the royal menagerie) who had climbed up there and had been unable to get down again. Apart from absurdities in both stories, such as Queen Elizabeth having ordered the door to be bricked up again — what possible reason could she have had for doing so? — we have the French Chronicler, Jean Molinet, writing many years later, saying they were 'shut up in a great dungeon, without air, food or water'[6]. This was a 'great' dungeon, not a small chamber (and therefore could hardly have been without air), and apparently in spite of their being deprived of food and water, it was still necessary to send in murderers to kill them.

Perhaps the one solid fact that can be drawn from all this is the power of suggestion that can lead people to make facts fit a known legend; a failing to which even scientists can be liable, as we shall see. The Princes had disappeared while they were in the Tower: bones are found there in approximately the place described by one source, though he himself withdrew it: therefore these bones must be those of the Princes. But if they were not the bones of the Princes, to whom do they belong? For they are still in their urn at Westminster Abbey supposed by the vast numbers of people who gaze at that urn, to be those of the Princes. Before going into the question of their possible identity as the Princes in detail, it may be as well to consider what sort of place the Tower of London was in the late fifteenth century.

It certainly was not thought of as a prison but as a palace where Kings traditionally stayed to await their coronation: the 'Bloody' Tower did not acquire that grim epithet until later Tudor times, when religious martyrs were kept there prior to their execution. In the last Plantagenet days it was still known as the Garden Tower, a porter's lodge with a pleasant garden in which the Princes were seen shooting and playing. It was above all a small town of busy families engaged in their various tasks, keeping the life of the community going; about six hundred people in all. Among them would be many children, some, no doubt, of the nobility whose parents might stay there briefly while engaged on business of the King's: playing in the gardens or on the river bank, watching the ships with their cargoes docking at the wharves and unloading their goods; reloading with the wool and other exports for foreign customers. There would be many outbreaks of slight as well as serious diseases, some of them perhaps brought by those very ships from foreign parts: many children would unfortunately die, but since so many children failed anyway to reach maturity or even puberty, their deaths would hardly cause much surprise or even horror. Some might have been buried hurriedly within the precincts of the Tower (perhaps as near as possible to the consecrated ground of the Chapel of St. John within the White Tower, marked as 6 on the accompanying map) because they had died mysteriously of some contagious or infectious complaint, curable today but alarming in those days of little or no medical knowledge. There had even been children killed in 'foundation sacrifices' in Roman times. There were also murders of children for revengeful reasons: there is the story that the two sons of the Earl of Desmond were killed in Ireland at the instigation of the Queen, Elizabeth Woodville, in revenge for an uncomplimentary remark alleged to have been made by their father the Earl to Edward IV on the subject of the King's marriage to Elizabeth.

Of course, like every mediæval castle in the country, the Tower had its prison, but if it had not been first and foremost a palace, Henry VII would hardly have sent his Queen there to have her last child. The fact that both the Queen and the baby died there has never been attributed to any sinister cause: damp and unhealthy though it may have been according to our standards, but no more so than most castles were in those days.

So, in order to try to settle the matter of identifying the 'supposed bones of the Princes' in the urn in Westminster Abbey, permission was sought and granted in 1933 for the urn to be opened and its contents examined by the most up-to-date methods known to science at that time. Dr. William Wright, Dean of the London Hospital Medical College and President of the Anatomical Society, and Mr. Lawrence Tanner, Keeper of the Muniments at Westminster Abbey, were given charge of the examination, while Dr. George Northcroft, late President of the Dental Association and British Society of Orthodontists, made a detailed examination of the teeth in order to try to establish the ages of the children[7].

Examination of the bones themselves led Prof. Wright to conclude that they were the bones of two children who could have been the right ages for the Princes in 1483, but too young to be those of the Princes in 1485. The presence of Wormian bones (which are extra isolated irregular small bones seen occasionally in the sutures which join the component bones of the cranium) was taken as evidence of consanguinity, as was the presence of unerupted teeth in the jawbones of the children. There was a stain on the jawbone of one child, which was taken to indicate possible death by suffocation or strangulation, and the elder child appeared to have been suffering from osteitis of the jaw. The two great questions which take precedence over all others are: When did these children die, and what was their sex? Although Professor Wright admitted in response to questioning that sex could not be determined before puberty, the identification with boys has been assumed throughout. When they were scientifically examined in 1933, no greater accuracy in dating with the methods then obtaining could be made other than to give them one hundred years either way. In other words, the skeletons could belong to any century up to the seventeenth. Even today, with the vastly improved radio-carbon method of dating, accuracy cannot be guaranteed nearer than fifty years either way. Nevertheless, the Wright-Tanner report[8] concluded that the bones were the right ages to have been the Princes in 1483, but not in 1485; that the elder was probably between twelve and thirteen and a half, and the younger nine or ten years old. Dr. Northcroft, having examined the teeth, agreed with the finding on the probable ages of the children.

But in 1963 Dr. Richard Lyne-Pirkis, a noted anatomist and the expert cited by Paul Murray Kendall in his Notes on the Appendix in his book 'Richard III', was asked to lecture to the Richard III Society. He illustrated his lecture with slides of the X-rays of the bones of 'the Princes', in detailing the growth of cartilage into bone in babies and children, and showed that there is a great deal of difference between the apparent age of a bone as seen on an X-ray plate, and the real age. He concluded that not enough is known about diet and its effect on teeth and bones in the fifteenth century accurately to pinpoint the ages of the skeletons within four years either way; that heredity must be taken into account (i.e. if their father was Edward IV, whose height was over 6 ft) they might well be taller than average, while the apparent osteitis in the jawbone of the elder might well have slowed down his growth, and the supposition that the stain on the jawbone of one child was due to suffocation was untenable because of the presence in the urn of three rusty nails, which could have caused the discolouration. No tests as to the possibility of the stain having been that of blood were carried out by Prof. Wright and Mr Tanner.

Since then many experts have queried the Tanner-Wright findings, and two of the most recent analyses follow:

On 29th June 1985, at the Glazier's Hall, London, the Richard III Society held a Symposium entitled 'The Fate of the Princes'. Dr. Theya Molleson, of the Department of Anthropology, British Museum of Natural History, gave an illustrated talk on 'the evidence of human skeletal remains, both general and particular': in effect, the bones of the Princes. By studying the X-rays of the bones, in the light of the report issued by Dr. Wright and Mr Tanner, and by comparison with the remains of Anne Mowbray and other examples from mediæval times, Dr. Molleson showed how, from close-up examination of unerupted teeth in the jawbones, as well as of bones in the skulls, a reasonably accurate estimate could be made of the age and the sex of the skeletons. She concluded that the younger one, although more advanced in skeletal and dental development than the older one, was that of a nine or ten year old, and the older that of a thirteen or fourteen year old. Both were, according to the size and position of the teeth, boys. Once again, no estimate as to the possible cause of death, or of the date when they died; even of the century they died in, and no more positive identification other than their being possibly male, was given.

In 1986 the Richard III and Yorkist History Trust published a book entitled 'Richard III: Loyalty Lordship and Law', edited by P. W. Hammond and containing an article on 'The Sons of Edward IV: a re-examination of the evidence on their deaths and on the Bones in Westminster Abbey', by P. W. Hammond and W. J. White. This article examines the whole controversy of the possible deaths or escapes from death of the two Princes, and includes material not discussed here, amongst which is a report in the *Divisie Chronicle* of the Low Countries[9] suggesting that the boys were starved to death or possibly murdered by the Duke of Buckingham, adding that 'some say' that Buckingham spared one of the children *'which he had lifted from the font and had him secretly abducted out of the country'*. The article by Hammond and White examines Sir

Thomas More's story that the bodies of the Princes were hidden in the Tower 'at the stayre foote, metely depe in the grounde under a great heape of stones'. As already mentioned, More goes on to say that they were subsequently moved to a 'better' location 'because thei wer a kinges sonnes' (or possibly thrown into the Thames in a weighted coffin); the actual course of events known only to a priest who was now dead — this latter point is presumably to explain why the bodies had not been dug up and exhibited by Henry. Attention is drawn to the inescapable fact that this has not prevented bones discovered almost anywhere in the Tower from being attributed to the sons of Edward IV; and the enormous turnover of residents in the Tower in mediæval times makes it inevitable that human remains should be found. Hammond cites the case of one Plantagenet whose remains have never been found; those of Henry Pole, son of Lord Montague and grandson of Margaret Countess of Salisbury (who was beheaded by Henry VIII at the age of 69). Henry Pole was 16 when he was thrown into the Tower in 1539; it was believed that he was starved to death, since he was never seen again. In 1977, says Hammond, during an excavation of the Inmost Ward of the Tower, a skeleton of a youth between the ages of thirteen and sixteen was found, and the bones dated firmly to the late Iron Age. This important find emphasises, continues Hammond, not only the continuity of human occupation of the site over the last two thousand years, but underlines the possibility of the so-called Princes' bones being in reality also of a much greater antiquity than popularly supposed. Who can doubt, he asks, that if the remains of this youth had been found three hundred years ago, here would have been Edward V? He also pinpoints another small mystery in connection with the 'Bones of the Princes', saying that the scraps of velvet which presupposed a royal or a noble occupant of the tomb, were apparently present at the opening of the chest or coffin in 1674, but absent from the urn when it was opened in 1933.

But two most vital points, potentially damaging to the long-held theory of the Princes' bones being in the urn in Westminster Abbey are:-

1. Measurement of the length of the limb bones in the urn with consideration of their skeletal age, indicates an age difference of between eighteen months and two years, instead of almost three years which would be the case with the Princes. Comparison of the bone lengths to try and

determine height and age again indicates a smaller difference in age than the three-year gap between the Princes.

2. The crowns of the teeth are generally larger in boys than in girls and the most important tooth for sex determination is the lower permanent canine tooth. This tooth survives unerupted in the jaw of the younger child, and if the published X-ray is to scale, as it is less than 7mm in diameter (contrary to Dr. Molleson's conclusions) there is the possibility that the owner of the skull was female. This possibility is further enhanced by the absence of a wisdom tooth in the jaw of the older child, which might tend to show that it was the skull of a female, since these teeth are more frequently absent in females than in males. This exciting possibility could obviously now be determined by a new examination of the bones, since Hammond states it is now possible to sex pre-pubertal skeletons; one expert having the enviable reputation of being able to sex with unerring accuracy even the bones of foetuses. The co-operation of the authorities at Westminster Abbey would, therefore, be of inestimable value in clearing up at least this part of the five-hundred-year-old mystery, but although in 1980 the Richard III Society made a further application to the Dean and Chapter of Westminster to allow the urn to be reopened for a more up-to-date examination, this has been refused on the grounds that the remains ought now to rest in peace. Yet on this supposedly scientific evidence is founded the case against Richard III for the murder of the 'little Princes in the Tower'.

Imagine if you will, bringing a charge of murder, even against persons unknown, for the deaths of these children in a modern court (or any court except possibly a Tudor one) given the facts: no evidence as to date of death within, say, two hundred years; no evidence as to age, sex or cause of death, other than supposition and hearsay. Imagine the protests of the media if the case were not immediately thrown out as an impudent waste of the magistrate's time.

Note:-
Readers who wish to go into the minutiae of all the points raised in the above Chapter cannot do better than to read the Tanner-Wright

report in Archaeologia LXXXIV; the excellent analysis of it by the late Audrey Williamson in her 'The Mystery of the Princes: an Investigation into a Supposed Murder' and the Hammond-White article 'The Sons of Edward IV: A Re-examination of the Evidence on their deaths and on the Bones in Westminster Abbey' in the book 'Richard III: Loyalty Lordship and Law. 1986.'

CHAPTER SEVEN

The Young Exile

'. . . Whereas the Prince of Wales, eldest son of Edward formerly King of England, was miserably put to death and I myself, then about nine years old, was also delivered to a certain lord to be killed, it pleased the Divine Clemency that that lord, having compassion on my innocence, preserved me alive and in safety, first, however, causing me to swear on the Holy Sacrament, that to no-one should I disclose my name, origin or family, until a certain number of years had passed. He sent me therefore abroad, with two persons who should watch over and take charge of me; and thus I, an orphan, bereaved of my royal father and brother, an exile from my kingdom and deprived of country, inheritance and fortune, a fugitive in the midst of extreme perils, led my miserable life, in fear, and weeping and grief, and for the space of nearly eight years lay hid in divers provinces. At length, one of those who had charge of me being dead, and the other returned to his country and never afterwards seen, scarcely had I emerged from childhood, alone and without means, I remained for a time in the Kingdom of Portugal . . .'*

The above is an extract from a letter, now in the British Museum[1] and addressed to Isabella, Queen of Spain, who was the great granddaughter of John of Gaunt. The letter is signed 'Richard', in what Sir Frederic Madden, F.R.S., F.S.A, a distinguished antiquarian and palaeographer of the nineteenth century, calls a bold and thoroughly English hand. It is written from the town of Dendermonde, (then in Austrian Flanders and under the jurisdiction of the Archduke Philip), on the 8th calends of September (25th August) 1493, and was in Latin. It is made clear that 'Richard' is Richard Plantagenet, second son of Edward formerly King; Duke of York, etc, who was also a great grandson of John of Gaunt. The writer addresses the Queen as 'My most honoured Lady and Cousin', and

*Given in full in Appendix II

goes on to ask for her help in persuading King Ferdinand of Spain to assist him to regain his kingdom.

It is of interest that, though historians who regard 'Perkin Warbeck', as Henry came to call him, as an impostor because 'it is well-known' that Richard murdered the Princes, the writer of this letter makes no such charge, merely saying that 'a certain lord' who had already murdered his brother, was about to kill him, but had mercy on his innocence. Critics have pointed out the unlikelihood of a murderer, having killed one boy in order to seize the throne for himself, leaving the second boy, now the heir to the throne, alive. This argument would appear to indict Henry Tudor or his partisans rather than Richard III. It must be remembered that the Pretender's claim, as the rightful heir of York, had to be based on the fact that Richard III was a usurper, and later references to his and his brother's fate, albeit reported by Tudor historians, naturally accuse Richard of the murder, which in any case made a better story. But in accepting the main gist of what the young man says about his youth, it is not necessary to believe all he says. It is highly unlikely that a nine or ten year old boy would be told all the plots, counter-plots and political motives around his brother and himself. If the plot was to hide him until he had grown up, it was necessary to keep him from betraying to anyone who he was or where he came from. There could hardly have been a better way to ensure a terrified boy's silence than to point out that his brother was no more, and that he would also die if he did not keep his mouth shut. It is not, unfortunately, possible to identify the 'two who had charge' of him, especially as he says one died. It is also of interest that, when he was of an age to come out of hiding and reveal more about those unhappy eight years, he still preserved that secrecy to the day of his death. But Bacon reports that he contrasted the behaviour of King Henry with that of his uncle King Richard, saying of the latter: 'Although desire of rule did blind him, yet in his other actions, like a true Plantagenet, was noble, and loved the honour of the realm, and the contentment and comfort of his nobles and people.'[2]

However, it is perhaps unwise to give the letter too much emphasis, apart from its 'typically English' signature, because it appears to have been an exercise in propaganda — trying to win Queen Isabella's sympathy for his cause — the first foray made by the young man into diplomacy. Sir Frederic Madden wrote slightingly of the 'indifferent Latin' in which it was written. Does he mean mistakes were made, such as using the words 'about nine' when he should have written 'ten'? But then, Madden himself gives the date of the birth of Prince Richard as 1472 instead of 1473.

It has been pointed out to me that one can never prove the validity of any birth certificate, and that we believe what our parents tell us. This must especially be true of a birth over five hundred years ago, yet I think one cannot carry cynicism to an absurd conclusion. The accompanying portraits of King Edward IV and the man who has gone down to history as 'Perkin Warbeck' deserve close study, because they reveal quite startling similarities, especially in the tips of the noses and the mouths. When one reflects that these portraits were executed in different countries, by different artists, and at least twenty years apart, and were certainly not intended to show likeness one to the other, one must concede, I think, that the younger man could certainly be a son of the older one. This, of course, brings us to the possibility that 'Perkin' was an illegitimate son of Edward IV, as history has decided he was, but it also overlooks two things. First, if that was so, why did Henry VII spend so much effort in trying to make out that 'Perkin' was only the son of Jehan and Nicaise Werbecque? King Edward IV's acknowledged bastard son, Arthur Plantagenet, was not similarly denigrated, and in fact served Henry VIII loyally until he died in the Tower, pardoned by the King for no other offence but that of being a Plantagenet, in 1542. Secondly, if 'Perkin' was the son of Edward IV by Nicaise Werbecque, he must have been conceived during the winter visit of Edward and his brother Richard to Flanders in 1470–1, which would make their child older than 'Perkin'; and there is no reason to believe that the Werbecques ever came to England. It could also be of interest that the portrait of 'Perkin', which is only an artist's first draft for a portrait, bears the notes for the future colouring of hair and clothes. The word 'Lon' on the hair is apparently interpreted as 'blonde', which is interesting in itself if he was the son of Nicaise Werbecque; she was of Portuguese extraction, a race not usually noted for blondness, whereas Elizabeth Woodville was what we would call 'platinum blonde' in these days. Horace Walpole, writing his 'Historic Doubts' in defence of Richard III, says: '. . . The Earl of Shaftesbury was so good as to inform me that his ancestor the Lady Ashley, who lived to a great age, had conversed with Lady Desmond (that Countess of Desmond who could remember Edward IV and Richard III), with this strong addition that Perkin Warbeck was remarkably like Edward IV'.[3]

Underneath the sketch of the Pretender, which is among the MS of the Arras Library, are the words: 'Pierre Warbeck native of Tournay taken for Richard Duke of York second son of Edward IV King of England, the year 1492, was hanged in London at the end of the year 1499'.

Beneath this portrait are photographs of two medallions which Dr. Desmons, an historian of Tournai who wrote an article on 'Perkin Warbeck' in 1910 in the 'Revue Tournaisienne' and which he entitles 'A Tournaisian pretender to the throne of England', describes as having been minted in the year 1492. But the silver gros (a small silver coin current in the North of Germany from the 13th to the 19th centuries) has the date 1494 on the reverse side. For a detailed description of these medallions, I cannot do better than to quote M. Longpérier, a noted numismatist of Tournai, who wrote in the 'Revue numismatique' of 1860:-

Obverse: DOMINE: SALUUM: FAC: REGEM. Within a garland of five arcs, an English écu [French silver coin] stamped with a royal crown and accosted [bordered] on the right with a fleur de lis, on the left with a rose, both crowned.

Reverse: MANI: TECKEL. PHARES. 1494. Within a garland of four arcs, a fleur de lis on the right, a leopard on the left, a closed crown above, a rose below. In the text, on obverse as on reverse side, a leopard rampant.

Regarding the second medallion, Longpérier describes it as a copper mark, struck at Tournai, and which probably refers to Werbecque.

On the obverse side one reads:- : † VIVE PERKIN. JETOIS DE TOURNAI around a cross capped with fleurs de lis, ornamented with four branches of a rose-tree.

On the reverse side:- † O MATER DEI MEMENTO MEI. A small tower completes the legend.

For the silver gros, described by M. Longpérier as 'an English écu', the legend on the obverse has been translated by an eminent Latinist as 'May the Lord save the King' [Richard IV], and on the reverse side Peter Hammond, Research Officer of the Richard III Society, has made the scholarly deduction that the legend is a fifteenth century rendering of the words 'MENE MENE TEKEL UPHARSIN' which are to be found, as knowledgeable readers of the Bible will know, in the Book of Daniel, Chapter Five, Verses 24–28, and which the Bible renders as: 'MENE: God hath numbered thy kingdom, and finished it. TEKEL: Thou art weighed in the balances, and art found wanting.' The word 'UPHARSIN' is not mentioned; instead the word 'PERES' is given, and translated as 'Thy kingdom is divided, and given to the Medes and Persians'. The second medallion, the copper mark, has as its legend on the obverse the words 'Long live Perkin. I was from Tournai', and on the reverse: 'O Mother of God remember me'. The purpose of these coins is somewhat obscure, because although the silver gros purports to acclaim 'the King', its reverse side bears such a very obvious and alarming warning to that 'King', that it is hard to believe it could have been minted at the instigation of the Yorkists in Flanders, as Dr. Desmons suggests. With regard to the second coin, its message would seem to be wholly antagonistic to the Pretender. Perhaps both coins are an early example of an entrepreneurial attempt to attract the tourist trade, and to establish a foot in both camps.

A homely clue, unconfirmed from any other source, as to 'Perkin's' identity, comes from an outlying member of the Werbecque family, one Nathaniel Osbeck, who responded predictably some years later to Henry's well-paid appeal for persons to come forward who had known 'Perkin' in his boyhood in Flanders. Nathaniel's 'testimony' bore out what Henry wished to hear: he averred that the boy was called 'Perkin' in the family because of his 'Effeminateness and Childishness'[4]. But Nathaniel's remark can be construed another way: the son of bourgeois parents in Tournai would excite little attention locally, but a fair boy with hands that were unused to work and ways that spoke of refinement, might certainly excite comment from the neighbours. And on 'Perkin's' own testimony we know that he spent the first years of his stay in the Low Countries in 'fear, and weeping and grief' — just the sort of behaviour which would earn the reproof of being 'Effeminate and Childish' from the stolid Dutch.

But from Henry's point of view, the fact of the boy's association with the Werbecque family was sufficient proof that he was born into their family circle, and he made the utmost capital out of it.

CHAPTER EIGHT

The Werbecques of Tournai

To try to trace the career of the man whom Henry VII called 'Perkin Warbeck' (in the way that English people habitually anglicise foreign names), we must first try to trace the real Perkin Warbeck, if there was one, or more properly Pierrechon, or Pierrequin, de Werbecque.

For those readers who wish to consult the Tournai Archives as they appeared in 1893, I have shown them separately in Appendix I, but for those who are not particularly interested in documentation, I give the somewhat sparse information on the family in a more digestible form.

In fact, the Archives of Tournai were destroyed by German bombing in 1940, but fortunately a copy, dated 1893, is preserved in an article by a local historian, Count P.A. Chastel de la Howarderie, entitled 'Notes sûr la famille de l'aventurier Perkin Warbeck'. Interestingly, he begins by saying 'Though all historians who speak of England and Tournai must mention Perkin Warbeck, *no-one has been able to say where this person comes from*' (my italics). It is a great pity that, having whetted our appetites for some amazing theory which he might produce to support this statement, he does not elucidate further. We must also beware because Chastel, as I shall call him for brevity, confesses that not all his information is obtained from the registers of Tournai: he gives as his main source of information the historian Lingard, the man whose comment on the 'imperfect and unsatisfactory' document of 'Perkin's' 'confession' is that one can see that Warbeck must have been born in Tournai because the name Jehan Osbeck is easily recognisable as Werbecque! It is therefore necessary to separate documented information from Chastel's personal opinions and comments, remembering that all historical opinion in those days was almost entirely Tudor-inspired. Dr. Desmons, in his article in the 'Revue Tournaisienne' somewhat after the turn of the nineteenth century, admits to having culled his comments from Gairdner and other pro-Tudor sources. A further difficulty appears in that the law to enforce registry of births was not always obeyed; deaths were registered at the time of probate of Wills, but even there, there is a slight confusion over the use of the word 'before' in the records. For instance, a death may be recorded as having taken place 'before May', when what is meant is 'before the end of May'.

But to pursue the facts about the Werbecque family:-

Grandfather Dieric (or Thiery), a carpenter and boat-builder, and a native of Berne-les-Audenarde, purchased the rights of citizenship of Tournai in 1429. His name is mentioned in an Act passed in 1442, when he was living in the parish of St. John des Cauffours on the bank of the River Scheldt in Tournai. He died in May 1474 and left one legitimate son, (Dr. Desmons says in his article, above-mentioned, that Dieric de Werbecque had two other children, presumably illegitimate: a daughter Jehanne, who married Jehan Stalyn, and a son, Noel). The legitimate son, Jehan de Werbecque (the 'de' was dropped later), took up his right of burghership at Tournai as the son of a native burgher, during the year of his marriage. This took place in 1473; he married Nicaise (or Caisine) Faroul or Faro, of a family long established in Tournai.[1] There is in fact a place called Faro on the South coast of the Algarve in Portugal.

Jehan was the father of four children, two legitimate and two natural. The legitimate were Pierrechon (or Pierre) Werbecque, born in 1474 (but this date is not registered; it may have been guessed at because of the date of marriage in 1473). Secondly, a daughter, Jehanne Werbecque (date of birth not registered), married during 1509 to Master Jehan Cambier, with whom she was still living in 1517.

The natural children were two sons:- Colin (or Nicolas) Werbecque, brought up at Pipais in the house of Mathieu Balguiem, and Innocent Werbecque, who received from his father the sum of ten pounds.

Jehan Werbecque died in December 1498, and on 20th December 1498 his widow Nicaise, accompanied by Pierre Flan and Adrien Carlier, tutors and guardians of her children Pierrechon and Jehanne, sold her house situated on the Scheldt at Cauffours to Jehan Vallois.[2] Nicaise then married Jehan de la Croix, who died in November 1509. She died on 12th April 1513, leaving as her sole heiress Jehanne Werbecque, married to Jehan Cambier. Nicaise also left small legacies to Colin and Innocent, the natural sons of her first husband Jehan Werbecque, and a legacy for perpetual Mass to be said for her soul in the chapel of the Hospice of

Marvis.[3] No mention is made of Pierrechon Werbecque, but Chastel
cannot resist giving a thumbnail sketch of 'Perkin's' imposture, leaving
the impression that these 'facts' are in the Archives of Tournai, but no-one
can now say with certainty that this is so, or, indeed, who 'Pierrechon'
was. Was he a legitimate son of the Werbecques who died as a child and
whose name was taken as a cover by the little Richard of York, to hide
him from Henry's agents? Why did Nicaise Werbecque employ 'tutors
and guardians' of her two children, if they were ordinary bourgeois
children born Werbecques? Was the money which Sir James Tyrell
brought over to Flanders payment for the guardians of the little Duke
of York? Was this money the source of the Werbecques' comfortable
way of living? Lastly, were the Werbecques recommended by Brampton,
whose trade with Antwerp and Bruges through Middelburgh was now
booming? Whatever the truth behind these questions, Brampton is
probably the link.

By way of throwing some light, but not much, on the time 'Perkin' (or
Pierrechon) spent in Tournai or thereabouts, we must now consult the
'confession'[4], the genuineness or otherwise of which will be dealt with
later, and which appears as it was taken down, in Appendix VII. This
then, purports to be the catalogue of the boy's movements:-

1. He first went to Jehan Stalyn who lived in the parish of St. Pyas
in Tournai, and who was married to an illegitimate sister of Jehan
Werbecque, by the name of Jehanne or Jane, for a 'certain season'.
2. He was taken by Nicaise Werbecque to Antwerp to the house of a
cousin of hers called John Stienbeck, who was an officer of Antwerp,
in order to learn Flemish. He was there for six months, after which
he was forced to return to Tournai because of the war which broke
out in Flanders at that time. Gairdner gives the probable date as either
1483 or 1484.[5] Dr. Desmons says that these wars occurred from the
end of 1483 to June 1485[6]. If we assume that the boy in question was
really the young prince and not 'Pierrechon Werbecque', the year 1484
is the most likely date for his return to Tournai, because he had already
spent six months or so with Jehan Stalyn, and this would accord with his
having left England some time in 1483. The young prince would have
been eleven years old in 1484, if it was indeed he who was in Antwerp
at this time. But the intriguing possibility remains that this account may
refer to the real 'Pierrechon' who may have died as a result of these wars,

or of the sickness mentioned below, and the prince may have taken over his identity at this point.

3. Within a year after this (probably just after June 1485, when the war ended), he returned to Antwerp with a Tournaisian merchant called Berlo, whose master's name was Alex, to the market there. He fell ill, and was ill for five months, so Berlo sent him to board at a tanner's house next door to the 'English House' — perhaps where the Yorkists could keep an eye on him? Thence he went to the Barowe Market. Chastelain, the Belgian author of a biography on 'Warbeck' entitled 'L'Imposture de Perkin Warbeck', says that no such place as 'Barrow Market' existed in Antwerp, and deduces that he probably means the neighbourhood of the Pont de Brouettiers or Cruyderbrugghe behind the Town Hall, where the house of the important corporation of the barrowers was built. In this neighbourhood, leading off from the bridge, is the Manstrate or street where there is the 'Old Man Inn' in which 'Perkin' says he lodged. The Manstrate or street is beside the Great Market and very near the Oude Beurs, where was situated the House of the Merchant Adventurers (perhaps what 'Perkin' meant in his 'confession' by 'The House of the English Nation')[7].

But in the French version of the 'confession' given by Dr. Desmons, there is no mention of 'Perkin' having indicated the Barrow Market, in spite of Dr. Desmons' production of the text in full, in French and English;[8], Dr. Desmons says he went to Bergen-op-Zoom. Such are the conflicting statements in the text of the confession, possibly due to hurried or wrong translations or misunderstanding, but Dr. Desmons should know his Antwerp. Yet one has to remember that the whole document was probably put together by Henry VII's agents, and 'Perkin' was forced to sign it. His movements as a child would have been fairly easy for Henry's agents to trace, since no other attempt at disguise was made, apart from the alias. As to the mistakes, which will be discussed later, Henry's spies may simply have been unfamiliar with Flanders or the places mentioned. 'Perkin' stayed at the Old Man Inn for two months, bringing us to the probable date of Christmas 1485.

4. Berlo then sent him with a merchant to do service with one John Strewe, to learn the language. (It is not clear which language is meant). Here he stayed from Christmas till Easter 1486. Chastelain says it was in the house of the Englishman John Strewe that 'Perkin' met Lady Brampton[9] and, while Henry would have us believe that the young

man was learning English, it is more likely that he was there in order to concert plans with the Yorkists for his future in which, as we shall see, Lady Brampton was involved. Brampton had remarried, but it is not clear whether his new wife was an Englishwoman. What is evident is that the youth spent very little time actually with the Werbecques in spite of his tender age on arrival: a little time in 1483, and less than a year from 1484–5.

5. From here he went to Portugal (his 'confession' only mentions the presence of Lady Brampton, but Dr. Cecil Roth, whose lectures on Brampton I have consulted, says that Brampton returned to Portugal that same year because he 'embarked at Middelburgh for Portugal, taking into his service as attendant upon his wife, a lad from Tournai named Perkin Warbeck')[10]. Dr. Roth stated that it was the late spring of 1486 when the three went to Portugal, but he later had evidence that it was 1487.[11] He also says that there is some evidence that Brampton paid a fleeting visit to England at about this time, trying to escape notice. If this is so, it suggests his activities had been highly unpopular with Henry VII, and it was not until 1489 that he won his way back into English favour by receiving with great charm and lavish hospitality an English embassy to Portugal that year.[12] Dr. Roth has an intriguing theory that Brampton won his pardon from Henry by 'ratting' on 'Warbeck'. As a result, Henry issued Brampton with a general pardon under the Privy Seal, and when his son came to England in 1500 Henry knighted him at Winchester.[13]

6. In Portugal 'Warbeck' took service with Sir Peter de Cogna, a one-eyed Knight who lived in Lisbon, and was with him for a year. Thus the youth would have been some fourteen years old, evidently beginning to feel his feet, and anxious to begin his challenge to Henry. He says that, because he wished to see other countries, he took leave of de Cogna and took service with a Breton called Pregent (Pierre-Jean) Meno, and eventually came to Ireland with him. This service with Meno must have lasted about three years, because it was not until the autumn of 1491 that he landed with Meno at Cork.[14] This Pregent Meno was evidently a man of importance, not the ordinary trader he has been made out to be. He was granted the privilege of Irish citizenship, awarded the rights of customs duties at Dublin and Drogheda in exchange for thirty sacks of wool and 300 livres, and he was even made Governor of Carrickfergus, in spite of his foreign birth.[15]

It is thus evident that, being a man of influence in Ireland, Meno had been carefully chosen by the Yorkists as being the ideal man to bring the young prince there and to launch him on his career. In spite of the failure of Lambert Simnel's attempt to start a Yorkist revival, the Irish were still ardently pro-Yorkist. We are told that the Pretender was wearing his 'master's' silks when he arrived in Ireland and the Irish, seeing in him the Plantagenet features, went wild about him.

With what joy, then, must the young man, pretender to the throne of England, have greeted the enthusiastic recognition of the Irish and their assurance of support: with what delight must he have welcomed the end of the lonely and wretched years of wandering and weeping in fear and grief of childhood. Now, with the advent of maturity, he could look forward to the realisation of his dream of re-establishing his House on the throne.

CHAPTER NINE

The Pretender in Ireland

There can be no doubt that the moment for the landing of the Pretender in Ireland and the launching of him on his bid to claim the English throne, was carefully chosen as being the most propitious time possible.

The state of Anglo-French relations had not varied much from 1488 to the autumn of 1491[1], but Charles VIII of France pursued a policy of aggression against Francis II, Duke of Brittany. Henry VII detested war, but he sent 8000 men to help Francis, though he delayed actually declaring war. Charles knew his man and gambled on the probability that Henry could be bought off; he was of course right.[2] At this point Duke Francis died, leaving his daughter Anne of Brittany as his sole heiress. Charles had been clandestinely supporting a move to put the Earl of Warwick, son of the late Duke of Clarence, on the English throne, but Henry had discovered the plot.[3] Naturally the French King would have been delighted to find a real Pretender to the throne whom he could support to Henry's embarrassment, and he lost little time in sending an embassy to the Pretender in Ireland, headed by a French envoy named Loyte Lucas, and Stephen Frion, who had been French Secretary to the King of England, but who had left his service and entered that of Charles. Frion was a Burgundian who was to serve the Pretender as his principal adviser. Henry's discomfiture must have been complete when Charles married the thirteen-year-old Anne of Brittany, thus eliminating an old foe, and a useful ally for England, by absorbing the independent duchy into the kingdom of France.

The absurdity of Henry's later claim that the Pretender spent these months in Ireland learning, not only English, but all the facts about his supposed father's court, and presumably how to recognise people he was supposed to have known when young and, more difficult, how to induce them to risk their lives by claiming to have known him, is only apparent to us in our day, since Henry was not interested in the truth, only in disproving that the Pretender was the Prince. Henry sought desperately to try to explain away how a young Flemish bourgeois could be so proficient in English and in detailed knowledge of the English court; but the one admission he could not make, naturally, is the only realistic one: that the Pretender was the person he claimed to be.

Bacon in his 'The Reign of Henry VII' makes out that the Pretender was a bastard of King Edward IV, which might have explained his startling likeness to his father: '. . . which might make a man think that he might indeed have in him some base blood of the House of York; so that at the least (though that were not) it might give the occasion to the boy, in being called King Edward's godson, or perhaps in sport King Edward's son, to entertain such thoughts into his head'.[4]

Bernard André, Henry's Poet Laureate, whom he commissioned to write a history of his life and times, does not mention King Edward as godfather to 'Perkin', but says he was the godfather of a converted Jew who took his name. He goes on to assert that 'Perkin' said: 'I was brought up by a converted Jew of the name of Edward, and before my pretence of being the younger son of the celebrated King Edward, I was a servant in England. The Jew was my master. He was in the intimate circle of the King and his children'.[5] This is the only account linking the Pretender with Brampton, the converted Jew, as his instructor in any way.

The Earls of Desmond and Kildare hastened to give the Prince their support, and it is evident that they had both been in correspondence with Margaret Duchess of Burgundy and other Yorkists before his landing in Cork, for he says in his 'confession' that it was by the assurance of support from these noblemen that he was emboldened to assume the character of the Duke of York;[6] as Kildare was then Lord Deputy of Ireland, he could not have had better patronage. Other Yorkists were also hastening to join him, and during that winter of 1491–2 at least, if not before, he was in correspondence with King James IV of Scotland: 'The secund day of Merche, gevin at the Kingis command til ane Inglis man callit Edwart Ormond that brocht letteris furth of Irland fra King Eduartis son and the Erle off Desmond, ten unicornis. . .nine pundis'.[7]

Naturally, the new prince would be the focus for dissident elements in England who resented the tyranny of the Tudor and who regretted having participated in Henry's usurpation. He was also of great interest to foreign powers who would send embassies to assess his possible value in their own political games.

In a speech which the Pretender is supposed to have made to the Irish nobles and gentlemen who gathered to support him, the young man gave instances of other 'distressed princes' who had had to flee from usurpers, such as the two sons of Edmund Ironside, who had fled from Canute when he seized the throne of England. Now, he said, this new usurper and tyrant had taken the throne, thanks to the King of France and the Duke of Brittany who had harboured him, in spite of the efforts of King Edward and King Richard to get hold of him. He revealed that the rebellion of his 'uncle' Lincoln (he was in fact his cousin) in 1487, and the putting forward of Lambert Simnel to impersonate his cousin the Earl of Warwick, had been only a ruse for his sake, who was then too young to be risked on the battlefield, and to 'make way to his fortunes'. He reminded his audience of Jack Cade of Kent, who had been induced by his own grandfather Richard, Duke of York, Governor of Ireland at that time, to style himself Sir John Mortimer.[8] Apparently the young man spoke with such fervour, and with such 'simulatory majesty', that his audience was overcome with desire to serve him, and to do him all reverence and honour. Though the speech is recorded by a Tudor historian, it is clear that his own personality and charm of address were beginning to cast their spell, as they were to do increasingly. Men would hasten to commit themselves to support him, once they had met him, and most of those supporters were willing to follow him to the death.

In view of the allegations made by Henry that the Pretender was only a humble Dutchman from Tournai who had had to learn English 'twice' (the second time in Ireland), it seems to have been a very remarkable coup indeed for a boatman's son who had apparently only had five months' instruction in English! Even if his speech had been written for him, what would the Irish have made of his foreign accent? and his later contacts of his probable Irish brogue?! Even so, could they have taught him to 'simulate majesty' so quickly and so adroitly? But if his audience was willingly duped, the same could not be said of the foreign representatives of embassies who were present. Even if it would profit their masters to have a puppet who would perform as an irritant to the English King Henry VII, they would surely have needed a better actor than a humble Dutchman who could deceive nobody, in order not to draw ridicule on themselves. English is surely one of the hardest languages for foreigners to speak perfectly, and Englishmen are notorious for their ridicule of foreigners who attempt to do so.

Nevertheless, the French King's emissaries must have reported favourably on the Pretender, for King Charles VIII invited him to go to France. Given that the French King's intentions were entirely self-interested and cynical, the swift acceptance of the invitation by the Pretender is nothing less than amazing if his lack of elegance and refinement could be quickly revealed by his behaviour in the French court.

In March, 1492, the Pretender sent Sir Edward Ormond as his emissary from Ireland to the French King, accepting the invitation to go to France the following May. Once there, he was received by Charles as a Royal Prince, and was given a guard of honour under the command of the Sieur de Concressault, an expatriate Scot by the name of William Monypenny. Sir George Nevill, Sir John Taylor, Rowland Robinson and about a hundred other English Yorkists joined him there and, understandably, tension between Henry and Charles became more acute. In the late autumn of that year, Henry had declared war, although overtures for peace had actually begun on 12th June. Henry's ships laid siege to Boulogne and he joined his army at Calais on 2nd October, but he was once again half-hearted about actually fighting. He gladly accepted Charles' offer of money, and the Treaty of Étaples was concluded between them on 3rd November 1492.

Henry returned to Calais on 7th November where, Polydore Vergil says, he first heard the news of the Pretender's claim. In spite of Vergil's statement, it is impossible to believe that Henry's army of spies had not reported to him the launching of the Pretender's claim in Ireland. Perhaps it was Henry's sudden realisation that here was no second Lambert Simnel who could be made to appear ridiculous and ignored, but a claimant who could become a real threat to him. Vergil says (quoting from Hall's Chronicle)

'. . . which sodeyne newes, more stacke and fretted in hys stomacke, than the battaile which now was late set forwards, and more paine he had (not without ieopardie of him self) to appease and quench this newe spronge conspiracy, then makynge peace with the French kynge hys enemy'.[9]

In accepting Charles' bribe to abandon military activities, Henry insisted on Charles' promise that he would cease to give aid to the enemies of himself.

The news of course was just what Henry had been dreading ever since the story was first spread in 1483, very possibly by Bishop Morton and his agents, that the Princes were dead, so as to clear Henry's way to the throne. It throws into perspective his remark about regretting the death of Lincoln at the Battle of Stoke, because he had hoped to learn from him what future danger remained. That his own chronicler should comment on his shock and displeasure is a good indication, not only of how deep the hurt went, but also of his own uncertainty about the real fate of the Princes.

But however anxious Henry was about the dangerous reality of the Pretender's existence, he was nothing if not an astute politician; he knew very well how to use the weaknesses and vanities of other people for his own ends, and he was beginning to discover the pleasant sensation of the desire of other European nations for England's friendship.

Charles VIII, too, was not less a skilful manipulator of his rivals, and he had, besides, his own schemes for the aggrandisement of France. The presence of the Pretender at his court had served to bring Henry to the peace table to sign the Treaty of Étaples, together with the offer of money: now Charles had no compunction in carrying out those peace terms, and politely asked his guest to depart.

CHAPTER TEN

The Duchess Margaret.

The Duchess Margaret of Burgundy, to whose court at Malines (Mechlin) the Pretender now repaired, was the older sister, by six and a half years, of Richard III, and the younger sister of Edward IV.

The civil war, erroneously known to history as the 'Wars of the Roses', came at the worst possible moment for her; she was only fourteen at the time of the deaths and horrible mutilation of the bodies of her father the Duke of York and young Edmund her brother, the Earl of Rutland, by the Lancastrian forces of Queen Margaret of Anjou after the battle of Wakefield in 1460. The horror of that tragedy must have inflicted deep and lasting scars on the adolescent girl: indeed, Tudor historians give that very event as forming the basis for her passionate hatred of the Lancastrians and her consequent espousal, first of Lambert Simnel and her nephew the Earl of Lincoln, whom she equipped and supported for the Battle of Stoke, as a curtain-raiser to her equally wholehearted commitment to her nephew, Prince Richard of York.

But in spite of Tudor historians such as Bernard André, Henry VII's chronicler, who described her as Henry's Juno, because she moved heaven and earth against him; and Thomas Gainsford, a gazette-maker of the late sixteenth century, who lost no opportunity to malign and denigrate her — calling her the prime mover of all the diabolical schemes launched against Henry on 'Perkin's' behalf, and asserting that she was activated by nothing but remorseless hatred for Henry — in reality the Duchess was another remarkable Margaret — a woman of vision and culture; charitable, vivacious and attractive.

Born on 3rd May 1446, at Fotheringhay, the sixth child of the Duke and Duchess of York, Margaret was evidently a true Plantagenet, with a lively, endearing disposition and a formidable intelligence. She had a special talent for languages, for she spoke no less than eleven by the time she grew up. She had auburn hair and large grey eyes, and with her happy temperament and gift for the 'bon mot', it is not surprising that she became widely loved and admired. She acted as the first lady of her brother Edward IV's court before he married, and in 1466 Edward sent his cousin Warwick and his old friend Lord Hastings to Flanders to negotiate a possible marriage between his sister Margaret and the Duke of Burgundy's son Charles, Count of Charolais. At the same time the French King sent an embassy to London with the same object of arranging a marriage with the King's sister, but Edward was anxious to bind Burgundy in an alliance in the hope of limiting the power of France. The next year, 1467, Charles of Charolais became Duke of Burgundy, and terms for the marriage were agreed. On 18th June, 1468, Margaret of York set out for Flanders, and embarked at Margate on 24th June. She was welcomed at Sluys the next day and the marriage took place at Damme on 3rd July. The Duke of Burgundy had been married twice before, and had an only daughter, Marie, who was only eight years younger than her new stepmother. Although Duke Charles 'the Bold' needed a male heir to succeed him, he appeared unwilling at first, even to agree to the marriage, in spite of the obvious dynastic and political advantages, but was won over by Margaret's tact and vivacity. Charles himself was a tempestuous and eccentric character, as his nickname 'the Bold' suggests (the French designated him 'the Rash', which certainly seems a more fitting epithet), and stories of his unreliability and erratic behaviour are numerous. There is certainly a story that he never consummated the marriage, perhaps borne out by the fact of their setting up separate establishments, though they were ceremonially 'bedded' on their wedding night, as was customary. This particular anecdote ends by claiming that even this one night of pretended conjugality nearly ended in disaster, with the bridal bed being set on fire by treachery, in a castle near Bruges.[1]

In contrast to her apparently unwilling and much older husband, Margaret was rumoured to have had many love affairs, and even to have had a son.[2] This story has been given some credence by the rumour put about by Tudor agents that 'Perkin Warbeck' was actually the son of Margaret of Burgundy by the Bishop of Cambrai, but, if this had been so, it is impossible to believe that Charles of Burgundy with his short temper, would not have put her away from him altogether. In any case, this solution would hardly account for the boy's likeness to Edward IV.

Whatever the true state of relationship between her and her husband, Margaret was soon enchanting her new countrymen by her gaiety and enthusiasm for all she saw around her. She had a deep interest in the arts, and it was she who encouraged William Caxton, who had set up his presses in Flanders, to go to England. A dance called 'La Marguerite' was invented and named in her honour, and the flower decorated every function which she attended. She had two tennis courts in the grounds of her palace at Malines, and she had the interests of her servants very much at heart, for she invented a system whereby they could 'clock on and off' for work, much like the present day, and she also set up a sort of canteen for their better feeding arrangements.

After Charles the Bold's death at the siege of Nancy in 1477, she virtually faced the French alone, but she acted fearlessly in pursuing a policy dedicated to her country's interests, and to the interests and happiness of her stepdaughter Marie, to whom she quickly became devoted. It was by Margaret's efforts that Marie was enabled to marry the Emperor Maximilian I of the Holy Roman Empire, and thus to place herself and her country under his protection against France. It has been asserted that the Duchess Margaret was in fact the founder of the 'buffer-state' known as the Low Countries — 'L'entre deux' — as they were then called.

In July or August 1480, in pursuit of her work for her new country, she came to England on a visit to her brother's (Edward IV's) court to discuss trade between the two countries, and to obtain from Edward her dowry on her marriage which had never been paid in full. She obtained an export licence beneficial to Burgundy,[3] but the major part of her dowry remained unpaid at the death of Edward IV three years later. She herself was thirty-seven at the time of her brother's death.

Such was the woman described by Tudor historians as a 'virago of hatred' because of her excessive devotion to the cause of the restoration of the House of York to the throne of England. Even her selfless devotion to her step-grandson, Marie's son Philip, is denigrated by Tudor apologists, who profess to read into it the possessiveness of a childless woman. This does not, apparently, deter them from trying to foist 'Perkin Warbeck' on her as her son in explanation of her whole-hearted support of him. She had certainly been instrumental in setting up the Lambert Simnel conspiracy to test what support there might be when the time came for her nephew to try to claim his throne: both Lord Lovell and the Earl of Lincoln (her nephew, named as Richard III's heir) had visited her at Malines before the Battle of Stoke, and she had provided the money to pay two thousand German mercenaries under the celebrated German army leader, Martin Swart.

Gainsford, the historian whose hostility to the Duchess Margaret bursts forth whenever he mentions her, says that she was stung to envy by the outcome of the Battle of Stoke, and therefore looked about for another 'idol of defiance' to take the place of Lambert Simnel: four years later she descried "Perkin Warbeck" as of "behaviour extraordinary and of manners audacious" and caused him to travel about in order to learn as many languages as he could, so that his English would be as near perfect as possible, that his real origins would be undetected, and those who met him would be persuaded into believing him to be of the House of Plantagenet. When 'her Youngling' returned from the French court to her own court of Burgundy at Malines, Gainsford says quoting Hall, she made him relate all his adventures to her and received him with embraces and tears, rejoicing in the superb performance he put up, wherein he neither stuttered nor stammered, so that the whole company believed him, and she immediately consigned him a guard of fifty persons in murrey and blue (the Yorkist colours), and honoured him with a cloth of estate[4].

The truth was, of course, quite different. We know from his 'confession', probably put together by Henry's agents, but also easily traced as his movements must have been, that he had spent the years since being brought to Flanders among the Werbecque relations, and had finally gone to Portugal with the Bramptons at the age of fourteen. There is the evidence quoted in Chapter Four above, that Margaret's brother King Richard III had kept her in touch with events and, undoubtedly, with the melancholy news of his own beloved son's death in April 1484. Bacon asserts that the Duchess had instructed him in the ways of the English court, and 'described to him the personages, lineaments and features of the King and Queen, his pretended parents; and of his brother and sisters, and divers others that were nearest to him in childhood, together with all passages, some secret, some common, that were fit for a child's memory, until . . . the death of his father Edward IV; his own imprisonment with his brother in the Tower; the murder of the latter and his own escape: gave him a smooth and likely tale of these matters, warning him not to vary from it; and finally taught him how to avoid sundry captious and tempting questions which were like to be asked of him.'[5] Gairdner, however, rightly says that, if she instructed him in anything, it was unlikely to have been very much, since she had left England before the birth of her nephew the Duke of York, and had been back at her brother's court only once for a few months twelve years before, so that her description of people there would hardly have been much use to the young man twelve years later.'[6]

In 'Annales, or a General Chronicle of England', begun by John Stow and 'continued and augmented . . . unto the end of this present year 1631', being Stow's life of 'Perkin Warbeck', probably adapted from Hall's Chronicles, themselves taken from Holinshed's 'Chronicles of England, Scotland and Ireland', there is a story that the Duchess of Burgundy 'espied Perkin' and, because he was of 'visage beautifull, of countenance demure, of wit subtill; this young man travelling many Countries, could speake English and divers other languages'; she began to 'instruct him both of the secrets and common affaires of the Realm of England . . . that like a good scholar he could tell all that was taught him without any staggering or staye in his words; And besides that he kept such a Princely countenance, that all men in manner did firmly believe that he was extracted of that noble family of the Duke of York . . .' This story is so like the one put out by Bacon that it is probably derived from the same source, namely that of Hall or Holinshed. What is of interest is that all accounts, however hostile they are to the young man, stress his good looks, his charm of manner and his princely bearing.

The truth was that the Duchess Margaret herself, when the Pretender arrived at her court, was at first sceptical of his claims to be Prince Richard; she wrote later to Queen Isabella of Spain, telling her that she had put him through a minute cross-examination to establish the truth, at which he never faltered or made a mistake in his knowledge of the court of King Edward, and that she was thus persuaded that he was who he claimed to be.[7]

Gainsford says that, as a result of the Duchess Margaret's recognition, all sorts of sedition began in England and 'no man was sure of his Friend, the Times grew to such distraction, and all sorts of people believed, not only of the better sort, but of the common people.'[8] Very much the same sort of sedition, in other words, which Henry and Morton had stirred up against King Richard III from 1483 onwards. Bacon, too, had to revise his opinion; he wrote 'The news thereof came blazing and thundering over into England, that the Duke of York was sure alive. As for the name of Perkin Warbeck, it was not at that time come to light, but all the news ran upon the Duke of York, that he was being entertained in Ireland; bought and sold in France, and was now plainly avowed and in great honour, in Flanders'.[9]

The Pretender was now surrounded with Yorkist exiles, and many more travelled to Flanders from England: to quote Buck: 'All those in a position to do so recognised him as Richard, Duke of York in every particular . . . and they went to him and viewed and considered him well and warily, and they had secret markings. And they found that by his face and countenance and other lineaments, and by all tokens known to them, that he was the younger son of King Edward. And they observed a princely grace and behaviour in him, and which was a good token of his princely birth. And he could readily account for many things he had seen and heard whilst he was in England, and some things that had been done and spoken very privately. And besides this he spake English very perfectly, and better than Dutch or Wallonish'.[10]

Prince Richard himself said at this time that 'he would prove before Henry VII himself, if the opportunity were only given him, by the evidence of three marks upon his person which those who had known the Duke of York in early years could vouch for, that he was no other than the person he claimed to be . . .'[11] It is a measure of his youth and political naïveté that he did not realise, apparently, that if he had been able to prove in Henry's presence that he was the real prince, it would have been his death-warrant, as indeed it was later to be.

If the Duchess Margaret had been unable, because of her long absence from the English court, to instruct her nephew in what in any case he already knew, she must surely have warned him that, among the supporters now flooding to her court, there must be some at least who were untrustworthy, possibly even spies sent over by Henry; and that many of the Heads of State now eager to recognise him as the rightful King of England were doing so for their own ends. She was, as a widow, under the protection of her step-grandson Philip, the new Duke of Burgundy since the tragic death of his mother Marie as a result of a fall from her horse in 1482. The people of Flanders had shown their preference for the young Philip by refusing to accept his father, Maximilian, at that time Archduke of Austria, when he came to the Low Countries to claim the Dukedom of Burgundy, and had even taken him captive. But Philip was still under age, and the affairs of Burgundy were in the hands of a Council who seem at this time to have condoned, if not supported, the activities of the Duchess Margaret on behalf of her nephew.

CHAPTER ELEVEN

The Kendal Plot.

In England, Henry was experiencing a wave of unpopularity, mainly due to the dual activities of Cardinal John Morton in raising taxes ('Morton's Fork' as it was called, being the simple yet brilliant device of extracting money from the rich because they had much to give, and from the thrifty because they must have saved much), and introducing reforms which alienated the clergy.

In Yorkshire, still loyal to their memories of King Richard, there had been an uprising in 1489 to protest against the excessive taxation, and the Earl of Northumberland, whose failure to support his King at Bosworth had probably never been forgiven by Yorkshiremen, was pulled off his horse by an infuriated mob and killed at Thirsk when he attempted to collect the taxes on Henry's behalf.

The discontent of some of the clergy resulted in the most bizarre plot, which was hatched in the beginning of 1493 by no less a person than Sir John Kendal, Grand Prior of the Order of St. John of Jerusalem, with his nephew John Thong or Tweng of the same Order, and Dr. William Horsey, Archdeacon of London. They allegedly met in Rome early in 1493 to discuss 'means and ways to undertake the killing of the King of England, his children, his mother and his near relations'. The conspirators were probably very early on in touch with the Pretender, who was to be referred to as 'The Merchant of the Ruby' in all correspondence. The incredible plot seems to have included a good deal of black magic; an obnoxious ointment produced by a Spanish astrologer which, if spread round a doorway through which the intended victim would pass, would induce his nearest and dearest to murder him! This part of the plot misfired early on, because the carrier of the magic ointment, one Bernard de Vignolles, a servant of Sir John Kendal's, luckily got cold feet and exchanged the foul contents of the magic box for innocuous ones. But the conspiracy continued for at least three years and involved some of the most influential clergy. It was not discovered until the same servant, Bernard de Vignolles, a Frenchman, having seen some secret correspondence between one of the Pretender's servants (Guillemin de Noyon, himself to be later a Knight of the Order) and Kendal, appears to have feigned illness in order to return to France and confess all to his King. Kendal apparently trusted him to return, which of course he never did. Instead, he revealed all he knew in a deposition which he signed at Rouen on 14th March 1496[1].

The most extraordinary part of the whole affair is that Sir John Kendal seems to have remained throughout entirely in Henry's confidence; yet he continued to plot and prepare for the day when the Pretender would invade. This seems to indicate that the French King did not pass on de Vignolles' information to Henry, who was apparently ignorant of the whole business. Kendal had not taken part in the defence of Rhodes when it was besieged by the Turks in about 1480; but he was designated Turcopilier, or General of the Infantry of the Order, which office was annexed to that of the Grand Prior of the Order of England, and he appeared on a medal struck to commemorate that event. On the medal's reverse is his shield of arms; viz, a fret, in chief a cross of Rhodes (the arms, impaled with those of England, are said to decorate the walls of an hotel in Rhodes). He succeeded John Weston as Prior of the Hospital of St. John of Jerusalem at Clerkenwell in 1491, and in this capacity was in Henry's confidence, being employed in political negotiations of great moment. His family probably came from Yorkshire.

In June 1492 Kendal was one of the Commissioners to treat of peace with France, and in February 1495–6 he held the same office in arranging the treaty with the Archduke Philip. In September that year he had a royal licence to import 50 casks of Gascon wine free of duty: at the same time he was busily plotting the overthrow of Henry and the instatement of Prince Richard, Duke of York, as King. No information is given of Kendal's nephew, Sir John Thong or Tweng, but Dr. William Horsey succeeded John Forster as Archdeacon of London soon after 1490, and did not resign until 1513. He was made Chancellor to Richard Fitzjames, Bishop of London, and Precentor of St. Paul's on 27th March 1514; which office he held until 1531. He died about April 1543. Each time that the Grand Prior, Kendal, received news from the Low Countries he communicated it to no less a person than the Bishop of Winchester[2] — that same admirer of King Richard, Thomas Langton, Bishop of

St. David's and in 1485 of Salisbury, and still another ardent but secret partisan of the Pretender.[3]

It was not to be expected that Henry would remain inactive in the face of so much unrest, although, surprisingly, he may never have known the full extent to which it had already grown. He had put down the Yorkshire rising with firmness, and he was certainly the man to deal with conspiracy and plotting, having triumphed from just such a rebellion himself. Gairdner quotes from Brewer's edition of 'Letters of Henry VIII':- '. . . The King that now dead is [Henry VII] . . . would handle such a cause circumspectly and with convenient diligence for inveigling, and yet not disclose it, to the party nor otherwise, by a great space after, but keep it to himself and always grope further, having ever good await and espial to the party . . . two or three years before he laid it to their charge, and kept it secret, and always gathered upon them more and more . . .' He wrote to Sir Gilbert Talbot on 20th July 1493 from Kenilworth Castle, complaining bitterly about the Duchess of Burgundy's schemes to subvert and destroy his realm and to instate 'another feigned lad called Perkin Warbeck, born at Tournay in Picardy' as King in his place, and he asked Sir Gilbert to have men, horses and equipment ready 'to resist her malice . . . with such diligence as that ye be ready with your said number, to come unto us upon our sudden warning.' His offer of financial reward for the 'discovery of Perkin's low birth' had not surprisingly borne fruit; the truth would presumably not have elicited any reward.

Henry next sent Sir Edward Poynings and Dr. William Warham (who afterwards became Archbishop of Canterbury), to the Low Countries to complain to the young Archduke Philip's Council of the support and countenance they were giving to the Pretender. The Council replied that they would preserve the peace with England, but that they could not interfere with the Duchess Margaret, who was free to do as she pleased.[4]

Sir Edward Poynings and Dr. Warham then received instructions from Henry to publish the 'details' of 'Perkin's low birth'. They were as follows:-

1. That the young man could not be Richard, Duke of York, because he had been murdered in the Tower,

2. That there was no likelihood that King Richard, having murdered his elder brother, would have spared him,

3. That Queen Elizabeth their mother was attainted* for surrendering her daughters into Richard's custody, when she knew he had murdered her sons,[5]

4. To desire Philip not to believe Perkin, and

5. To remember how Henry had helped and relieved Maximilian (Philip's father) when oppressed by the French King, and it would be ungrateful if he now assisted anyone against himself (Henry).[6]

Gainsford gives an account of the meeting between Henry's envoys and the Duchess Margaret, at which the Pretender was present. But Gainsford does not mention a remark, attributed to Dr. Warham by Dr. Desmons, himself an avowed supporter of Henry, and whose article 'A Tournaisian pretender to the throne of England' has already been quoted, in which Dr. Warham 'audaciously jested that, in spite of her declining years, she had just brought to birth successively two princes aged one hundred and eighty months' — by which he meant her support for both Lambert Simnel and for 'Perkin'. Gainsford merely describes Warham's peroration as 'well-penned', but Dr. Desmons rightly castigates him for his remark as being 'ironic and unseemly', and it certainly does not enhance his reputation as a diplomat. Not surprisingly, it drew a spirited and erudite rebuff from the Duchess although, being reported by Gainsford, it contains malicious and unsubstantiated attacks on her brother Richard which she would have been most unlikely to make since, as we have seen, they were in correspondence as late as 1484. She refuted each one of the points made by Henry in his 'details of Perkin's low birth; saying it was 'well-known that the Cardinal himself [Cardinal Bourchier, presumably, who had stood surety to Elizabeth Woodville for the safety of the Duke of York] was deceived and the Child conveyed away'. She reminded them that 'sons are to be preferred before daughters' and assured them that they would not deter her from assisting her nephew or from being the Protectrix of 'this every way distressed Prince': she would always be an enemy to Lancaster. In answer to their taunt about ingratitude on the part of Maximilian, she said that Maximilian knew it was but folly to help them in their designs on France, for 'as fast as you got it one way, you would lose it another, so that you cannot now show any Town or Port, either of King Edward's conquests, or Henry the

*Note: Elizabeth Woodville was not attainted by Henry: Vergil is the only Chronicler who uses the word 'atteyntatus'.

Fifth's enterprises except Calais, which lying so near to you, you cannot for shame but defend'. She then told them to go back to their 'politick Prince' and tell him that she intended to arm 'ourselves and this Prince' and defy him in his own Kingdom to make an equal combat the decider of both their titles. She then arose, says Gainsford, and swept out of the room taking 'Perkin' with her, leaving the envoys who were known to be 'invincible for their courage and exploits, amazed at her heroical speech and delicate manner of obstinacy'[7]

As a result of the reply of the Archduke Philip's Council to Henry's complaint about the Duchess Margaret's activities, Henry angrily broke off trade relations with Flanders, and instead set up a market for English goods at Calais. This trade embargo proved to be a double-edged weapon: so many London apprentices were thrown out of work that many of them attacked the Steelyard of the Easterlings (the headquarters of the foreign merchants in London), and the ensuing riots were only quelled by the appearance of the Lord Mayor and his magistrates. But in the end it was far more damaging to Flanders, and as soon as Philip came of age he hastened to repair the damage.

In August 1493, the Pretender wrote his letter to Queen Isabella of Spain (already quoted in Chapter Seven, and which can be found in full in Appendix II), imploring the aid of herself and King Ferdinand in restoring him to the throne of England which was rightly his.

But there was no reply from the Spanish monarchs; the Pretender was not to know that their own diplomatic and secret efforts were directed towards seeking Henry's help against the designs of the King of France on Naples. The overthrow of the English King by a Pretender, however genuine, would disrupt and perhaps utterly confound these plans, and they could not afford to gamble on the doubtful possibility of the Pretender's success. But time would show that they also acknowledged in secret that the Pretender was Richard, Duke of York.[8]

RICARDVS · III · ANG · REX ·

King Richard III *National Portrait Gallery, London.*

Elizabeth Woodville wife of Edward IV. *Queens College, Cambridge.*

King Edward IV

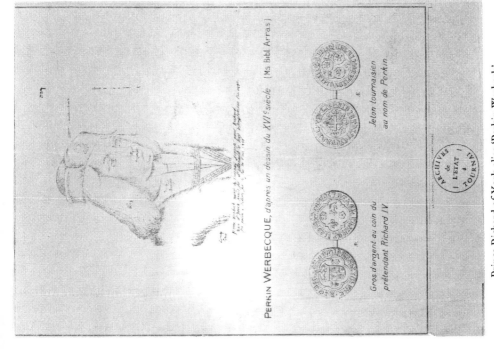

Prince Richard of York alias 'Perkin Warbeck'.
Jacques le Boucq, State Archives of Tournai.

ELIZABETHA · VXOR
HENRICI · VII ·

Elizabeth of York wife of Henry VII. *National Portrait Gallery, London*

CHAPTER TWELVE

Support and Betrayal

The Pretender's hopes were burgeoning; he spent the summer of 1493 with his aunt the Duchess Margaret of Burgundy at her court at Malines.

She threw the full weight of her influence and energy into support for him; she bore the expenses, not only of his clothes but also those of his attendants who were dressed in the murrey and blue livery of the House of York. Among those attendants were Hugh de Melun,* who later became a Knight of the Golden Fleece and Governor of Dendermonde in the Austrian Netherlands (under the jurisdiction of the Archduke Philip), and Anthony de la Forsse, whom the Pretender later revealed in a letter to Anthony's father, Sir Bernard de la Forsse (himself Richard III's Ambassador to Spain), had been attendant on him for many years and in many different countries.[1] The Duchess was also instrumental in bringing her nephew to the notice of all the princes of Europe who recognised him as the rightful King of England, with the exception of the Kings of France and Spain.[2]

In November of that year the Pretender was present in Vienna at the funeral of the Emperor Frederic III of the Holy Roman Empire (Maximilian's father), in the company of the Duke of Saxony, where he was given a place appropriate to the King of England. Jean Molinet, the chronicler, who refers to him at all times as an impostor, nevertheless lists him among the mourners for the Emperor Frederic as 'Richart, son of Edward IV, made offertory with the orators of the Archduke Philip'.[3]

At this time Sir John Kendal's conspiracy in England to overthrow Henry and replace him with the Pretender was at its height, and many of Henry's nobles were either actively engaged in correspondence with or

---

*In 1513 the Prince de Ligne in a letter to Henry VIII complained that de Melun (the courageous defender of Dendermonde against the Ganton's in 1512) was 'The person who directed all Perkin's affairs in Flanders'. The Prince de Ligne was at the court of Francis I. See also p.98)

preparing to join the Prince in Flanders, or secretly awaiting his expected invasion with sympathy. Kendal received a secret letter from one of the Prince's attendants, Guillemin de Noyon, who called himself a servant of the Prince, but who was described in the correspondence as 'cavaliere de Rhodes' and who later became a Knight of the Order of St. John of Jerusalem. The letter informed Kendal that the 'Merchant of the Ruby' (the Pretender) had been unable to sell his wares in Flanders for the price asked, and was going to the King of the Romans (Maximilian) to see if he could get more.[4]

By the following summer (1494), the Prince was holding court in Flanders, and kept his state at the 'Hotel des Anglais', or the House of the Merchant Adventurers in Antwerp. There he hung out his arms — three leopards and three fleurs de lis, with the legend 'Arms of Richard, Prince of Wales and Duke of York, son and heir of Edward the Fourth, by the Grace of God late King of England and France, Lord of Ireland', in Latin.

At Malines on the 24th August (St. Bartholomew's Day, and a week after the Prince's own twenty-first birthday), the Emperor Maximilian rode to church with his son the Archduke Philip and the Pretender, splendidly dressed in cloth of gold as befitted the King of England, with thirty halberdiers dressed in the murrey and blue livery of the House of York in attendance on him, and with Hugh de Melun beside him. Once again, Jean Molinet records his presence as 'The Duke of York of England'.[5]

Maximilian thus openly declared his full support for the Pretender; it was all the more of a snub to Henry, who had a month previously sent Garter King of Arms to remonstrate with both Maximilian and the Duchess Margaret against their support for the Pretender, and to tell them both by word of mouth that he was only the son of a burgher of Tournai. His protest being rejected by both Maximilian and the Duchess, the herald proceeded to proclaim it aloud in the streets of Malines, which brought him the threat of imprisonment.

It is odd how apologists for Henry, when faced with unpalatable facts, react by denigrating and belittling those whose actions give the lie to the Tudor story, and this they attempt to do in the case of Maximilian. Gairdner reports mistakenly the fact that when Maximilian asked his Tyrolian subjects for 16,000 florins to promote an enterprise on behalf of the Pretender, they refused him. Gairdner believes this implies that the Pretender was not recognised as King of England, but he ignores the fact that Maximilian was habitually short of money and his rebellious subjects were always refusing him grants on one count or another. Even Henry, certainly a more autocratic monarch than Maximilian, often had great difficulty in extorting sums of money from his subjects: dislike of paying taxes is not limited to the fifteenth century, nor even to one country alone.

Maximilian has been, at least partly on account of his support for the Pretender, belittled almost to the point of ridicule by many historians, who delight in outlining his failures, both as a child and as a man, and argue that he has left very little trace of greatness or success.

But the truth is that nothing about Maximilian was ordinary or pedestrian; he battled against, and usually overcame, setbacks and disasters, and never lost his romantic outlook on life. His parents were distraught at first, believing him to be an idiot because he was unable to speak before he was six years old, but he was soon amazing everyone with his speech; he learned to speak Latin, French, Italian and Flemish fluently, and could boast some knowledge of Spanish, Walloon and English. He became the favourite among poets and scholars, but he also excelled at the tournay and at hunting, and was known to be one of the finest swordsmen of Europe. His love of the chase became so great that, in order not to have to delay unduly, he learned the blacksmith's trade and shod his own horses for the hunt.

His marriage to the little Marie, only child of the late Duke Charles of Burgundy, seems to have been a true love match: she chose him out of the many princes who aspired to her hand on her father's death, and after her tragic death after a fall from her horse in 1482 Maximilian could not hear her name without weeping and sighing: 'belle, bonne, douce, aimable, pieuse, respectée de tous' was her epitaph, and a most fitting one.

Maximilian's worst fault was that he had so many great and grandiose schemes that he was chronically short of money — generous to a fault, however much he had, he always overspent. On one occasion, having been granted 150,000 ducats from the Pope, and another 100,000 from France, he had to allow the opportunity for a great victory in Italy to pass by, because he was kicking his heels in Innsbruck, again without sufficient funds to pay his troops. Yet Machiavelli said it was because the Germans, who formed the major part of his fighting men, were a free people and would not serve in the army unless overpaid: he described Maximilian in generous terms:- 'He governs his country with great justice; he is also a good general, skilful and successful in war:', and 'if he could get over two qualities — weakness and his easy nature, he would be a perfect man.' His whole life seems to have been not far removed from one of his own favourite epic poems; rich in romance and chivalry, and by turns steeped in sorrow.[6]

Waas says of him: 'He was able to estimate a person's abilities at a glance, so that he could immediately assign each person for the task for which he was most suited'; and 'He was the most accomplished Prince the House of Habsburg has produced; he had energy and a strong desire to reform abuses, and inherited a striking personality from his vivacious mother'[7]. Jean Molinet praised him fulsomely and Waas quotes a story that someone once remarked to King Louis XI of France that Maximilian was nothing more than the Mayor of Augsburg, and that Louis replied 'Yes, but every time the Mayor rings the bell, he makes all France tremble.'[8] The 'Weisskunig' and 'Teuerdank', the two books on his chivalric exploits, read like stories from the Arabian Nights, and reveal him as a man of the highest ideals and noblest feelings; one who was as much at home in the idealistic world of poetry and music as in the realistic one of politics and fighting.

This, then, was the man who publicly recognised the Pretender as the true Prince and who entertained him at his court as though he were about to become the de facto King of England, and who never lost faith in him or reviled him for failure. Political necessity cannot account for the fact that in such an intellectual court as Maximilian's, the Pretender was never found wanting in any princely charm or grace: Maximilian was not the man to put up with false pretensions or posturings by an ill-bred upstart: if the young man had so behaved, he would quickly have been dismissed. Maximilian did, however, after Henry's representations to himself and the Duchess Margaret, cause enquiries to be made of 'good authorities' in England, through the medium of Philip of Nassau and the Provost of Utrecht, as to what was thought of the Pretender in England,[9] and this Gairdner has interpreted as meaning that Maximilian was unsure what to believe, but it might equally imply that a prudent man was enquiring what success the Pretender was likely to meet with, if and when he would invade. Even so convinced a romantic as Maximilian would be unlikely to throw his money away for a hopeless cause. The reply he received must have been satisfactory, because he not only continued to support the Pretender fully, but through his efforts the Pretender gained the additional support of the King of Denmark and the Duke of Saxony.

The French King Charles had already sent an embassy to Maximilian, from whom he received news of the Emperor's faith in the Pretender; faith which would shortly be backed with money and arms to promote the Pretender's enterprise against England. Charles was at the moment on friendly terms with Henry, so he sent him news of Maximilian's intentions, offering to supply Henry with ships from Brittany and Normandy (Brittany now being part of the Kingdom of France through Charles' marriage to Anne of Brittany). The French King further assured Henry that he would allow Frenchmen to volunteer as mercenaries; he took the opportunity to remind Henry that he had originally assisted *him* to obtain the English crown.

Henry's reply was cordial; he thanked Charles for his offer, which he would take up if the necessity should occur; but he stressed that he took no account of the affair of 'le garçon', since everyone in England knew him to be the son of a burgher in Tournai. These were brave words from Henry, since he must already have had a good idea of how many of his nobles either accepted the fact that the young man was the true Prince, or perhaps secretly sympathised with his cause. He also knew that the French King intended the conquest of the Kingdom of Naples, and this displeased him greatly on account of having bestowed the Garter on Alphonso, King of Naples. He offered to mediate between them in order to preserve the peace, but Charles was not to be deflected.

On 6th October Maximilian rode with the young Pretender to the Church of Our Lady (now the Cathedral) at Antwerp, to witness Maximilian's son Philip, now sixteen years old and of age, take the oath as Duke of Brabant. The Pretender had a bodyguard of gentlemen with twenty archers wearing the badge of the White Rose on their livery. The occasion was obviously of great importance for the Pretender, and when two of the observers sent over by Henry attempted to throw mud at the procession and at the coat of arms of the Prince at the 'Hotel des Anglais', they were set on by the angry mob, and had difficulty in escaping from the town. A third man, an innocent bystander, was unlucky enough to be killed by the mob.[10]

All this indicated that the affairs of the Pretender were rapidly coming to a head; time would show that, if the young man and his advisers could have concerted their plans and taken advantage of the tide that was running swiftly in his favour at that moment, he might well have brought down Henry. As it was, he was certainly no match for the Tudor — 'a King both wise, stout and fortunate', as Bacon would later describe him in his 'History of the Reign of Henry VII'. Henry could certainly not afford to have the Emperor of the Holy Roman Empire conspiring with a Yorkist-Burgundian Princess to encompass his overthrow, and he moved swiftly and cunningly to defeat their plans.

Amongst the flood of Yorkists streaming from England to join the Pretender in Flanders were Sir Robert Clifford and Sir William Barley. Whether they were in fact agents sent by Henry to spy on the Prince's entourage and to discover his adherents in England, is not entirely clear; but Sir Robert wrote home that he knew the Pretender to be the real Prince, since he had known him as a boy and had seen 'secret markings' which convinced him that Richard, Duke of York and the Pretender were one and the same person.[11] The Yorkists at Duchess Margaret's court seem to have been unaware of the danger of infiltration of their ranks by Henry's spies; Clifford and Barley were treated as welcome adherents to the Yorkist cause and entrusted with all their secrets. Henry certainly had other spies in the Low Countries, to whom he gave secret assurances of pardon and financial reward if they would come home and reveal all. Clifford and Barley fall under the gravest suspicion of being double agents, by the alacrity with which they took up Henry's offer and returned home to England: Clifford received his pardon on 22nd December and a reward of £500 from the King on 20th January 1495. But Barley did not make his submission until two years later, but was also pardoned: if they were not actually Henry's agents from the beginning, perhaps the value of what they were able to disclose was sufficient to melt Henry's otherwise unforgiving nature.

Clifford's alarming revelations of the vast extent of the Pretender's support among Henry's entourage virtually put paid to the young man's chances of success. It had been the promise of active support, not on account of King Richard's unpopularity, but on account of the promise of the fusion of the Red Rose with the White, which had ensured Henry's own successful rebellion: now it was vital for the Prince to be able to rely on the support of the majority of the nobles, due to Henry's unpopularity, in order to have any hope of seizing Henry's throne.

Among those accused by Clifford were Lord Fitzwalter, Sir Simon Mountford, Sir Thomas Thwaites, William Daubeney, Robert Ratcliffe,

Thomas Cressener, Thomas Astwood, William Worsley, Dean of St. Paul's, and many other priests and friars.[12] Sir John Kendal and his associates were apparently not mentioned, in spite of Clifford's wholesale denunciations, and his conspiracy on the Pretender's behalf continued in secret.

It seems likely that Sir Robert Clifford had written his accusations privately to Henry before his arrival back in London, or else that other spies sent to Flanders by Henry had anticipated Sir Robert, for when Clifford returned, Henry came up to the Tower of London from Greenwich where he had been keeping Christmas, to give Sir Robert a private audience in 'a place where any important person in the court could be arrested without suspicion or noise or sending abroad of warrants.' Henry's Lord Chamberlain and step-uncle, Sir William Stanley, whose treacherous intervention at Bosworth had gained Henry his throne, was in attendance at the Tower. He must have been completely without suspicion that the man whom Sir Robert Clifford would next accuse would be himself[13]; surely he would have put a safe distance between himself and the King if he had had any idea of his coming betrayal. Henry was dumbfounded; according to Gainsford he burst out: 'What, my bosom Friend? My Counsellor? My Chamberlain? I see there is no trust in men'[14]. Other sources do not put words into Henry's mouth; they state that he refused, for some time, to believe Stanley's treachery.

There is no record of Sir William Stanley's trial in the 'Baga de Secretis' (the 'classified information' of those days, which it was treason to reveal), but Bernard André afterwards wrote that Sir William had said to Clifford that if he knew for certain that the young man was the son of King Edward, he would never bear arms against him, and that he had promised him financial support.[15] This statement surely proves that it was still not accepted, even among Henry's own courtiers, that the Princes had died in the Tower. Historians less charitable to Henry have suggested that Sir William had been pestering Henry for greater rewards for his services to him at Bosworth, and that Henry was only waiting for an excuse, such as his remark reported only by Clifford, to get rid of Sir William and to appropriate all his considerable lands and goods for himself. Bacon reports that Henry's rejoinder was that though Stanley had saved his life at Bosworth, he had delayed long enough to endanger it.[16]

Most of the plotters were tried as early as November 1494, bearing out the probability that other spies had accused them before Clifford's return;

towards the end of January 1495 Mountford, Ratcliffe and Daubeney were beheaded and others were hanged at Tyburn. The churchmen were pardoned and Lord Fitzwalter was spared, but after a year in prison at Calais he tried to escape and was beheaded.

Sir William Stanley was executed on 5th February 1495. Sir George Buck confirms that there were 'many wise and signal persons, who, like Clifford, had served King Edward IV and 'knew the younger son of King Edward IV *and were privy to the conveyance away from England'* [my italics].[17] Buck lists even more of the Pretender's supporters: he gives the names of Sir John Taylor, Sir Thomas Challoner, Thomas Bagnol and many other gentlemen of quality, and also sundry prelates and priests who had been chaplains to King Edward his father, 'or otherwise occasioned to attend his court'; namely, Dr. Rocheford, Dr. Poynes, Dr. Sutton, Dr. Leyburn, Dr. Lessey and other learned professors of divinity who 'would not endure to hear that he who was called "Perkin" was a counterfeit, but that he was Richard of York'. 'In the same faith, the King's Serjeant Ferior, for the knowledge that he had of Richard (alias Perkin), leaving the King's service, was executed as a traitor.'[18]

Sir Thomas More says:- 'Not only for that Perkin Warbeck, by many folks' malice and more folks' folly so long space deceiving the world, was as well by princes as the poorer people reputed and taken for the younger of those two [the Princes]'[19].

Chastelain records that on 11th February 1495 the Milanese Ambassador to Flanders wrote to Ludovico Sforza, Duke of Milan from Bois-le-duc, saying that Maximilian had alleged that Clifford said on his return to England that the Duke of York was the son of the Duchess Margaret and the Bishop of Cambrai.[20] This is far from saying that this was Maximilian's opinion, for he continued to show his complete faith in the Pretender: it may well have been an attempt by Clifford to curry favour with Henry, and a sign that he was not, after all, a double agent for Tudor. Clifford was certainly trying to hedge his bets, for Sir Hugh Conway wrote to Henry reporting that Sir Robert Clifford had told a lady at Calais that 'Perkin Warbeck' was King Edward's son.[21]

Both sides were severely shaken by the plots and the revelation of them.

Henry sent Roger Machado, Clarenceux King of Arms to France at the beginning of the year 1495, with instructions dated at Greenwich the 30th December 1494, giving Charles a good report of his situation at home and playing down the importance of 'Perkin'. In reality Henry was becoming increasingly nervous, for the attitude of the French King was changing slightly towards him as a result of the indifference shown by Henry over Charles' offer of help, which had included a promise not to assist the Scottish King, James IV, if he should invade England. Henry's agitation about the young man he always sneeringly referred to as 'le garçon' or 'le lad' betrayed itself in the revelation to the French King that 'things change from day to day; where the said youth is, and who he is.' Only five months previously, Henry had certified that none of his subjects had any doubt about the identity of the Pretender.[22] Although he must have known that some of his subjects were still at heart ardent Yorkists, the extent and ramifications of the plots on the Prince's behalf evidently surprised and shocked him. But he reacted with characteristic speed and severity, and his promptitude certainly saved him his crown.

In Flanders the reactions were equally those of shock and dismay: Maximilian retaliated against Henry's execution of Sir William Stanley by banishing English merchants from the Low Countries and forbidding his subjects to traffic in 'English clothes, yearne, tynne, leade and other commodities of this Realme'[23]. But the blow was to be mortal: it did indeed 'quail the designs of Perkin and his complices'.[24] Henry's move had wiped out the very men who were to aid him on his landing: only Sir John Kendal's conspiracy remained undiscovered.

All this time Sir John, Grand Prior of the Order of St. John of Jerusalem, was in Bedfordshire at a religious house belonging to the Order at Milbourne, Meldburn or Mechelburn, a Preceptory of St. John of Jerusalem given to the Order in the reign of Henry I — 'a right fair place of square stone, standing much upon pillered vaultes of stone', according to the description by the historian Leland. Here Kendal was having a certain number of 'jacquettes' made for his attendants; the stockings to be of two colours, green and red in stripes (the Yorkist colours being blue and murrey). Beneath the belt were two stripes, one in front and one behind, the width of about four fingers, which was to carry the emblem of the Red Rose (but Bernard de Vignolles was to disclose in his deposition at Rouen the following year that the Red Rose was to be replaced with the White, presumably once the Pretender had landed.) Kendal also had tunics made of the same colour to be worn with the jacquettes; he ordered each Knight to carry it on the bow of his saddle. A servant of Guillemin de Noyon, the Pretender's close associate, whose name was Peter, came

to Kendal with letters supposedly warning the King of the Pretender's
coming invasion of England, but instead he brought letters of which the
King had no knowledge, and later told de Vignolles that he had letters
for Thomas Brandon (Sir Thomas Brandon was Master of the Horse to
Henry VII, and became Ambassador to Maximilian in 1502), which he
said he was afraid to deliver. Kendal himself apparently delivered them to
Brandon, and was in the habit of showing all such letters to the Bishop of
Winchester, Thomas Langton, John Heusse (Horsey), Sir Thomas Tirrel
and Archdeacon Heusse (Horsey), giving them news of the Pretender;
and they in turn passed on news to Kendal whenever they received it.

Their own informant was probably James Kething, Prior of St. John
of Jerusalem in Ireland, who had apparently been with the Pretender for
some years and who accompanied him in his small invasion force.

Kendal had also visited the house of Sir Thomas Tirrel several times.
It is not clear who this Tirrel or Tyrell was; he was not mentioned by the
Chroniclers or in the Act of Attainder, and the name in the original MS is
not certain either: Sir James Tyrell had a son of the name of Thomas who
was condemned with him in 1502, but who was later pardoned and had
his attainder reversed, but he was not then a Knight; he had been with
his father in Guisnes. There was also a Sir Thomas Tyrell who was a
first cousin of Sir James[25]. According to de Vignolles' deposition, it was
Kendal who had remarked to Sir Thomas that King Edward had formerly
been in the said house (again, it is not clear whether it is the Tyrell home
at Gipping in Suffolk, or the home of Sir Thomas at Heron which is
meant); to which Sir Thomas replied that it was true and that he hoped
King Edward's son would make like cheer there; he said the house had
been built with French money and that some day he hoped to have enough
to build another as fair.[26] During this discourse apparently de Vignolles
and Sir John Thong (Thweng?) were also present. Kendal's secretary,
William Outon (Wotton?), a servant of Archdeacon Horsey named Lilly,
and another man named John Watre [obviously the same man who had
been among the first to join the Prince in Ireland, and who was finally
arrested and hanged with him in 1499] 'were', said de Vignolles, 'all three
acquainted with the whole treason as meditated by the said persons, and
Lilly and Watre knew the astrologer originally involved in the plot to kill
Henry and his family, for they were both living in Rome'. De Vignolles
expressed the view that the King ought to prevent them from leaving the
country.[27] In view of this comprehensive denunciation, it is amazing that

Kendal escaped, apparently undetected, though Prior Kething, who was with the Pretender, must have been aware of Kendal's plans.

In the same year that de Vignolles made his deposition against him, Kendal continued to act normally, making claims for lands on behalf of the Order of St. John, while still secretly sending letters, all of which apparently were intercepted, to Guillemin de Noyon, Bernard de Vignolles himself, Étienne Maranecho (the Sardinian who lived near the astrologer in Rome) and the Prior of the Order of St. John of Jerusalem in France. On the 17th April he wrote to de Vignolles asking him to undertake the valuation of some stones and then to return, after which the conspirators were to receive further instructions. He ends 'I have given the bearer three' and then follows an inverted triangle, which is presumably of some significance. The letters to Maranecho and the French Prior are in the same vein; the reference to 'stones' being the efforts to raise money for the Pretender's support. Bernard de Vignolles had pleaded the illness of his brother, in order to escape to France, where his treachery revealed the whole plot.[28]

As a result of Henry's wholesale executions in England of the Pretender's adherents (Buck says there were over two hundred, at least, such executions)[29] it was obvious that his plans for invasion would have to be put back, although by that time they had reached a high state of maturity.[30]

But in the month before Clifford's betrayal, and in the euphoria of the expectation of imminent success, the Prince had signed deeds (witnessed by both Clifford and Barley) promising his aunt compensation in money and estates for the dowry which had never been paid in full by her brother Edward IV on her marriage to the Duke of Burgundy in 1468. Of the 200,000 crowns of gold promised, 81,666 crowns still remained to be paid when the Duke died in 1477. For all the losses which she and her adoptive country had suffered, in spite of the grants she had won from Edward IV in 1480, and the manor of Hunsdon which had been taken from her after Richard III's death, the Prince undertook to recompense her; to give effect to all his father's grants and to reimburse her for all the expenses she had had in mounting Lincoln's and Lovell's offensive against Henry in support of Lambert Simnel. In reward for her hospitality to himself he gave her the town and castle of Scarborough as well as the manor of Hunsdon. These deeds were drawn up in the name of Richard Duke of York and witnessed by notaries, as well as by Clifford and Barley.

After the devastating blow of Clifford's betrayal, the Pretender signed at Malines on 24th January 1495, in his aunt's presence and that of the Archbishop of Mayence and two of the Archduke Philip's Councillors, a document which looks almost like a Will. In it the Pretender made over to Maximilian and his son Philip his rights to the English throne should he die without male issue, and he swore not to seek absolution from the Pope from these oaths for any reason, even that of being under age. (This document is given in full in Appendix III).[31]

The notary who drew up this document was Francis de Busleiden, Provost of Liège and afterwards Bishop of Besancon, who may well have had more the interests of the Archduke Philip in mind than those of the young English Prince whose fortunes were, to say the least, questionable. The signature, 'Richard of England', is once again remarkable, according to Madden, for its boldness and thoroughly English character. The seal shows a shield quartered, bearing in the first and fourth quarters the lilies of France and in the second and third, three leopards, covered with a royal crown, enclosed. Within the circle of the crown are lilies and crowned leopards, holding ostrich feathers above them.

All in all, the document threw down the gauntlet to Henry in trying to ensure that, if the Pretender failed in his attempt to regain the crown, Henry would then have to deal with the claims of both Maximilian and his son. Tudor protagonists see in this a readiness of the Duchess Margaret to sacrifice her nephew for her excessive love for her step-grandson Philip, whom she wished to see on the throne of England. But these protagonists, by maintaining also that the Pretender was really a son of Margaret by the Bishop of Cambrai, are in effect saying that she would sacrifice her own son to gratify her hatred for Henry and her love for Philip, a young man who was only her relative by marriage.

On the 8th May the Duchess made a formal appeal to the Pope on behalf of her nephew, but the Pope's reply is not documented.[32]

The French King had gone to Italy to achieve his conquest of Naples, having circumvented Henry's attempt to prevent him. Henry sent Clarenceux King of Arms to him in Italy, and a flowery exchange of compliments and reminders of the debts each owed the other, followed: Henry's real objective was to discover through Clarenceux as much as he could of the affairs of the Pretender and of the opinions of him of the Pope, the King of Naples and the other lords of Venice, Florence etc.[33] The Pretender's name is not to be mentioned: Henry was making it clear he was not worried by 'the lad' from Flanders. Naturally the French King understood that the sending of such a high dignitary to him in Italy betrayed Henry's nervousness about the Pretender and his plans, and was a plea to him to help in cutting off support for the young man.

The state of Henry's nerves, however, can have been as nothing compared with the dismay and misgivings in the Yorkist camp, knowing what little support there could now be for the small invading army on its arrival in England. Chastelain lists four Englishmen who accompanied the Pretender: Wight, Bell, Corbett and Mountford, son of Sir Simon Mountford executed by Henry; there was also presumably Anthony de la Forsse, Prior Kething and John Watre. Hall says there were eight captains, two of whom were Spanish and whom Hall names as Don Fulano de Guevara and one as Diego the Lame. There was much youthful enthusiasm but no single military leader of repute. The Pretender himself was totally without either military training or, as it was to be demonstrated, taste or zeal for military adventure.* In any case, his chance of success had gone with Sir William Stanley's head.

But mercenaries and stores cannot be kept waiting indefinitely, and it was now time to justify the hopes of Maximilian and the Duchess Margaret. With his flotilla of fifteen ships, fitted out by Maximilian and full of vagabonds and murderers (says Chastelain, quoting Hall), Prince Richard of York set sail at the beginning of July 1495 from the Low Countries to begin his attempt to gain the English throne.

*Except for some possible military tutelage from Hugh de Melun (see p.77 above also p.98)

CHAPTER THIRTEEN

Initial Failure

On 3rd July 1495 Prince Richard, Pretender to the throne of England, arrived with his small flotilla of fifteen ships off Deal in Kent. Chastelain alone has an extraordinary story that 'Perkin's fleet, arriving in the outskirts of London, found the population antagonistic towards him: he thought it better to try another part of the island'.[1] and so arrived off Deal. Chastelain's story sounds most unlikely: if the populace of London had been so unfriendly, it is doubtful whether any of the ships would have escaped from the mouth of the Thames estuary.

Margaret, Maximilian and Philip anxiously awaited the outcome: Maximilian was presiding over the Diet at Worms when the news came that the landing had been successful and that the Prince had been received with enthusiasm by a crowd of partisans. Maximilian spoke to the Venetian Ambassadors as though the regaining of the throne by Richard of York was already a *fait accompli,* and envisaged the army of the new King marching with his own against France.[2]

Six days later the real story arrived in Worms and Malines, where the Duchess was waiting. The truth was horribly different.

Some three hundred of the Pretender's men had indeed landed at Deal, and had managed to plant three standards, but the men of Kent, always sturdily independent, after asking who they were and inviting the Pretender ashore (which invitation he rightly suspected was a trap), set on the invaders and killed one hundred and fifty of them and took eighty more prisoner, all of whom were afterwards hanged and their bodies strung up along the coast to deter others, having first been handed over to Sir John Peachey 'railed in ropes like horses drawn in a cart'[3]. The rest fled back to the ships and told their sorry story. Not one of Henry's soldiers had been required in the defeat of the ill-conceived and ill-managed adventure, and the unhappy Pretender decided to cut his losses and sail on to

Ireland, whence he believed he would be able to mount another attempt.

Gairdner and Chastelain scornfully report this set-back to the Prince's first attempt to invade; taking the view that this episode, reflecting most ill on the Prince's personal courage and his 'contemptible abandonment of his men' (Gairdner) proves that he was no Plantagenet Prince. But surely it only proves that he lacked any military experience whatever; if he had landed with his men, his whole enterprise might well have ended there and then, and he was not to know that another day would not bring a different result. Henry himself, when attempting to land at Poole to link up with Buckingham in the autumn of 1483 on his own first invasion attempt, also refused an invitation to come ashore, and sailed on to try again another day, and I do not know that anyone has blamed him for it. Neither Richard II nor Henry VI were noted for their martial exploits, but their Plantagenet blood has not been questioned because of it. Plantagenet blood, it is hardly necessary to point out, is apt to be diluted from the mother's side, and in consequence may produce offspring of completely different character and temperament from that of the father.

In the Calendar of Venetian State Papers, dealing with events in England from 1495–1498, stress is laid on the efforts of the Emperor Maximilian to induce Henry VII to join a league against the King of France, who was invading the Kingdom of Naples; pointing out that Henry and other European monarchs were using 'Perkin' as a pawn: while 'Perkin's' small force was making the assault on the coast of Kent, Maximilian was reported to have remarked that 'he could dispose of this Duke of York at his pleasure' (dated at Worms, 15th July 1495). It will be noted that Maximilian calls the Prince 'Duke of York' and not 'Perkin' and, as we shall see, Ambassadors in foreign countries often reported gossip as fact.

Henry was evidently not expecting the Pretender's invasion at that time, for he had left on a Northern progress and on 4th July, the day after the Prince's ill-fated attempt off Deal, Henry was at Worcester, having been to visit his mother, the Lady Margaret Stanley, at Latham on the way. He must have been overjoyed to hear the news, and in October that year he sent Sir Richard Guildford into Kent to thank the people for what they had done.

King Ferdinand and Queen Isabella of Spain wrote to their Ambassador, who was negotiating the marriage between their daughter the Infanta Catalina of Aragon and Henry's son Arthur:- 'as for the affair of him who calls himself duke, we hold it for a jest'.[4] They certainly did not want to have their negotiations for Henry's friendship broken up by a change of rulers in England. On the other hand, at the time the Venetian Ambassador was reporting Maximilian's alleged remark disparaging 'this duke of york', the Emperor was writing to the Pope, backing up the Duchess Margaret's appeal to him on behalf of the Duke of York.[5]

But the prince found that the situation in Ireland had changed drastically. It was not to be supposed that Henry would allow that country to become once again a thorn in his side; the belligerent Irish had supported first Lambert Simnel at Stoke and had then welcomed and flocked to join Prince Richard in 1491. Clifford's betrayal had probably revealed the names of many other Yorkist supporters lying in wait in Ireland as well; but even before that Henry had sent an army to Ireland under the command of Sir Edward Poynings, who was appointed Lieutenant of Ireland on 13th September 1494, and who gave the Irish very short shrift. Every town and place where the Pretender had been received, helped or honoured, had been purged by Poynings, and the country had paid horribly dear for its former adherence to York. The Earl of Desmond still welcomed the Pretender but other nobles lay low, and the Irish people were cold.

With Desmond in Munster, the Pretender and his advisers considered their future plans. They must have concluded that the coasts of England would now be too heavily defended against him after his abortive raid on Deal. One report says he went to France at this time, but was forced to leave because of the terms of a Treaty Henry had made with Charles, but since this Treaty was not made until 24th February 1496, and the Prince's movements at the end of July are known, this report must be confused with the Prince's earlier visit to France in 1492.

King James IV of Scotland, who had been in touch with the Pretender over the last three years, sent at least one ship, *The Keke-out*, (the Spy) to aid Richard and, with Desmond's help, the Pretender captured an English vessel called the *Christopher of Plymouth*, at Youghal. Whoever advised the Pretender at this time, certainly gave him the worst possible counsel, for, with a flotilla of eleven ships he sailed up the harbour and laid siege to Waterford — the one town which had remained loyal to Henry when the Irish had given aid to Lambert Simnel nine years before.

The siege began on 23rd July and continued for eleven days, but Waterford's cannon, firing from Reginald's Tower, stove in the side of one of the Pretender's ships and, making no headway, having lost three of his ships, one of which was the Scottish *Keke-out*, he was advised to raise the siege, which he accordingly did on 3rd August.

In the Royal MS are all the details of the siege: the Deputy Lieutenant took the field with the King's standard displayed, on 23rd July. The Captains of the Gunners who were responsible for the defence and who captured the ships, were Adam van Edyngton and William Warrewick; they were rewarded with £4 on 26th August. The captured ship the *Keke-out* was sold to Henry Wyot for £26.13s.4d: another was sold to John Clerc for the same sum and the third, called *le Mare*, was sold to the same man for cloth to the amount of £40.[6] The foregoing shows the smallness of the Pretender's ships.

According to a Spanish report the men of Waterford pursued the Pretender and his followers to Cork, where his friend John O'Water (or Walters) was Mayor; but the name may be confused with the John Watre who appears to have been his companion all along; the story continues that the Prince's vessel was wrecked, and that he and his friends were forced to cross the mountains in disguise, reaching a small seaport (unspecified), where three Spanish ships were waiting for them.

Madden says that 'Perkin' now returned to Flanders [7], but this is most unlikely, because the situation there had also changed. Henry's trade ban on Flanders had hurt the Low Countries badly and, now that the Archduke Philip had come of age, he had thrown off the advice of his Council and, at the end of 1495, opened negotiations for peace with Henry. The English Ambassadors appointed were Richard Fox, Bishop of Durham, Viscount Welles, and none other than Sir John Kendal, Prior of the Order of St. John of Jerusalem, who was still evidently unsuspected by Henry. The Treaty was finally concluded on 24th February 1496, and the two parties agreed not to help one another's enemies. It is most unlikely, therefore, that Philip would have welcomed the Pretender into Flanders while the negotiations were proceeding, or even contemplated, in London, and his step-grandmother, the Duchess Margaret, was now subject to his jurisdiction.

Chastelain makes out that, now 'Perkin' had had two failures, the Princes of Europe tossed him aside like a sucked orange, having in any case only used him as long as he could be of any advantage to them in their own schemes, but Maximilian, as we have already seen, wrote to the Pope as late as the 22nd September, backing up the appeal on the Pretender's behalf, which the Duchess Margaret had already made.[8] Even the Archduke Philip, who had had to forbid the Pretender to return to Flanders as a result of the Treaty he was negotiating with Henry for the restoration of trade between the two countries, also wrote to the King of the Scots recommending that he help the Duke of York.[9]

Accordingly it was to Scotland and the Scottish King James IV that Prince Richard now appealed for aid and sanctuary.

CHAPTER FOURTEEN

The Court of Scotland

King James III of Scotland had been killed at Sauchieburn in 1488 during an uprising of his people protesting at his friendliness towards Henry VII: tragically, his young son James had been persuaded to join the rebels by an appeal to his patriotism, and the young man blamed himself bitterly ever afterwards for his father's death, which he had certainly never intended. Now, as James IV, he sought an excuse, possibly any excuse, for a renewal of the old hostility towards England. In any case, it was the most popular policy which he could possibly have adopted to unite his warlike people and to engage and keep the love of his lawless subjects.

Both James and Henry were conspiring to deceive each other, even though a new truce was being debated at the same time. Henry's agents were Sir John Cheney and Sir William Tyler, but he had also gained a most valuable ally in the traitorous Duke of Bothwell, who had fought for James III against his son and had never forgiven that son for the father's death. Bothwell agreed to spy for Henry against his own King, and with Sir James Tod proposed to try and capture not only the King but his younger brother the Duke of Ross, who was himself conspiring to usurp his elder brother's throne. The Earl of Angus and his son George Douglas made a pact with Henry's agents that if the King would not agree to a new truce, they would join the conspiracy against him.

A new truce was, however, made at Coldstream in 1492, to last until 30th April 1494; and on 25th June 1493 a peace treaty was drawn up to last for seven years, ratified a month later by both James and Henry. By this treaty Henry agreed to pay James an indemnity of 1,000 marks for all past injuries inflicted by land and sea. But in the spring the warlike Scots were again threatening to invade the Northern counties; and the Earl of Surrey, who had ultimately been pardoned by Henry for fighting against him at Bosworth, and was now Vice-Warden of the West and Middle Marches, was commissioned to array men between the Trent and Tweed to resist the Scots army.

James was at this time in correspondence with the Duchess Margaret of Burgundy, making preparations to help fit out ships and supply men and money for the Pretender. The town of Aberdeen alone was asked to supply one month's pay at five shillings and fourpence a day for eight Englishmen to serve the Pretender: James granted them licence to remain at home when he should invade England on the Pretender's behalf. It is thus clear that, although it suited the hawks among the Scots to make use of any excuse to attack England despite any truce or treaty made between their King and Henry, in James' own mind his support for the Pretender was a separate issue not covered by the treaty.

The Spanish State Papers of this time, translated by the scholar G.A. Bergenroth, contain a lively description of King James by the then Spanish Ambassador to the Scottish court, Pedro de Ayala.

He writes:-

'He is twenty-five and some months old. He is of noble stature, neither tall nor short, and as handsome in complexion and shape as a man can be. His address is very agreeable. He speaks Latin very well; French, German, Flemish, Italian and Spanish. . .besides the language of the savages who live in some parts of Scotland on the islands. He fears God and observes all the precepts of the Church. He does not eat meat on Wednesdays and Fridays. He says all his prayers. . . after Mass he has the cantata sung. . . he gives alms liberally, but is a severe judge, especially in the case of murderers. . .he has a very good memory'. De Ayala goes on: 'He is not avaricious nor prodigal, but liberal when occasion requires. He is courageous even more so than a King should be. I am a good witness of it. I have seen him often undertake most dangerous things in the last wars. . . he does not take the least care of himself' [here Bergenroth inserts the note that de Ayala, in spite of his clerical character, occasionally took part in a little fighting on the Borders during his frequent travels between Edinburgh and London.] 'He is not a good Captain, because he begins to fight before he has given his orders. He said to me that his subjects serve him with their persons and their goods, in just and unjust quarrels, exactly as he likes, and that therefore he does not think it right to begin any warlike undertaking without being himself the first in danger. His deeds are as good as his words. For this reason, and because he is a very humane Prince, he is much loved. He is active and works hard. When he is not at war he hunts in the mountains. I tell your Highness that God has worked a miracle in him, for I have never seen a man so temperate in eating and drinking, out of Spain. . . He lends a willing ear to his counsellors, and decides nothing without asking them; but in great matters he acts according to his own judgment, and in my opinion he generally makes a right decision. I recognise him perfectly in the conclusion of the last peace, which was made against the wishes of the majority in his kingdom. When he was a minor he was instigated by those who held the government to do some dishonourable things. They favoured his love intrigues with their relations in order to keep him in their subjection. But as soon as he came of age and understood his duties he gave up these intrigues. When I arrived he was keeping a lady with great state in a castle. . .it may be about a year since he gave up — so at least it is believed — his love-making, as well from fear of God as from fear of scandal in this world, which is thought very much of here. I can say with truth that he esteems himself as much as though he were Lord of the World. He loves war so much that I fear, judging by the provocation he receives, the peace will not last long.'

That de Ayala allowed his obvious affection for James to cloud his judgment slightly about the King's love-life is of little importance: he had his reason. In another dispatch he counsels his Sovereigns to match their third daughter with James:- 'he would always be a faithful ally, near at hand and ready to assist. . . the kingdom is very old and very noble, and the King possesses great virtues and no defects worth mentioning.'

Of the Scottish people, de Ayala says:- 'They spend all their time in wars, and when there is no war they fight with each other. The Scotch are not industrious, and the people are poor. But since the present King succeeded to the throne they do not dare to quarrel so much with one another as formerly, especially since he came of age. They have learnt by experience that he executes the law without respect to rich or poor. I am told that Scotland has improved so much during his reign that it is worth three times more now than formerly, on account of foreigners having come into the country and taught them how to live. . .The Scots like foreigners so much that they dispute with one another as to who shall have and treat a foreigner in his house. [The King had an English court jester, Jolly John, according to the Accounts of the Lord High Treasurer]. They are vain and ostentatious by nature. They spend all they have to keep up appearances. They are as well dressed as it is possible to be in such a country.'

In a description of de Ayala, who was not only Spanish Ambassador to Scotland, but also accredited to London, Bergenroth says he was no great scholar, but a charming man who made friends everywhere; his admiration and respect for the Scottish King was evidently returned, for James called him 'Father'.

Henry well knew of de Ayala's reputation and his great flair for business: he flattered him and tried to win him over, but he never succeeded.[1]

This was the King who now invited the Pretender to his country, and received him both as a friend in distress and as a cousin, welcoming him to his family circle; he paid for his clothes, his servants, his horses, and was even prepared to stage an invasion into England on his behalf. Taking into account the convenience of an excuse, any excuse, for attacking and annoying Henry, it is surely unreasonable to imagine that the canny Scottish King would have continued to pay for the young man's court within a court, if he had not believed in him as a prince. They were very much of an age, and probably had many interests common to young noblemen as added reasons for friendship, but temperamentally they could hardly have been more different: the Scots King had been trained from a small boy in warlike exercises, and had been involved in the pitiless and bloody fighting during the rebellion against his father, when he was only fifteen, but Richard had led a cosseted life until the age of ten, and had then spent his formative years in disguise as a wandering merchant's assistant, when he should have been learning military and political arts. The only hint that he may have imbibed some military training and knowledge when he was in Flanders at the age of about twenty, is in a letter addressed by the Prince de Ligne to Henry VIII in 1513. In it the Prince de Ligne complains of the conduct of Hue de Mellum, Hugh de Melun, or Hugues de Meleun, as his name is also spelt, who, he states, was the person who directed all 'Perkin's' affairs at that time. De Meleun was Vicomte de Gand, Knight of the Golden Fleece, and Governor of Dendermonde. He enjoyed the confidence of both Maximilian and his son Philip, and the previous year (1492) had defeated the Gantois who had sent troops to surprise the town of Dendermonde. All the more tribute to the Pretender, therefore, that in manners and bearing, as well as fluency in many languages, he was able to hold his own with James.

The Scottish King, though he found fault with the Pretender's lack of experience and zeal for martial matters, was never to discredit him, even after his failure and death.

The Pretender landed on the West coast of Scotland, dressed as splendidly as possible in order to impress the people with his appearance which, as he resembled his handsome father, Edward IV, so closely in looks and figure, must have been quite outstanding. Arras work had been carried from Edinburgh to Stirling in preparation for the official reception, but James did not wait for this and hurried to meet him at Stirling on 20th November 1495. The Scottish Accounts give details of the presents given by the generous King to his impoverished guest: 'a pair of hose' of 'risillis blak' at thirty-five shillings; lining and points to cost five shillings more, and twenty shillings for 'half an elne of purpour dammas to begare the sammyn' (embellish it with stripes): a 'hogtoun' or cassock for the Prince 'against the tournay'; a 'pair of arming hose': later, 'a spousing gown (for his wedding); a great coat and various other articles for his personal use and that of his servants.[2]

The official reception seems to have taken place a week later, on 27th November. Polydore Vergil, Hall and later, Gainsford, all give an account of the Prince's speech to King James on that occasion, and since they are all Tudor accounts it is difficult to say what, if any of it, is factual. It will therefore be sufficient to summarize it because much of it is a repetition of his wanderings and misfortunes the account of which readers will by now be familiar with. He accuses his uncle Richard of having murdered his brother Edward V and of attempting to murder himself; but in doing so he says that the murderer, having had pity on him, nevertheless reported to King Richard that both boys were dead, so that 'this report was accordingly believed and published generally, so that the world hath been possessed of an opinion that they were both barbarously made away'. He goes on to say 'For the manner of my escape, it is fit it should pass in silence, or at least in a more secret relation, for that it may concern some alive and the memory of some that are dead'. But he reserves the full force of his recriminations for King Henry, his 'extreme and mortal enemy', who was trying to procure his destruction by bribing his servants to poison him and suborning others such as Sir Robert Clifford to betray him, and by spreading false stories that he was 'a feigned person.' He ends his speech by praising both his aunt, the Duchess Margaret, for her help and support, and his present host,

King James, for his willingnes to assist him to regain his throne, and 'I do faithfully promise to bear myself towards your Grace no otherwise than if I were your own natural brother and will, upon the recovery of mine inheritance, gratefully do you all the pleasure that is in my utmost power'.[3]

Once again, though pouring scorn on the Pretender's claims and assertions, Hall (quoted by Gainsford in his own flowery style) notes: 'His audience was so touched both by his manner and gestures, no less than by his youth and bearing, that the King cheered him by telling him that he would assist him so that he would not repent him of his coming thither.' Tytler, the Scottish historian, while calling him an accomplished impostor, also draws attention to his noble appearance and the grace and unaffected dignity of his manners, and says the air of mystery and romance which his misfortunes had thrown around him, contributed to persuade the King of the identity of his person and the justice of his claim upon the throne of England.

He was welcomed to Scotland with great state and rejoicing. The King addressed him as 'Cousin' and arranged tournaments and other courtly festivities to honour his arrival, conducting him in a progress through his dominions 'in which by his handsome appearance and popular manners he [the Prince] concentrated to himself the admiration of the people'.[4] One can partly explain the Scots' enthusiasm by remembering that it needed very little excuse in Scottish minds to fight the English: nevertheless this still cannot satisfactorily explain how a young man, allegedly not only a foreigner but one of extremely humble birth, should have not only a striking resemblance to Edward IV, but how he acquired in such a short time the grace, manners and art of self-expression in at least three other languages besides perfect English. In the accomplished, chivalrous and intellectual courts of Charles of France, Maximilian and the Duchess Margaret of Burgundy, as in that of James IV of Scotland, he was never to be found wanting in any way in refinement of manner or feeling.

King James called his Council together and it was agreed to help the young man, who was to be known as the Duke of York. Further, the King arranged to pay him not only a pension, but money for clothes (white damask for his 'wedding gown' the following January), with dresses for the tournay for himself and six servants, with a banner of murrey and blue, the Yorkist colours, to be borne before him on the expedition into England.[5] James was able to persuade his Council to vote the money for the Prince's expenses by pointing out the future benefits to Scotland.

'As a result of this the young man's behaviour became much more cheerful, and he hawked and hunted with the nobles, while the young ladies of the court vied with each other to get his favours; he was young, handsome and witty, and might become one of the mightiest kings in Europe. They thought themselves happy, if his fancy should fasten upon any of them. So he dallied with some, danced with others, jested with the rest, and was acceptable to all. At last he met and fell deeply in love with the Lady Catherine Gordon, the elder daughter of the Earl of Huntly; her mother probably being his second wife, the Princess Annabella, daughter of James I and his Queen, Jane Beaufort, by which descent Lady Catherine was a cousin of King James IV. It is not certain when the Pretender first met her, but it cannot have been long after his arrival, for they were married the following January.' Gainsford has a lyrical account of the wooing of the Lady Catherine by Prince Richard who, after declaring his undying love and beseeching her to take pity on him by trusting her fate to his, 'with a kind of reverence, after he had kissed her thrice, he took her in both his hands cross-wise and gazed upon her, with a kind of putting her from him and pulling her to him, and so again and again rekissed her, and set her in her place with a pretty manner of enforcement.'[6]

It was obviously mutual love at first sight, for the young lady lost no time in accepting him and assuring him of her devotion. We have the Scottish historian Tytler's description of her as 'a lady of extraordinary beauty and accomplishments' whose effect on men was as devastating as that of the Pretender on women. He was to love her with a consuming passion which Henry may have used later to contribute to his downfall: she loved him with a true devotion which refused to denounce him even when he was forced to confess to imposture. It is therefore impossible to believe that they had any secrets from one another, given their obvious feelings of love. He had already made public the circumstances of his escape from the Tower, together with his wanderings meanly dressed for his own safety, until he grew old enough to lay claim to the crown. Her own proximity to King James would ensure that she knew the stories that King Henry was circulating about the Prince.

But the Earl of Huntly, like most fathers, was less enthusiastic; he apparently thought little of the Pretender's chances of reclaiming the

English throne, whatever he thought about his identity. However, his daughter and his Sovereign combined to put pressure on him, and he gave way. He and his wife were certainly mollified when they saw that King James was prepared to treat him as the future King of England.

The Scottish Treasurer's Accounts state that the Pretender was with the King on St. Nicholas' Day (6th December), when both made offerings in Church; and they were again together in Edinburgh on Candlemas Day (2nd February) in early 1496. There are no Edinburgh Marriage Registers for the reign of James IV, but another Scottish historian, Dickson, says that, after the King and Pretender met at Perth for 'wapping-schawing' (arming of men in preparation for war), at which the Northern lords were summoned to levy men for military service: 'Early in January 1496 the King returned to Edinburgh, where probably the marriage of 'Perkin' took place about the middle of the month. There seems reason for supposing that the Tournay referred to in the Accounts was held on St. Mungo's Day (13th January) in honour of this event'.[7] We already know that the King had paid for the Prince's 'spousing gown' and a length of white damask, presumably for his wedding clothes.

Among the Spanish State Papers discovered and translated by the nineteenth century German historian G. A. Bergenroth at the Castle of Simancas in Spain is an ecstatic love-letter which he concluded had been written by the Pretender to the Lady Catherine Gordon. The original was in Latin written, Bergenroth says, in his own hand. He comments: 'As regards refinement and chivalrous feeling, the Pretender had few if any equals among the Princes and nobles of his time.'

For readers of a romantic disposition, I give an English translation of the letter in full in Appendix IV. After reading so many words which may or may not have been put into the Pretender's mouth by historians, it is refreshing to feel that here we are glimpsing the real man.

CHAPTER FIFTEEN

Henry's Dilemma and the Abortive Raid

Soon after the Prince's arrival in Scotland, Henry sent Clarenceux King of Arms on a third mission to France with instructions dated at Shene the 5th March 1496. Henry's message was full of artful dissembling: he referred to a possible meeting between the two Kings; hinted at a possible marriage between the Dauphin and his daughter Margaret; mentioned the monies he had lent Charles; referred to his Queen and the French Queen being pregnant and a possible marriage between the two children if a boy and a girl (but Elizabeth of York was not pregnant, unless she lost the baby), and he ended by saying that the Pope, the King of Spain and Maximilian were all trying to persuade him to join the League of Venice in protest at the French King's attempt to invade Italy. Henry's real message, however, was contained in the private instructions he gave Clarenceux: if the French King inquires how he and the King of Scotland accord now that James is supporting 'le garçon' ('Perkin'), Clarenceux is to assure the French King that Henry is completely unconcerned; he says James IV is unable to hurt him, and that if he attempts it, he reminds Charles of his promise to aid England; in particular if James made an attempt to capture Berwick. A similar message was sent through Clarenceux to the Cardinal of St.Malo, Guillaume Briconnet, who had held the rank of General under Louis XI; Henry disclosed that, in secret overtures, the French King Charles would permit the son of the Duke of Albany (James IV's uncle) to be used against the Scots in the event of James making war on England.[1]

Meanwhile the Spanish Sovereigns were continuing their efforts to provide parents for 'Perkin', while maintaining their public insistence that he was of no interest to them because of his humble birth. Their Ambassador in London, Roderigo de Puebla, revealed in one of his letters to them that their desire to capture 'Perkin' was in order to force Henry thereby to join the League against Charles. In his turn, Charles sent Henry a private message referring to 'Perkin' as the son of a barber (probably a mistake for 'boatman') and offering to send his parents over the Channel. The affair of the 'unimportant garçon' was bordering on the farcical, with the Spanish Sovereigns vying with the French King in offering to produce 'Perkin's' parents: they wrote to Henry saying they could produce several people, including a Portuguese gentleman by the name of Ruy de Sousa who knew the Duke of York well, having been Portuguese Ambassador in England, where he had seen the Duke of York, and two years later had seen 'the other person' in Portugal. But the last occasion on which Ruy de Sousa could have seen the little Duke of York would have been before his father's death in 1483, and the man whom he called 'the other person' did not arrive in Portugal until after Easter 1487. The relevant passage is:- 'We could send the father and mother of Perkin, who are living in Portugal and are our subjects'.[2] Ruy de Sousa's evidence may be interpreted in any one of four ways:-

1. That he did indeed see the real Duke of York in England two years before seeing 'Perkin' in Portugal in 1487, which means the young Prince was alive after the date the two Princes were supposed to have been murdered;
2. That 'Perkin' had arrived in Portugal with Brampton before 1487;
3. That he really was convinced that the Duke of York and 'Perkin' were two different people, or
4. That he was anxious to ingratiate himself with the Spanish Sovereigns, having recently entered their service and quit that of his own country, Portugal.

One must also take into account the fact that the little Duke of York was of such tender years before 1483 that he is unlikely to have been very frequently seen by foreign Ambassadors at his father's court, and that he would have changed considerably in appearance in his teens, so one must obviously allow for a genuine mistake in identification by the Portuguese Ambassador. In any case it is highly significant that Henry never made any use of any of these offers to produce 'Perkin's' parents: he contented himself with saying he had 'witnesses', but he never produced them and there is no hint of their having been brought over to give evidence, by any inclusion in royal accounts. Of much more pressing importance to Henry at this time was the French King's disclosure that James intended to attack

Berwick, three miles from the Scottish border. It was known to be a thorn in James' side (he told the Pretender that it was a centre for Henry's spies), and it was also the place where the letters of Sir John Kendal to Bernard de Vignolles and Guillemin de Noyon were intercepted on 17th April 1496,[3]. Two months later, in June 1496, the Scots were busy with preparations for invasion of the border.[4]

France, Spain, Maximilian and Venice were all now watching to see if Henry could keep his throne. Historians who reason that, because the Princes of Europe made what use they could of the Pretender, they therefore considered him to be an impostor, ignore the fact that all the Princes of Europe made use of rival claimants to embarrass their enemies whenever they could. In James IV's case it was his younger brother the Duke of Ross, certainly no impostor, who was being used by Henry to embarrass James, and was later discarded when it suited Henry to do so. If the Pretender had won the throne from Henry, that would also have suited the Princes of Europe; they would then have brought pressure to bear on the new monarch while he was trying to establish himself. The Pope, Spain, Venice and Milan all joined in asking Henry to join the Holy League of Venice, and now even Maximilian added his voice to theirs.

On the arrival of the Venetian Ambassadors, Piero Contarini and Luca Valaresso in London, Henry gave Contarini audience at once, and went out of his way to impress and welcome him. Contarini reported to the Signory that Henry received him 'in a small hall hung with very handsome tapestry; leaning against a tall gilt chair covered with cloth of gold. He was wearing a violet-coloured gown lined with cloth-of-gold, and a collar of many jewels, and on his cap was a large diamond and a very beautiful pearl. Prince Arthur, aged twelve [he would actually have been nine and a half] was present, also the Duke of Buckingham and other Lords and Prelates. The King remained standing throughout. Subsequently Henry gave Contarini private audience, and as a special favour presented him to the Queen, who was wearing cloth-of-gold, and on one side of her was the King's mother; on the other side the Prince.'[5] Contarini was suitably impressed: he wrote to the Emperor Maximilian advising him to copy Spain and 'lay aside the affairs of the Duke of York'. But a little later Contarini was reporting to the Signory that King Henry was in dread of being expelled from his kingdom by the Duke of York, then in Scotland, whose King meant to assist him and had given him his niece [sic] in marriage.[6]

Maximilian's reply to the Venetian Ambassador was forthright: 'The King of the Romans made answer that he had recently received letters from the Duke of York, informing him that his affairs were prospering and that, through the disturbances imminent in England, he hoped for victory. . . . That it would be unfortunate, as the Duke had embarked on the undertaking at his [Maximilian's] persuasion and placed hope in him — if, through the negotiation for bringing Henry into the League, the Duke of York's success should be impeded, by so much more as, were the Duke of York to obtain the crown, the King of the Romans and the League might avail themselves of England against the King of France as if the island were their own.'[7] It is interesting that the Pretender is reported in the above letter as having mentioned 'disturbances imminent in England', which is some evidence that he was in touch with dissidents. Both Bacon and Gainsford record that the following year he was invited by the Cornish rebels to lead them.[8]

But by that time his temporary good fortune would be in decline: the invasion from Scotland would have turned out to be nothing but an abortive raid, and the opportunity to co-ordinate plans would be gone. . . . Truly, good fortune must be taken at the flood, as Shakespeare has pointed out. The tragedy for the Pretender was that he was fated always to miss the tide.

Meanwhile preparations for the invasion of the North of England by King James on the Pretender's behalf went ahead in Scotland.

Henry's spy at the Scottish court, the Earl of Bothwell, was busy learning all the details. There are two letters extant, written by Bothwell to Henry[9] telling him that the 'feynit boy' and James intend making another expedition into England on 17th September with 1,400 men, and that two vessels had arrived from the Duchess Margaret in Flanders, with sixty German men-at-arms, harness, crossbows and other necessary military stores under the command of Roderick de la Lane. Bothwell advises Henry to make an immediate descent on Scotland to stop the invasion, and says that if he himself had a fleet he could sail northwards and destroy all James's ships. He gives details of the provision of Ordnance for Edinburgh Castle: 'ij great curtaldis of war sent from France, x falconis [small field guns] or little serpentinis [old cannon]; thirty cart gunnis of iron with chaumeris and sixteen clos carts for spears, powder, stanis and other stuff for gunnery'.[10] Bothwell had also persuaded the Duke of Ross, James's younger brother, the Earl of

Buchan and the Bishop of Moray to promise Henry their utmost support; Ross even undertaking to 'place himself under the protection of the King of England the moment his royal brother crossed the borders.' Bothwell even entered into a plot at Henry's suggestion, with Buchan and the English envoy, Wyot, to seize 'Warbeck' in his tent at night. 'Please your Grace', Bothwell wrote to Henry, 'anent the matter that Master Wyot laid to me, I have been busy about it, and my Lord of Buchan takes upon him the fulfilling of it, gif it be possible; and thinks best now: in this lang night within his tent to enterprise the matter; for he has no watch but the King's appointed to be about him; and they have ordanit the Englishmen and strangers to be at another quarter lugit [lodged] but a few about him'.[11] Only the vigilance of the Royal Guard keeping ceaseless watch, is assumed to be the reason why this project failed.

'While many of the most powerful Scottish barons thus secretly lent themselves to Henry, and remained with the army only to betray it, others endeavoured to dissuade James from the enterprise; but the glory of restoring an unfortunate Prince, the last of a noble race, to his hereditary throne; the recovery of Berwick which he had engaged to place in the hands of the Scottish King, were motives too strong to be resisted.'[12]

The Lord Treasure's Accounts record that on 10th September a payment of 'two hundred of gold party to the Duke of York's banner' was made; on the 14th, a sum of fourteen shillings for the Duke of York's offering; and a present of £36 in his purse by the King's command'. On 21st, at Coldstream, 'when the Duke of York come hame', there was a further sum of £74.8s. also given him by the King's command.[13]

Henry made a last desperate attempt to prevent the invasion from getting under way. He commissioned Bishop Fox, Bishop of Durham, to suggest a marriage between James and Henry's daughter Margaret: at the same time Thomas Savage, Bishop of London, was sent to Spain to urge on the negotiations between Henry and the Spanish Sovereigns to secure the marriage of their daughter Catherine with Arthur, Prince of Wales.

But James also had his spies, who intercepted letters from Ferdinand and Isabella to their Ambassadors who were travelling to Edinburgh from London, in which their Majesties instructed their Ambassadors to offer King James the hand of one of their daughters (Catherine), whom Henry had already revealed was contracted to marry Prince Arthur. The consequent embarrassment of the Spanish Ambassadors can be imagined, and Henry's offer therefore fell on deaf ears as far as James was concerned; but he did remark to Blacader that if the child Margaret kept on growing and he himself stayed unwed long enough, Scotland might yet have an English consort for lack of any other mate. . .[14]

Charles VIII of France, too, was playing a double game; he sent as his Ambassador to Scotland the Lord of Concressault (the same William Monypenny who had formerly commanded the Pretender's bodyguard while he was at the French court). Ostensibly Concressault was to act as mediator between Henry and James, but he had orders to try and persuade King James to send the Pretender back to France, yet secretly to encourage the invasion. Bothwell reported to Henry that 'the Sieur de Concressault had orders to enquire about "Perkin's" birth, and that he [Bothwell] showed him a document from Meautes, the King of England's French Secretary . . . and he plainly said he never understood it, but rather trowed the contrary'. Gairdner suggests this may have been the document Charles had sent to Henry saying that 'Perkin' was the son of a barber and offering to send over his parents[15], but there is no confirmation of this and if it was so, Concressault evidently did not believe its contents. On the whole Bothwell thinks the French Ambassador's coming had done little good, 'for he [James] and the feynit boy are every day in Council'.[16]

The Venetian Ambassadors in London were now reporting to the Signory that King Henry was in danger of being driven from his throne[17], and Bacon later commented that 'Perkin' would have won the crown if he had been in Cornwall when the rising there was first mooted.

Kendal, as we have seen, was busily hatching his plots in Berwick, and was presumably on the point of declaring himself for the Pretender, when his letters were intercepted and exposed by Bernard de Vignolles. Kendal was extremely fortunate, or perhaps particularly astute, in escaping the consequences of his treasonable activities. The Pretender had also written to the Earl of Desmond in Ireland asking for his help, but Desmond had been disciplined by Henry and did not dare to reply.

On the eve of invasion, the Pretender issued a Proclamation which Chastelain quotes in full, and which those readers who are interested may find in Appendix V. It contained a long recital, once again, of his escape from the Tower; of Henry's seizure of the throne which was rightly his; of Henry's attempts to have him killed and his betrayal by Clifford; of Henry's cruel taxation of his subjects and his execution of a number of courtiers: he castigates Henry for his imprisonment of the young Edward of Warwick, his cousin, and many others in order to prevent them from helping him, and for forcing 'certain of our sisters' to marry inferior people. He accuses Henry of intending to send abroad the treasure of the realm with the intention of following it, and he promises large rewards to any who will join him, or capture Henry, or even who will desist from their support of Henry and return to their allegiance to him. He will ensure that justice, such as it has always been administered by his ancestors, will once again be equitably apportioned to any who would now lend arms to his force.[18]

No Englishmen responded to this appeal, although many of the Border barons, notably the Nevills, Dacres, Lovels and Herons, had been in secret touch with the Pretender. Nevertheless, the Scottish King confidently expected that the disposition in the Pretender's favour would become general the moment he penetrated into England. Tytler says of the Proclamation:- 'It was judiciously drawn up, yet it gained no proselytes. So long as 'Warbeck' had attempted to assert his pretended rights to the throne by the assistance of the English, whom he claimed as his own subjects, he had some chance of success; but such was still the hatred between the two nations, that his appearance at the head of a Scottish army at once destroyed all sympathy and affection for his cause. Instead of a general uprising of the people, the Scottish Monarch found that the English Border barons who had joined him were avoided as traitors and renegades, and the large force of German, French and Flemish volunteers who marched along with the army, only increased the odium. . .'

It is indeed hard for us to understand, from this distance in time, how the canny James could have thought for a moment that the Pretender's cause could possibly be furthered by the appearance of the hated Scots army in the Northern counties, but presumably his desire to give his beloved Scots what they most enjoyed — the opportunity of fighting over the Border — must have acted as a spur, together with the Pretender's promise, on the advice of his chief Counsellor, Sir George Nevill, to cede Berwick to James and to pay an indemnity of 50,000 marks over the next two years,[19]. One must also recall that James was laying out a considerable sum of money in support and maintenance, all of which he would lose if his 'Cousin of York' failed to gain the throne. It would certainly be to his advantage to have a friendly monarch on the English throne, indebted for that throne to himself. It must also have weighed with James that the young man had refused the soft option of living out his life with his beloved wife as a nobleman of Scotland, in order to put all to the touch again. Privately, King James must have been grateful that the Pretender had chosen the thorny path, for the 'soft option' of remaining in Scotland would undoubtedly have been at James' expense. Impostors usually give up after failure; persistence, moral courage and the ability to inspire enduring loyalty are not normally their most remarkable characteristics.

The preparations which James had been making for the invasion were intensified; he rode round the country himself with his usual energy, superintending the equipment of the rude train of artillery which had to be collected from various forts and castles. Andrew Wood was despatched to the North with letters to the barons of that district, and a general muster of the military force of the Kingdom was ordered by letters of 'weapon-schawings', which were followed by an order to the whole body of the lieges, including the men of the Isles, to meet the King at Lauder. A communication was sent to the Irish and Anglo-Irish barons who supported the Pretender's cause: when all the preparations had been completed the young Monarch placed himself at the head of his army. He was accompanied by the Pretender under his title of Duke of York, and whom he treated with distinguished honours and equipped for war with a magnificence hardly inferior to that of the King himself.

The siege guns for use against the English Border fortresses were sent in advance. Heralds went forth from Ellem to proclaim in the English counties that King Richard IV was upon his way to reclaim the crown for the Plantagenets. Messages of support were received from the English Border lords, but James with his native realism must have begun to doubt how much actual as opposed to verbal support would be forthcoming. Secrecy was now too late; deeds, not words, were needed.

King James sent across the Border a force of cavalry mustered especially from the borders, to stir the English North. They returned with the expected answer that they had met neither opposition nor welcome. The Pretender probably assured the King that it would be different when the 'trew King' showed himself in England, and so the word to advance was given.

Tytler says, 'Once below the Tweed, where the land was bare and desolate, the peasants, apprised of their coming, withdrew into the towers of their feudal lords, knowing that their own poor hovels would be set ablaze and their cattle stolen.

'In answer to the demands of the invading army to come out and join their English King, there was nothing but a hail of arrows.' A realist could hardly have expected anything else, seeing the hated Scots with a motley army of foreigners with an unknown Englishman advancing on their defenceless homes.

James gave the inevitable order for the cannon to raze the towers: ricks, barns and homes were set alight and the Scottish cavalry charged through the farms, driving the terrified cattle before them, killing anyone foolhardy enough to try to escape the flames. As the realisation dawned on the wild Scots that here was neither battle against English opponents of the Pretender nor support for them to continue a glorious advance South, their fury mounted, and they resorted to the usual pillage and rape. For James it was a routine of war; he allowed what he did not approve, because he knew his Scots and felt he owed it to them for their allegiance. But for the Pretender, who had not been brought up for war, and had probably never seen bloodshed, and never imagined what it meant to the poor and helpless people who had to suffer for no fault of their own, it was horrific; appalling. He cried out to James to have mercy: to stop killing his poor subjects: to which James angrily retorted that his Cousin of York seemed to him to be too solicitous of a nation which hesitated to acknowledge him either as King or subject: at which the Duke mounted his horse and spurred it away in the direction of Scotland, calling out that he would rather renounce the crown than gain it at the expense of such misery. [20]

The spilling of blood and the stupidity and barbarity of war was to be the Pretender's Achilles heel; the weakness which would bring him down. Nathaniel Osbeck's reference to him (if this was not invented by historians such as Gainsford) as 'Effeminate' may have been more than just a reference to fair complexion and delicate hands that had not known work. [21] Gainsford gives his own account of the Scots' invasion: he says that when 'Perkin' protested to James about the brutality he was showing to 'his' [the Pretender's] subjects, James remarked that it was ridiculous of him to resent what was done to another man's possessions: that, as to calling them his people, he had seen no signs that anyone of worth was prepared to join him, and it would take a Herculean effort to win him his rights. 'Perkin' defended himself, according to Gainsford, by trying to lay the blame on the failure of the King of France to help him as he had promised; to the failure of the help promised by the Duchess Margaret to materialise, and to the fact that Henry had had time to strengthen his defences.[22] This is probably Gainsford's invention, since we know that the French King had sent help, and the sixty volunteers in James's army was proof that the Duchess had not failed him. In these days the Pretender would probably be honoured for his merciful and pacific views: in his day it was despicable: the fatal flaw in a man. Perhaps he really did mean that he would rather throw away his chance of gaining the crown than ask others to pay such an unbearable price for his sake. Perhaps that is the real reason why history has judged him an impostor, though other Plantagenet princes come to mind who have not cut martial figures.

James was furious and humiliated. The great invasion had turned out to be nothing more than a border raid, giving England the excuse of bloody reprisals, which would cost him and his people dear. He saw his beloved Scots behaving like savages; stealing, killing and driving herds of cattle before them, with carts piled high with hay and loot; more like a gypsy caravan than an army. He was sickened and grieved for them, but he could never find it in his heart to blame them. He knew where the true blame lay, and he must at that moment have seen the ill omens for the future of his Cousin of York. But neither then nor at any future time would he denounce him as an impostor, and he steadfastly refused all Henry's offers of bribes to hand him over.

Now there was nothing to do but to give the order to retire.

King Henry VII. M. Sittow. National Portrait Gallery, London. c.1505

Lady Margaret Beaufort mother of Henry VII. *National Portrait Gallery, London.*

Margaret of York, Duchess of Burgundy. *Society of Antiquaries, London*

King James IV of Scotland. *National Galleries of Scotland.*

Emperor Maximilian I. *A. de Predis. Kunsthistorisches Museum, Vienna. c.1502*

CHAPTER SIXTEEN

The End of the Honeymoon, and the Cornish Rebellion

Prince Richard of York was back in Coldstream by the 21st September, just four days after the beginning of the invasion which was to have started him on his triumphant road to the throne.

The feelings of King James can be imagined when he himself returned home at the head of his pillaging army with their spoils, to find his cousin (this was the conventional address employed by royalty: King James and Richard were not cousins except in the sense that Richard had married a cousin of the King) at home enjoying his little court within a court, paid for by James himself. He was continuing to pay the Pretender a monthly sum of £112, besides paying for his retainers and for those of his wife, the Lady Catherine, who had now taken the title of Duchess of York, and was widely known as the White Rose of Scotland.[1] But even this large pension did not prevent the Pretender from falling into debt; in the Accounts of the Lord High Treasurer of Scotland there is an entry for the payment of thirteen shillings for the brown horse of the Duke of York. Perhaps King James, an experienced leader, realised that, lack of belligerence apart, his cousin of York was not to blame for the lack of timing of his first attempt to invade Kent too late by a few months to make use of those nobles who would have supported him had they not been betrayed by Clifford. Soon James would realise that his own invasion had been staged too early by nine months, to co-ordinate with the uprising of the Cornish rebels. If his cousin would not give up his attempt now, he would almost certainly be killed by Henry and he, James, would have to make the best terms he could with the English King.

Henry was so enraged by the invasion of the North that he made preparations for a retaliatory raid into Scotland, but he delayed carrying his plans into effect because of the pacific influence of the Spanish Ambassador in London, Roderigo de Puebla; though he irritably told de Puebla that the Spanish Ambassador to Scotland, de Ayala, had shown himself over-credulous in believing what James told him.[2]

In October 1496, the Pretender wrote a letter in his own hand (Appendix VI) to Sir Bernard de la Forsse, Knight, who was then at Fuentarabia in Spain. Sir Bernard had been employed by Edward IV and was a friend and Counsellor to Richard III, who selected him as his Ambassador to Spain in 1483, with the mission of concluding a peace treaty first begun between Edward IV and Henry of Castile. Sir Bernard's son Anthony had been the Pretender's constant companion, attending on him in various countries when he travelled from Flanders into France, Portugal and Scotland, as he reveals in his letter. He asks Sir Bernard to help him obtain the support of Ferdinand and Isabella, reminding him of his connection and service with his father King Edward. As the letter was addressed to Sir Bernard, it is possible that it was intercepted by the Spanish Secretary of State Almazan, because there is no record of a reply from Sir Bernard, though Almazan endorsed the letter 'To Their Highnesses [the Spanish Sovereigns] from the Duke of York'.

Henry summoned a Parliament on 16th January 1497 to levy a subsidy of £120,000 and two ships to prosecute the war against Scotland. A powerful army was assembled under the command of Sir Giles Daubeney, the Lord Chamberlain. The Scottish historian, Tytler, records that the anguish shown by the 'English Prince' during the raid of Ellem appeared to have shaken James' confidence, not in the Pretender's identity, but in his qualifications as a man of action and as a firm enough King for his country: a deduction only too well borne out by subsequent events. But Henry's own outburst shows that the Pretender had a good deal of right on his side, for in the terms of a commission by Henry on 13th February, commanding Sir Thomas Dacre, his Lieutenant of the West March (one of the Northern Lords who had secretly supported the Pretender, but whose discretion had proved greater than his valour), to make an array against the Scots, it is stated 'since our enemy of Scotland, with a great array of our rebels and traitors, has hostilely invaded our Kingdom of England, and cruelly slain our subjects, neither sparing age nor sex, and has burned and destroyed without remorse castles, fortalices and towers, and intends further mischief.'[3]

The French Ambassador in Scotland was authorised to offer King James £100,000 if he would deliver up his guest to the French King: James indignantly refused, and neither then nor thereafter did he repudiate the husband he had bestowed on his cousin the Lady Catherine.[4]

The tax which Henry imposed on the whole country in order to pay for the punitive expedition into Scotland aroused widespread anger and resentment, nowhere greater than in Cornwall where it was flatly refused. Even as Daubeney's army began its march towards the Scottish border, rebellion against the tax broke out in the West; particular execration being levelled at Morton, the Archbishop of Canterbury and Lord Chancellor, Sir Reginald Bray and even the King himself.

An extract from the Sanuto Diaries for 14–15th July states that letters were received saying that. . .'20,000 men had taken up arms in the North under certain chiefs and were in the field some twenty miles from London: that they had made a demand for the surrender to them of five individuals, including the Cardinal Archbishop of Canterbury, Lord Chancellor; Master Bray, Master Lovel, and the Privy Seal; no mention being made of the fifth, who was however supposed to be King Henry. . .' Sanuto comments: 'And I have heard that King Henry, on perceiving these assemblies, determined to oppose them and ordered one of his captains to come to London against these men from the North, and was answered by him that he was of the opinion that when they demanded those four they made a just demand, and that he did not think it fit to come.' But, as so often when foreigners record events they do not fully understand, there is a mixture of fact and wild rumour in Sanuto's message. The reason that John Morton, Archbishop of Canterbury and Lord Chancellor, was held in such execration was on account of his 'Morton's Fork' system of harsh taxation. The men of the West grumbled that they should have to pay anything for a force being sent against Scotland, with which the Cornishmen felt they had nothing to do. A messenger was sent to the Pretender in Scotland, asking him to lead the men of Cornwall in their revolt, but he arrived too late for the Pretender to be of any practical use. James advised him that this might indeed lead to success, but pleaded that he himself would need many ships to transport his army into any part of England where they could be of use, but he agreed to invade England once again.[5] Gainsford describes the scene as one of chaos; rebels were marching from the West on London: France was wavering: Flanders was threatening and the Scots King was backing the Pretender.

But the Cornishmen wanted action; they could not be restrained long enough to wait for the Pretender's arrival. Thomas Flammock, a lawyer, and Michael Joseph, 'a notable talking fellow' and a blacksmith from Bodmin, were the chief rebels who stirred up resentment and resistance to the tax. Finally a large body of malcontents marched through Devon into Somerset where James Tuchet, Lord Audley, assumed command. Numbers variously estimated at sixteen to forty thousand men marched through Taunton, killed the Provost, the principal Commissioner for the collection of the subsidy, and went on to Wells. The 'army' went on to Winchester and Salisbury, gathering numbers but little in the way of arms as they went. They joined the men of Kent and in June the motley army encamped on the outskirts of London at Blackheath.

Henry appointed Thomas Howard, Earl of Surrey, and John, Lord Dinham, High Treasurer of England, to muster the forces of the County Palatine of Durham to deal with the Scots; he had to recall Daubeney from the North and put him in command of his army in the South, to deal with the Cornish rebels. Rumours were flying thick and fast, and foreign Ambassadors were busily reporting to their Sovereigns and Signories all that they heard.

The garrisons of Calais and Guisnes were much augmented, and the Navy was prepared for any possible invasion from Flanders. The Earl of Essex and Lord Mountjoy offered their services to prevent the invasion of 'Perkin'.[6] Henry also sent the French Ambassadors to Dover, to keep them out of danger, which may have given rise to the rumour that he had sent 'the Queen and his children to a castle on the coast, with enough treasure and valuables to aid their escape. . . . He wanted to attack the King of Scotland for the overthrow of the Duke of York, and under pretence of this he amassed much money, and the people complained of paying; and it was said that the King had placed all his property in a tower nearest the coast, that he might escape if necessary.'[7]

The ragged army, encamped on a hill at Blackheath, were quickly surrounded by Henry's much larger and well-armed force in which were the Earl of Kent, Lord Abergavenny, John Brooke, Lord Cobham, Sir Edward Poynings, Sir Richard Guildford, Sir Thomas Bourchier, Sir John Pechy, William Scot and many other gentlemen. Guns were positioned at Southwark, and the forces mustered at the Tower. John, Earl of Oxford, Henry Bourchier, Earl of Essex, Edmund de la Pole, Earl of Suffolk, Sir Rhys ap Thomas, Humphrey Stanley and others, were sent with a company of archers and horsemen to surround the hill; and Henry himself, with the main army and much Ordnance, took St. George's-Fields, where he quartered himself on a Friday night, and very early on Saturday morning he posted Lord Daubeney to Dartford, where he took the bridge in the Strand in spite of the arrows which met him. At the start of the battle Daubeney had apparently been taken prisoner by the rebels, but they released him for want of good advice: the armies then closed in from all sides and the battle was quickly over. On the King's side the losses were rated at about 300, most of them shot with arrows, but about 2,000 of the rebels were slain. The date was the 17th June 1497.

Audley was drawn to Tower Hill from Newgate in a coat of his own arms painted upon paper reversed and all torn, and there beheaded on 28th June for 'levying war against the Crown': Thomas Flammock and Michael Joseph were hanged, drawn and quartered and their quarters sent into Cornwall for display there. The rest were pardoned under Proclamation.[8] Those who got safely back to Cornwall 'dared to say to their neighbours and countrymen that the King did well to pardon them. . . (as) he knew he should leave few subjects in England if he hanged all that were of their mind. . . .'[9]

Meanwhile Henry had issued a warning to men north of the Trent to be ready at an hour's notice to serve against the Scots. But he was still unwilling to begin hostilities. The efforts of the Spanish Ambassador in London, Roderigo de Puebla, and those of de Ayala in Scotland, were having effect on both Henry and James. James had refrained from troubling the English border again during the Cornishmen's rebellion, though he must have greatly regretted that the Pretender had not had much earlier information on the Cornish revolt, so that he could have been there to lead them.

In the end Henry commissioned Bishop Fox, Bishop of Durham, Warham (afterwards Archbishop of Canterbury) and John Cartington on 4th July, to treat for peace with James. James' envoy was the Earl of Angus. Henry's instructions, dated at Shene Palace on 5th July 1497, were to demand first of all that James should hand over 'Perkin Warbeck'. He pointed out that James might very well give him up without staining his honour, on the grounds that he was not the person he claimed to be.[10]

Evidently King James and his guest had been reviewing their positions very realistically, and had agreed that time was running out for the Pretender, and that he could no longer expect the King to keep and entertain him now that his chances of success were so obviously reduced. Gainsford reports (and probably distorts) a speech made by the Pretender in which he thanks the King for all he has done for him, and declares his unwillingness to trespass further upon his kindness. He asks only James' leave to 'rig and caulk up' his ships (supplied by James), and to gather together those who will voluntarily attend him. One must assume that preparations for his departure had been going ahead for some time, since ships cannot be caulked up, provisioned and men made ready for a voyage in only two days, which some accounts imply, arguing that Henry's demand made on 4th July for the hand-over of the Pretender made him depart hurriedly on 6th. Gairdner suggests that the only reason James did not hand him over was because he had already gone. But Tytler makes it clear that James did not for a moment consider the idea of handing over his guest, whom he continued to treat with honour and to pay him his handsome pension and the salaries of his retinue. The last payments were made on 27th June, when the sum of £112 was paid to the Pretender (Scots pounds are not specified); but the young man seems to have been overdrawn in spite of the King's generosity.

The Scottish Treasury Accounts show that on 6th July 1497, Roland Robinson received five pounds to pay 'two carts going to the town of Ayr with the Duke of York's gear'. But this does not reveal how long it took for the carts to get there. Three days earlier in Edinburgh 'enough Rouen Tawney and Risillis black cloth' was purchased on the King's order for a gown and cloak for the Duchess of York. These garments would have taken some days to make and deliver to Ayr.[11] Besides this, the King generously supplied large quantities of beef, mutton, oatmeal, biscuits, wine, ale, beer, cider, peats, coal and candles to provision the ships.

The ship in which the Duke and Duchess of York sailed was *The Cuckoo*, owned by Robert and Andrew Barton, renowned seafaring brothers who often chartered their ship to the King. Gainsford writes of five small ships in the Duke's fleet; it is reasonable to suppose that about 120 men, with their gear and provisions could not have been carried in one small ship. There is an anonymous English ballad entitled 'A true relation of the life and death of Sir Andrew Barton, a Pirate and Rover on the Seas.'[12]

The Scottish King came in person to bid farewell to his guests: there is an entry in the Accounts 'Item: for walking of the Kingis hors' in Ayr, and immediately following 'Item: the ix day of Julij the

King passit to Kingorne and gave largesse to the boatmen and to the poor'.[13]

At last all was ready, and the Duke and Duchess sailed away from Ayr on 6th July, bidding farewell to Scotland forever. One of the other ships in the fleet was commanded by Guy Foulcart, a Breton merchant, who wrote afterwards to King James complaining that the voyage had been disastrous for him, for he had been captured and fined by the English and had lost all his goods. However, James sent his reply to Anne of Brittany (now Queen of France) saying that Foulcart knew that he could apply to the Scottish courts where he would have obtained justice, and that in any case he had known the risks and had accepted them in advance for adequate payment.[14] Gairdner says that the Pretender first intended to land in Cornwall, but even allowing for the slowness of communications, it was improbable that he did not know the Cornish revolt was over.

The citizens of Waterford wrote to Henry telling him of the Duke's arrival there on 1st August; Henry was at Woodstock when he received the news on 6th. Gairdner reports that the captain of the ship had been told to land the Pretender in England, but that, because it was not a war vessel and he was accompanied by his wife and children, it was decided to go first to Ireland, where they reached Cork on 26th July.[15] But there is certainly no corroboration for the story that the Duke and Duchess had any children; later historians who mention them give Bernard André as their source. Unless they had twins, it was hardly possible that they had more than one child and, since nothing further is heard of it, it may well have died during what must have been an extremely hazardous voyage. Henry's subsequent refusal to allow the Pretender to sleep with his wife, although they were allowed to meet in captivity, argues that he was determined to see that there would be no heirs to trouble him in the future, and implies that none was alive at that time.

There is some confusion about what happened after the Duke and Duchess' arrival in Cork; the Prince had relied on help from the Earls of Desmond and Kildare, but they had been punished by Henry and were too afraid to help the Pretender again. There is a story that the Pretender had arranged to go to Ireland in a Spanish fishing smack, and to send for a safe-conduct from the Spanish Sovereigns, but that the ship had been wrecked and the Pretender and a young Spaniard called Don Pedro de Guevara had to cross the mountains in disguise to reach three Spanish ships which were waiting to go to Spain. But this story sounds so unlikely, containing no reference to the Duchess, and being an identical story to the one which was current two years before, when the Pretender had left Ireland for Scotland, that it can safely be discounted on the grounds that the source for it, a Spanish historian called Zurita, had got his dates wrong.[16]

Henry wrote to the citizens of Waterford on 6th August 1497, offering a thousand marks sterling for the capture of 'Perkin Warbeck', and as a result, when the Pretender's ship landed at Cork, it was chased by the Waterford men. The Pretender, having heard that the Cornishmen were still in a ferment over Henry's severe taxation and the loss of their army at Blackheath, was advised by his faithful friends John Heron, a bankrupt London merchant, Edward Skelton and Nicholas Astley, to make his attempt on England in Cornwall. Accordingly, he sailed with his wife and a small retinue (two small ships and a Breton pinnace, perhaps Foulcart's vessel, mentioned in Henry's letter to Sir Gilbert Talbot), and the men of Waterford fitted out their own ships and gave chase.[17]

The Spanish Ambassador in London, de Puebla, has a slightly different version. In a letter to his Sovereigns dated 28th August 1498 (this must be a mistake for 1497) he relates that the vessel, which he describes as Biscayan, was intercepted by the English fleet sent forth for that purpose by King Henry, who was anxious to get 'Perkin' onto English ground, there to be broken and overwhelmed: 'The Commander of the said fleet called the Captain and crew of this ship into his presence and told them that, as the Kings of Spain and England were living on terms of intimate friendship; that the Prince of Wales has now married the Princess Katherine [they were married by proxy but had not yet met]. . . as faithful subjects of your Highness they must deliver up Perkin if he were hidden in their ship. . . The Commander of the fleet promised them 2,000 nobles [then equal to 1,000 marks or pounds] in the name of the King, besides many other favours, and showed them letters patent under the royal signature, signed with the royal seal. . .The obstinate Biscayans, however, swore in spite of all this, that they had never heard of such a man. 'Perkin' was all the time in the bows of the ship hidden. . .'[18] This story may also be read in Polydore Vergil and Hall, and in curious letters from the King, the Earl of Devon and the Bishop of Bath, printed by Sir Henry Ellis, and to be found among the papers of the Plumpton family. Among these letters is a paper giving an account of the Pretender's landing, signed by Sir Henry Wentworth and dated 16th September 1497.[19]

Whatever the precise details of the Pretender's narrow escape thanks to the trustworthiness of his crew, it is surely a great tribute to his personality that these tough men of the sea, to whom 1,000 marks would have been a very great sum indeed, refused to betray him. The incident gave him confidence in the future and in his own powers of persuasion; he had been able to speak to them in their own language, and he saw in his escape the promise of being able to command the loyalty and love of his own countrymen when he could appeal to them.

The final test lay ahead, and the young Pretender landed with his wife and some 100 to 120 men on 7th September 1497, at Whitesand Bay in Cornwall.

CHAPTER SEVENTEEN

The Third Failure

The many foreign Ambassadors in London, continually sending back
their own versions of events to their Sovereigns and masters, including
all manner of rumours, counter-rumours and mis-judgments aimed,
naturally, at proving their own indispensability to their employers, now
transmitted widely divergent views on the situation.

Before the news of the Pretender's landing in Cornwall had reached
London, the Milanese Envoy in London wrote on 8th September to
his master the Duke of Milan (Ludovico Sforza): — 'This kingdom is
perfectly stable by reason, first, of the King's wisdom, whereof everyone
stands in awe; and secondly on account of the King's wealth, for I am
informed that he has upwards of six millions of gold, and it is said that
he puts by annually 500,000 ducats, which is of easy accomplishment,
for his revenue is very great and real, not a written schedule, nor does
he spend anything'.[1]

The Venetian envoys in London, Piero Contarini and Luca Valaresso,
who the year before had written that King Henry was in dread of being
driven out of his Kingdom by the Duke of York[2], wrote six months later:
— '. . . the island was in a disturbed state, and it had been reported that
the English and Scots had fought a battle in which 15,000 men were
killed, and the cause of the war was that the Duke of York had taken
for wife the kinswoman of the King of Scotland, and meant to invade
and seize the kingdom of England, as he was the son of King Edward'.[3].
— a somewhat exaggerated view of King James' abortive raid over the
border.

Gutierre Gomez de Fuensalida, the Spanish Ambassador to Germany,
Flanders and England from 1490 to 1507, wrote what almost amounted
to a rebuke to his Sovereign, King Ferdinand: — '. . . it is certain that
there is nobody in England who does not marvel at what they have seen:
for at a time when the whole Kingdom was against the King, and when

Perequin had entered the country calling himself King, and the King of Scotland was coming in by another way, and the whole country was in rebellion, and the men of Cornwall were giving battle at a short distance from London; when, had the King lost the battle he would have been finished off and beheaded; that at that very moment a marriage should have been arranged on conditions disadvantageous to your Highness, filled everyone with amazement.'[4] It must be noted that the Ambassador telescopes events which he is reporting, so that it appears that they took place simultaneously, which is very far from the truth, as we know. If matters had stood as he described, the Pretender would almost certainly have toppled Henry. But perhaps the Ambassador was only being pessimistic in order to underline his own evident disapproval of the marriage of Henry's son Arthur to the Infanta Catherine of Aragon.

In Scotland, in spite of the commission for peace which Henry had sent, King James, true to his promise to the Pretender, once more invaded the borders of England. Obviously, this plan had been concerted between James and the Pretender to coincide with the latter's landing in Cornwall but again, ill-luck dogged the Pretender's timing; with his hostile reception in Ireland and the chase by sea, his own plans were delayed and King James' second invasion was too early to have any effect on the ultimate result. James attempted to besiege Norham Castle, but its occupant, Bishop Fox, had fortified it strongly, provided a Navy of ships under the command of Lord Brooke, and had time to send for the Earl of Surrey to come to his rescue, so that James had to retreat across the Border. Surrey then invaded Scotland and caused damage to four of James' castles and demanded the delivery to him of Haiton (Aytoun?) Castle. James, only a mile away but with an inferior force, dared not come to the rescue, but he sent Surrey a typically bold and daring challenge to engage in single combat; both armies to abide by the result, and the town of Berwick to be surrendered to James if he won. Surrey made the excuse that the combat would be unequal in that he, as a subject, if he won, would have to release so great a man as the King, but that if he lost, James would take his life. It was a clever move by Surrey: James was a renowned fighter and might well have won; it would have been a severe blow to Henry. Yet another hope for success for the Pretender's cause was extinguished. All other options being closed to the loyal James, he was forced to sign a peace treaty with Henry at Aytoun on 30th September, to last for seven years, but even now he insisted on inserting a clause which would allow possessors of a safe-conduct to be entertained in either realm; a clause which would have enabled the Pretender to seek sanctuary in Scotland if he could have escaped there.[5] The Treaty also contained a contract of marriage between James and Henry's elder daughter Margaret.

The Pretender, having installed his wife and servants in St. Michael's Mount, marched inland to Bodmin. Here he set up his standard and proclaimed himself Richard the Fourth, King of England and Wales and Lord of Ireland. The humble Cornishmen, still smarting from their overthrow at Blackheath and Henry's retribution, nevertheless flocked to answer his call, but most of the great lords played their usual waiting game.

On 17th September the Venetian envoys reported that the Duke had raised from six to eight thousand insurgents and had marched sixty miles inland, leaving his wife and children at a place on the coast called Penryn[6] — a good example of rumour being reported as fact. In two more similar effusions, the same envoy reported that the King had sent a fleet to Cornwall to prevent 'Perkin's' escape by sea and next, that the Duke had 35,000 followers and the King had sent his wife and eldest son to safety on the coast with ships to take them overseas[7]. Polydore Vergil and Hall put the Duke's numbers at Bodmin far more realistically at between three and four thousand.[8]

With this ragged army the Duke marched to Exeter and laid siege to it. Once again, the lack of proper military advice and direction extinguished any real hope of success: according to tradition, it was customary to call upon the inhabitants and state one's cause and terms, so that the garrison would be able to consider what their reaction would be. In this case, with no such declaration, the citizens closed their gates and prepared to offer a spirited defence, hoping that Henry's army would speedily come to their rescue. The Pretender assaulted the North and East gates, throwing ladders over the walls to gain entry; but without guns to breach the walls, the position was hopeless. The commander of the Exeter garrison was the Earl of Devon (whose son, William Courtney, had married Catherine of York, daughter of Edward IV, one of the Prince's sisters), and with the determined action of the citizens, the Duke's assault was quickly thrown back. The Earl reported to Henry 'when our guns were felt, Perkin and his army gathered themselves together and departed'.[9] However, the Earl had somewhat surprisingly, granted the Duke a six-hour truce, provided that no inhabitant of Exeter joined him. A secret letter to the Earl of Devon from King Henry which came to light recently, reveals that the King wished 'Perkin' to be taken alive; hence the granting of a truce. Whether any citizens of Exeter actually joined the Pretender or not is unclear; baskets were certainly let down by them over the walls, ostensibly to fetch help, but when the Pretender and his army marched away, reports put his numbers at seven thousand. Another account of the siege says that 'Perkin's' army, lacking guns, resorted to battering rams. Lighting a fire at one of the gates, they burst into the narrow streets, where about two hundred of the Pretender's men were slain; the Earl and several others having been wounded by arrows. The citizens threw all manner of missiles at them, and the difficulty of fighting in narrow streets and becoming separated, made the Pretender decide to withdraw. Henry later rode to Exeter to thank the inhabitants; some he knighted and granted many petitions, and afterwards proceeded to 'exemplary punishment of divers refractary Cornishmen.'[10]

Henry wrote to the Bishop of Bath and Wells on 20th that 'Warbeck' would find 'Our Steward of the Household the Lord St. Mourice' and many other nobles arrayed against him, and at their back the citizens of Exeter, 'And wee with Our hoost royall shall not be farr, for the final conclusion of the matter.'[11] He sent Lord Willoughby de Broke to secure the sea ports, and then joined the army himself beyond Taunton, staying discreetly in the background.

The Duke reached the outskirts of Taunton on 20th September, leading his 'army', now said to number about eight thousand, 'howbeit poor and naked [unarmed]'[12]. Chastelain insists that, although his army was a rabble with no great lords to support him, seven to eight thousand men were prepared to follow him to the death, if need be, and all was not lost. Translated, his comment reads: 'As he faced Henry's army at Polden Hills, did he not feel that it was now or never? He seems to have stiffened his resolve; it was reported that his bearing took on an added grandeur: with calmness he repulsed the announcement from the King's army of a royal pardon to any of his troops that would desert him, with the reply that he had established connection in intelligence with several English lords; [the Duke of Milan's envoy affirms that the Pretender cited the existence of an Apostolic Bull confirming that he was the son of Edward IV, an extremely unlikely supposition], and announced his intention of raising money to distribute to the people. During the 20th and 21st he prepared himself calmly for the fray, disposing his battalions with a perfect calmness, inspiring all with confidence. Did he wish to prove to these rude peasants that the role he had played since 1491 was not too heavy for his shoulders?'[13]

In any case he must have realised that he could not trust Henry's promise of pardon, certainly not for himself; and one is tempted to wonder if history's assessment of him would have been kinder if he had lost his life in the battle that was to come. But, alas, the fatal flaw: the indecision, the want of firmness and above all, the lack of military training (or, apparently the stomach for it), once again surfaced and betrayed him. He had not scrupled to denounce Henry; he had invaded his realm and taken up arms against him: did he believe that he would escape a traitor's death in Henry's hands? History has judged him a coward and an impostor, but has he been judged an impostor because he was a coward? It seems that cowardice is the one failing not permitted to princes; as though the lack of courage proved him to have been no prince. Yet there are examples of unmilitary figures, even amongst Plantagenet princes; Richard II, Edward II and Henry VI to mention only three. Studying afresh the unfinished sketch of 'Perkin', is there not an indication of weakness in the rather full and flaccid face with the fleshy, almost womanly lips; the jaunty set of his cap which betokens the young man of the bon mot rather than the warrior? So many of the writers on the subject of 'Perkin Warbeck' have pointed out what a tragedy it was that he inherited the features of his father Edward IV (whose weakness lay in another direction altogether), and perhaps those of his mother Elizabeth Woodville (though no writer to date allows him to have been the Prince), but not his military genius.

However that may be, when dawn came on the morning of 22nd September, to the general stupefaction, the standard of Richard IV was nowhere to be seen. The 'King' had fled during the night with his followers Heron, Skelton, Astley and a dozen mounted men to Beaulieu Abbey, where they begged the Prior to give them sanctuary. Gairdner, quoting here the MS City Chronicle Vitellus, says there was a small company (other accounts say sixty) on horseback his principal captains leaving his host entirely without leaders.[14] Polydore Vergil and Hall say that 'Perkin' saved himself by seeking and obtaining sanctuary, but that so large a number of horsemen could not be admitted, so that the captains were taken captive by Henry's men and brought to the King:

Lord Daubeney having sent 500 spears in pursuit, who surrounded the sanctuary.

Piero Contarini, the Venetian envoy, reported the débacle to the Doge and Signory: '. . . but when he [the Duke] was about to contest the place [Exeter], Chamberlain [the Lord Chamberlain, Lord Daubeney] came up with a large army, so that the Duke retreated with his troops . . . and fled by night with a few followers for sanctuary into a monastery. . . . His troops were put to flight, routed and dispersed; and there was a report that he had been taken by the King and hanged for being in his dominions'.[15]

'"Perkin's" now leaderless followers had to submit without striking a blow . . . his army melted away in disbelief and despair'[16]. A number were hanged and the rest heavily fined in the counties of Somerset, Dorset, Wiltshire, Hampshire and a portion of Devon: the fines amounted to £9,665.10s, besides a large sum levied in Cornwall.[17] In 'The History of Taunton in the county of Somerset', written at the end of the 18th century by Joshua Toulmin, D.D., there is a note confirming the above, but the author also quotes from Granger's 'Biographical History', to the effect that the arguments of Horace Walpole 'to prove that Perkin Warbeck was the real Duke of York, had the appearance of being conclusive'[18].

King Henry wrote a long letter to the Mayor of Waterford, describing the siege of Exeter and 'Perkin's' flight from Taunton. He says it was 'Perkin' who first sued for pardon as he desired to be sure of his life; and that in the presence of the Abbot he and his men swore to come to Henry without any manner of constraint, to 'put themselves in Our grace and pity, in trust of Our grace and pardon aforesaid.' He also says that 'Perkin' declared his name to be 'Osbeck', and to have been born in Tournai.[19]

Two things are of interest here; Henry's sudden change of 'Perkin's' name from 'Warbeck' to 'Osbeck', and his assertion that 'John Osbeck', his supposed father, had died in Tournai. As we know, the family name was Werbecque, with one relative at least who was Osbeck. Why Henry should choose to complicate the issue, remains a mystery, although of course he may have had his own reasons for discouraging too close an investigation of the Werbecque family. Secondly, 'Perkin's' supposed father did not die until November 1498, as will be seen.

If we blame the Abbot of Beaulieu for his abuse of sanctuary in delivering up his charges to the King, we must concede that, to be surrounded by 500 of Henry's mounted spearmen was a powerful argument in Henry's favour: also perhaps he believed Henry's word that he would grant 'Perkin' his life. The young man did likewise, and surrendered.

'At Exeter', wrote Bacon, an admirer of Henry VII, 'the King had consulted with his Council about how to treat the rebels . . . and did appoint Lord Darcy and other Commissioners for the fining of all such as were of any value, or had had any hand in the partaking in the aid or comfort of Perkin in the field or in the flight. These Commissioners proceeded with such strictness and severity as did much obscure the King's mercy in the sparing of blood.'[20]

In an official document on St. Michael's Mount, the Rev. T. Taylor gives a list of those fined by the Commissioners. It includes many good old family names from Cornwall and the West Country: 'These, and others of solid worth', says the Rev. Taylor, 'are most unlikely to have come out in response to the Proclamation of Richard the Fourth unless they saw in him, or thought they saw, the true son of Edward IV'.[21]

Two volumes of Henry's accounts for his Household are still extant: every word on the first four pages of one volume is written by the King; the other entries, written by a clerk, are checked and initialled by the King, and endorsed in the King's hand 'Fynes off the Counties of Somerset Dorset Wiltes and Hampshire, whereof William Hatteclyffe is Receyvor and must answere the mony'. Henry's signature is large and aggressive.[22]

Now Henry's triumph was almost complete; all that remained was the extortion, by all and any means, of a confession of the Pretender's imposture. The pressure was easy; Henry offered fair terms for both the Pretender and his wife — the most powerful incentive for a young man in love. Chastelain alone has a story that 'Perkin' begged Henry at this juncture to send his wife back to Scotland, but that Henry preferred to keep her near him.[23] The young man was probably already too far gone in misery to realise that Henry would not keep his promise.

Once again, there are several differing accounts of what happened to the Lady Catherine, Duchess of York. Holinshed says Henry's soldiers chased her from Beaulieu to St. Michael's Mount 'lest', he says 'if she gave birth to a son, yet another claimant should arise.'[24] Bacon says that Henry sent some horse men to get Lady Catherine where she was left by her husband 'whom in all fortunes she entirely loved, adding the virtues of a wife to the virtues of her sex.'[25] Gainsford says that she had disguised herself as a serving-maid, but was betrayed to the King's men, to whom she said 'I know you will use me like yourselves, and understand that I am a Prince every way'. She was allowed to dress herself, but was brought before the King like a 'Bondswoman and captive'.[26] But there is no evidence that she was at Beaulieu. On the contrary, Henry's letter to the Mayor of Waterford, quoted above, ends by saying 'Perkin's wife is in good surety for Us, and trust that she shall shortly come to Us to this city of Exeter, as she is in dole [distress]'[27]. Also dated from 'Our citie of Excestre the xvjth day of Octobre the xiij yere of Our reigne' is an order of 'Henry, by the Grace of God etc etc.' to Thomas Stokes, one of the tellers of the Exchequer, for the 'diete of Katherine daughter to therle [the Earl] of Huntlye' and for her to be taken 'unto Our derrest wife the Quene wheresoever she bee'[28]. On 23rd October the King wrote in Latin to the Spanish Ambassador, de Puebla, that he had 'sent the wife of Perkin to the Queen, and holds Perkin in his own keeping.'[29]

The King was amazed at her beauty, and 'some say' says Gainsford, 'he fancied her person himself, and kept her near him as his choicest delight; yea, so doated on her that he forgot all things but the contentment which he received by her . . . some say, he durst not let her marry, for fear of tumours [pretensions] in such as could attain to such a fortune . . . she scorned all others in regard of herself . . .' [she thought herself too good for any but, presumably, royalty]. Henry sent her to his Queen majestically attended, as if she had been a Queen herself.[30] Holinshed confirms the effect she had on the King, where he says: 'her beautie was such as King Henrie thought hir a more meet prie for an empereur than for souldiers and therefore used hir verie honourablie appointing hir to remaine in the court with the Quene his wife, where she continued so long as the said King lived'.[31]

Foreign Ambassadors, usually so verbose on so many, and often trivial, matters, are maddeningly silent about scenes which might easily light up an otherwise inexplicable situation. Did the Queen, Elizabeth of York — kept in subjection by her mother-in-law, we are told, and possibly also by her husband — greet the lovely captive as if she were truly her sister-in-law, which she well may have been? Did she wonder if she was about to see again her long-lost younger brother Richard, supposed to have been murdered fourteen years before? In the months to come, when Henry kept him at court, no hint is allowed to us that they ever met; but the two young women must often have glimpsed him as he walked in

the gardens. The Queen might not know for certain that he was her
brother, but she might very well have known if there was no possibility
of his being so. If he was really a son of a Tournaisian boatman, as
Henry insisted, his features were unlikely to bear the remotest hint of
a Plantagenet sire. In that case, why did she not tell Henry so? Even
though he kept her in subjection, it would have been a great boost to his
story of 'Perkin's' low birth. That we hear nothing, is perhaps revealing,
when we remember how Henry ensured Elizabeth Woodville's silence at
the time of Lambert Simnel's insurrection by sending her to a nunnery,
so this was surely a time when he could have made use of his wife's
corroboration. And when Henry saw the Pretender for the first time
— he who was so prolific in letter-writing — why do we hear nothing
of his spontaneous reaction? If the young man was only the bourgeois
Warbeck or even Osbeck, why did not Henry burst out laughing, and
dismiss him as of no interest, as he had done Lambert Simnel eleven
years before? Henry's letter to the Mayor of Waterford also revealed
that 'Perkin' threw himself on his knees and repeated that he was not
the Duke of York, and asked for pardon. Indicating the nobles round
him, Henry asked him if he could identify any of them; some of them
had known Richard of York in childhood. It is doubtful how many of
the nobles he would have seen before he was ten years old, and fourteen
years would have left their mark on them as it had on him. No noble
would have been so foolish as to have recognised him. 'Perkin' was not
yet so foolish either; he said that he had accepted the role of the Duke of
York at the instigation of the English and Irish, but had wanted for the
last two years to give it up. He added, in answer to Henry's questions
that, except for the Duchess of Burgundy, all the princes who supported
him were persuaded of the legitimacy of his rights. [32]

Hall says that the Duchess of York was taken from St. Michael's Mount
a few days before 18th October: that the King caused her to be brought
before him and, having addressed a few words of sympathy to her called
forth no less by her beauty and youth than by her tears and affliction,
made Perkin confess to her. [33] Again, it is a little unclear who is being
taken in by this: Catherine knew very well from the Pretender himself the
details of his early life in the Low Countries and of his connection with the
Werbecques. Nor could she have been so ingenuous, however youthful,
at this stage, as to believe that there was any use in her husband's resistance
to Henry's demands. She certainly knew of Henry's accusations, because

the Pretender had referred while in Scotland, to Henry having 'ridiculed us with soubriquets'. In fact, it is most likely that the Pretender was still relying on Henry's promise of fair terms for them both, in return for the Pretender doing what Henry demanded. It must have provided some crumbs of comfort to remember that Lambert Simnel had escaped somewhat lightly in a similar situation (he had been made a scullion in the royal kitchens, later a falconer.)

What is surprising is that, far from joining in Henry's condemnation of 'Perkin', the foreign Ambassadors in London were writing to their Princes and Senates advice of a different sort: the Spanish Ambassador de Fuensalida wrote to King Ferdinand: 'Your Majesty ought to form a fleet in Biscay or elsewhere . . . and forces should also be held in readiness in Flanders with the intention of attacking the King of England, to liberate the Duke of York Pierrequin and the Duke of Clarence [Warwick] who are prisoners'. He goes on to hint that others may be willing to liberate 'Perequin' and cause disturbance in that kingdom 'in spite of the marriage which Your Highnesses have arranged with England.'[34]

It appears from the foregoing that de Fuensalida did not attach much importance to 'Perequin's' confession: presumably he knew too well how confessions were obtained in his own country.

CHAPTER EIGHTEEN

The Confession and the Letter

The Pretender was taken before Henry at Taunton on 5th October 1497, where he made his submission to the King and declared his real name to be Piers Osbeck, or Warbeck, of Tournai; and stated who his father was.[1] He was then taken by the King back to Exeter, where he was forced to repeat before his wife the whole story of his 'imposture'[2].

The whole 'confession' is given by Henry's chronicler Bernard André in his 'Life of Henry VII' and is also given by Hall, Polydore Vergil and later historians Molinet, Ulmann and Bacon. But it is not clear whether the 'confession' was actually written out by the Pretender himself, or was taken down at Exeter by Henry's secretaries from the Pretender's verbal account. It was certainly stated by Henry and copied by his secretaries that the Pretender said his name was Osbek; but, as we have seen, the Tournai records refer to the de Werbecque family. Henry ordered that transcripts of 'Perkin's' interrogation at Taunton should be taken and these were then widely distributed. The original and early copies were made in French, for the Milanese Ambassador wrote to Ludovico Sforza that Richmond King of Arms had shown him a paper printed in French giving all the details of his family and of Tournai, and the Ambassador said it was signed by 'Perkin' himself, yet the signature was Osbeck. One must take leave to doubt, of course, that the Milanese Ambassador would have known whether 'Perkin's' signature was genuine or faked. Still more confusing in a situation which surely called for Henry to be most clear and specific for his case to be credible, is the fact that the articles sent to Dublin for the arraignment of John O'Water on the charge of high treason, were made out for his 'communication with Parkyn Wosebeck'.[3] Against all this it has to be remembered that Henry was an autocrat, and therefore he could afford to write his own rules for his own historians to follow. He was fortunate, perhaps, in not having to face insistent and aggressive questioning by self-important television interviewers.

A copy of the 'confession' is in the Tournai records, and is given in full in Appendix VII. It is also given in French and English by Dr. Desmons in his article at the beginning of this century, entitled 'A Tournaisian pretender to the throne of England' with some of his comments which may be found of interest. For the sake of those who dislike documents, and because the main facts of 'Perkin's' movements as a child and as a teenager in the Low Countries and Portugal have already been given in Chapter Eight, it will be sufficient here to summarize his enforced statement.

He begins with the surprising admission that his father's name was John Osbeck, Controller of Tournai, although he says one of his 'grandsires' names was Deryck Osbeck; another was Petir Flan who was Receiver of Tournai and Doyen of the boatmen. He refers to his mother as Kateryn de Faro. He traces all his movements among the family, saying his mother took him to Antwerp to learn Flemish, but that he had to return from there because of the wars in Flanders. He then went back to Antwerp within the year following; fell sick and was sent to board for five months in a tanner's house next door to the 'House of the English Nation'. Later he went from Middelburgh to Portugal in the company of Sir Edward Brampton's wife in a ship called the *Queen's ship*. In Lisbon he worked for a year with a one-eyed Knight called Peter de Cogna, but left him because he wanted to see other countries. Three years are unaccounted for (though he does not say so), but he says he arrived in Cork in Ireland with a Breton merchant called Pregent (Pierre-Jean) Meno, whose silks he was wearing. He says the Irish immediately insisted that he was the Duke of Clarence's son (Edward, Earl of Warwick, whom Henry had imprisoned in the Tower because he was a Yorkist heir.) It is probable that the continued interest of the Irish in the Earl of Warwick, in spite of the Lambert Simnel fiasco, was because he was the son of the Duke of Clarence, who had been born in Dublin. The Pretender denied identity with Warwick and was made to swear on the Eucharist that he was not the Duke's son, nor a relation of his. After this, an Englishman called Steve [Steffe] Poytron and another man called John Water swore that they knew he was King Richard's bastard son (John of Gloucester). He again denied this under oath, and they then told him not to be afraid, and that they would assist him against the King of England, with the help of the Earls of Desmond and Kildare, who were anxious to do all in their power against the English King. They forced him to learn English, and taught him what he should do and say. And then they called him the Duke of York, the second son of King Edward IV, because King Richard's bastard son was in the hands of the King of England. A short time later the French King sent an embassy to him in Ireland, whose names were Loyte Lucas and Steve [Steffe] Frion, inviting him to go to France. He then went to France, and thence into Flanders; from Flanders into Ireland and from Ireland into Scotland, and so into England.[4]

The first thing that must strike us about this hotch-potch of fact and fiction is that the Pretender says his father's name is John Osbeck, although there is no mention of such a name in the Tournai Archives; it is only the Tudor historians who say it is easy to recognize the name 'Osbeck' because of its likeness to 'Warbeck'. Thus it must be Henry or his agents who give 'Perkin' the name 'Osbeck'; but whoever did so changed it to 'Werbecque' and back again to 'Osbeck'. Perhaps Henry's secretaries, in taking down 'Perkin's' statement, were unfamiliar with the French language or merited Chastelain's taunt that, if one considers English pronounciation, 'Warbeck' might easily be mistaken for 'Osbeck'. But Henry certainly did not have that excuse; his long years at the Breton and French courts must have made him bi-lingual in French and English.

Secondly, 'Perkin' says his mother's name is Kateryn de Faro. The Tournai Archives give it as Nicaise or Caisine: whether this can possibly be turned into a Portuguese version of Kateryn it is impossible to say, but the young man had stayed with the family and should have known what his own or his adopted mother's name was.

Next, there is the account of the young man's wanderings from the time he was about ten until he came to Ireland at eighteen, going on to France, Flanders, Ireland again, Scotland and England. These details he had already made clear in his speeches and Proclamations, so they were not hard for Henry's agents to get down correctly. But the reference to his coming to Ireland with Pregent Meno, and to the fact that the citizens of Cork, with an Englishman named Steve Poytron and another man called John Water 'forced him against his will to learn English' — and even more amazing — 'taught him what to do and say' — is too absurd for belief. It would be hard enough for a boatman's son from Tournai to learn sufficient English in few months to be tolerably fluent, so that other Englishmen could be so persuaded of his genuineness as to risk their lives for him — but to learn a difficult language 'against his will' — is really straining the imagination. And that two men, utterly unconnected with the court of any country, could teach him what to do and say so that he might be mistaken for a prince of the blood, has all the makings of a first-rate farce. But Dr. Desmons in his article in the 'Revue Tournaisienne', while expressing some doubts about the 'confession', because it was obtained when he was in Henry's hands and was written by a 'poor tortured devil who saw no way of saving his head but that of doing what his conqueror willed', nevertheless accepts it because he says none of the contemporary chroniclers objected to it! He ignores the fact that Henry's chronicler, Polydore Vergil, did not come to England until after 1500, at least a year after 'Perkin' was dead, and can hardly be described as a contemporary chronicler since he was not in London at the relevant time; and the other chroniclers he mentions, with the exception of Bernard André, all lived and wrote about it much later. Bernard André, whom Dr. Desmons misquotes (but later corrects himself in his 'Errata') as saying that André described Pregent Meno as the 'converted Jew who was Edward's godson' (André wrote only that the converted Jew was Edward's godson), was commissioned by Henry to write his (Henry's) life, and would hardly have been so foolish as to have disagreed with his patron's opinions.

To sum up his view of the 'confession', Dr. Desmons allows himself the realistic if not cynical reflection that, if the fortune of arms had smiled on him, the Pretender would have become Richard IV, and his adventures between 1474 and 1497 would have been admitted as history. Defeated, he was only his own man; if he had won, he would have been York. What a superbly wounding judgment on all historians! Sir John Harington put it at least more poetically, if none the less realistically, in his well-known couplet:-

'Treason doth never prosper: what's the reason?
'For if it prosper, none dare call it treason'.

Henry VII's treason certainly prospered; Richard of York's did not, but it does not follow that he was an impostor. It is puzzling to know why Henry chose, of all lies, to try to pin on the Pretender foreign birth, when he looked and spoke like an Englishman, and like a son of Edward IV, as we know. Would it not have been easier, besides being more credible, to have branded him as a bastard son of Edward

IV, whoever his mother was? We know that he was indeed bastardized by the Act of Titulus Regius, but naturally Henry could not admit that the Pretender's mother was Elizabeth Woodville, since he had destroyed, or believed he had destroyed, the copies of that Act in order to legitimise his wife Elizabeth of York, after which it became vital to try and prove that her brothers, the Princes, were no longer alive.

Having obtained what he wanted, Henry sent the Pretender's wife to his Queen at Richmond; the Queen having just returned there from Walsingham on 21st October.[5] The Lady Catherine, as she was now to be called, was evidently honourably treated, for in Henry's Privy Purse Expenses there occurs the payment of £7.13s.4d. to Robert Suthewell for horses, saddles and other necessaries for conveying her to the Queen.[6] Desmons quotes Hall as saying that she was 'accompanied by a goodly sorte of sad [respectable] matrones and gentlewomen'.[7]

Henry then returned to London, but the Pretender was kept in Exeter, from where he is said to have written a curious letter in French to his 'mother' in Tournai, and which I give below in modern English with its errors and distortions:-

'My Mother,

I recommend myself as humbly as I can to you, And may it please you to know that, by chance, under the pretext of an imposture, certain Englishmen made me take upon myself to be the son of King Edward of England, called his second son Richard Duke of York; I now find myself in such perplexity that if you are not in this hour my good mother, I will be in great danger and inconvenience on account of the name which at their instance I took on myself and because of the enterprise which I have made. And so that you hear and recognise clearly that I am your son and none other, may it please you to remember that I parted from you to go to Antwerp with Berlo; you wept when you bade me goodbye, and my father brought me to the gate at Marvis. And also of the last letter which you wrote me in your hand, to Middelburgh, that you had given birth to a daughter and also that my grandfather and my sister Jehanne had died of the plague at the procession of Tournai, and how my father, you and myself went to live at Lannoy, outside the town, and you will remember the beautiful (pig-keeper's wife?). The King of England has me in his hands, to whom I have declared the truth in the matter, and begged him very humbly to pardon the offence which I have done to him, agreeing that I have never been his native subject, and that I pretended to be such at the instigation and wish of his own subjects. But I have had no good response from him, nor expect any, and I am therefore in great dole [distress]. And however, my mother, I beg you and require you to have pity on me and purchase my deliverance. And I recommend myself humbly to my godfather Pierre Haes, to master John Stalin my uncle, to my friend Guillaume Rucq and to John Bourdeau. I hear that my father has departed this life, God rest his soul, which is heavy news for me. And God be with you, my mother. Written at Exeter the 13th day of October, by the hand of your humble son, *Pierrequin Warbecque*. [It will be noted that not only the name 'Osbeck' has been changed back to the original Werbecque, but that it is now spelt with an 'a' instead of 'e'].

'My mother, I beg you to send me a little money to help me, to ensure that my guards are more amiable to me and in order to give them something. Recommend me to my aunt Stalin and to all our good neighbours.

'To Mademoiselle my mother, *Catherine Warbecque*, living at St. Jehan on the Scheldt'.

If Henry's purpose in having this letter written to the Pretender's 'mother' (and as we shall see, no original of this letter has ever been found) was to prove that he was her son, as the letter endeavours to do by recalling small events in their lives, it actually proves no such thing: the only thing it establishes is that he was the boy who was with her on those occasions.

Next, there is no mention in the Archives of the birth of another daughter to the couple when 'Perkin' was in Middelburgh, unless she died soon afterwards. He cannot mean Jehanne or Jenette, because in the same letter he mentions her as having died of the plague at the procession of Tournai; whereas we know she was still living with her husband in Tournai in 1517. Dr. Desmons casts further fog over the whole story by saying that there was no plague in Tournai between 1425 and 1513; he cites the Belgian historian Cauchie who, writing about the very procession which 'Perkin' mentions, says that no plague occurred there at any time between 1484 and 1499. He therefore asks pertinently, how the death of Jehanne in about 1487 could have been referred to when she was still alive in 1517? Faulty translation into English has also presented the Werbecques with another son: in 'Perkin's' letter to his mother appears the phrase 'my brother Thayon', but as Dr. Desmons points out, the expression 'mon père Thayon' in French means 'my grandfather'; he lists it under the words 'mon aïeul' [which appears in any good French dictionary and is translated as 'grandfather']: 'le père taïon et la mère taïe' are 'grandparents', says Dr. Desmons.[8] We have already discussed the strange naming of his 'mother' as Kateryn when the Archives give her name as 'Nicaise' or 'Caisine': Dr. Desmons notes this also, and further draws attention to the spelling of the family's surname as 'Warbecque' instead of the usual 'Werbecque', which he says completely alters the pronounciation of this name from the way in which it has been pronounced in Tournai for the last half-century. Next, he refers to the expression 'living at St. Jehan on the Scheldt'; no Tournaisian, he says would have omitted the correct designation of that parish, which is 'St. Jehan des Cauffours'. The most extraordinary mistake, in my view, is surely the passage in 'Perkin's' letter which refers to his 'father' having died recently (in 1497), when, as Dr. Desmons especially confirms, Jehan Werbecque died in December 1498! Dr. Desmons, who gives as his main sources Vergil and Hall's Chronicle, and from the French angle Molinet, finally sums up the letter as not having the style of the century in which it is supposed to have been written, but this he believes is the fault of the transcribers who modernised the text. In fact, no original of the letter has ever been found. Two copies are extant in Belgium; one is in the MS de Goethals at Courtrai, and the other is in the MS du Fief in the Library of Burgundy in Brussels. This latter copy, Desmons thinks, may have been 'drawn up according to the terms of the confession and passed from hand to hand until Canon de Fief copied it into his collection of manuscripts'.[9]

This Nicolas du Fief was born at Tournai in 1578, the son of a Recorder of an Aldermanry of Tournai. Becoming Canon of Tournai in 1611, and dying in Brussels in 1651, du Fief left numerous works and various MSS, extracts of parts of documents relevant to his studies. These lie in the Library of Burgundy in Brussels, with copies in Tournai. But as a method of recording history, it is not only thoroughly unreliable, it is in this case actually misleading. Dr. Desmons sums up his opinion by finding that the letter is a fake.

It is therefore a matter for conjecture why Henry's agents, if it was they who produced this clumsy effort, should have thought it necessary to Henry's case to write it at all. Was it supposed to prove that the young man had turned in extremis to his real mother? And if so, was he so desperate that he could not get his mother's name and address right? And who, precisely, was expecting an answer, if indeed the letter was ever sent to anyone? It inevitably leads one to believe that the letter was written neither in October 1497, nor by 'Perkin Warbeck'.

Note: On the Continent at that time, only noblemen's wives were designated 'Madame': lesser ranks were still addressed as 'Mademoiselle' after marriage.

CHAPTER NINETEEN

Final Humiliation

The Pretender was brought to London on 28th November. Nothing is known of what happened to him between the 5th of October when he submitted himself to Henry, and the end of November when he was sent for to come to London, but from his instant submission to Henry's will, we can assume that his first and only thought was to protect his wife who was now in the hands of his enemy. No further torment, or threats of torture, would be needed to extract from him whatever Henry desired him to say, than the belief that Henry might harm the Lady Catherine. In his desolate position it may not have occurred to him that Henry would never have harmed such a valuable weapon as had fallen into his power.

On 23rd of October Henry wrote to Dr. Roderigo Gonzales de Puebla, the Spanish Ambassador in London, and told him of 'Perkin's' capture, adding that the Scots were sending a delegation to him.[1] But King James was to remain steadfast to his 'Cousin of York', refusing to give up the clause which would allow possessors of a safe-conduct to find 'entertainment' in the Scottish realm.

From Exeter the Pretender was brought to London, and on the way 'great crowds were permitted to come and gape at and abuse him. . .and would have carried things further if the King had not been there'.[2] But there is no evidence that the King was with him on the way; Hall only says that 'Perkin' was brought to London and paraded through the streets there: he continues that people flocked to see him 'as if he were a monster, because he being an alien of no ability by his poor parents (although it was otherwise talked and dissimulated), durst once invade so noble a realm'. In an MS of Cotton Vitellus there is the statement that he was 'conveyed about the city and Westminster with many a curse and wondering enough'.[3] And in 'Excerpta Historica', a collection of writings quoting Hall, Vergil and André, put together by Samuel Bentley in 1831, there is a note on 'the expenses of Perkin's horsemete, accounted for to the end of April 1498, at 5d. a day, and on 23rd May 11s. were paid for his riding-gown'.[4]

The Milanese envoy, Raimondo de Soncino, writing to Ludovico Sforza, says: 'Perkin has become a spectacle for the crowd: every day he is led across London, so that all the world can judge his false past. To my mind, he bears his lot courageously'.[5]

In the Sanuto Diaries on 31st December 1497, there is a note stating that the Venetian Ambassador in London, Andrea Trevisano, went to the King, who gave him a gracious greeting, and chose to give an audience to an Ambassador from the King of Scotland who had come to negotiate an agreement in the presence of all the Ambassadors, including the one from the King of France. 'The King was well arrayed with a very costly jewelled collar.' Has also seen that Perkin, who was in a chamber of the King's palace and habitation. 'He is a well-favoured young man, twenty-three years old [he was actually twenty-four], and his wife a very handsome woman; the King treats them well, but does not allow them to sleep together.' But there is also a slight criticism of the Pretender's otherwise universally admired good looks; Chastelain reports that Clarenceux King of Arms did not consider him handsome because he had had a slight accident to his left eye which left it lustre-less, but he told the Milanese envoy that he was intelligent and expressed himself to perfection.[6] It is odd that no other historian mentions this defect of the Pretender's appearance, but the renowned historical novelists Philip Lindsay and Rosemary Hawley Jarman certainly refer to it, and a renewed study of the draft sketch for the portrait of the Pretender by Jacques Le Boucq, and now in the Archives of Tournai, does appear to show the left eye differing in expression from the right one, as if to accentuate its lack of lustre. It would indeed be fascinating to know if this slight defect was one of the three marks which the Pretender claimed to have on his body, by which anyone who had known the little Duke of York would know that he and the Duke were one and the same person. What an opportunity the Pretender neglected here to prove his own identity, by the failure to elaborate on what those marks were:- unless, of course, he did so, and his remarks have been conveniently ignored by historians of his time.

Bacon does not agree that Henry's treatment of his prisoner was good; he confirms that Henry caused the young man to be conveyed on horseback 'through Cheapside and Cornhill to the Tower, and from thence back again through Candlewick Street to Westminster, exposed to a thousand taunts and reproaches'.[7]

Soon after this, the Pretender was 'diligently examined and an extract made of such parts of his Confession as were thought to be divulged'. This information is likely to be the source from which both the 'confession' and the letter have been formed. Yet Henry appears to have doubted that he had obtained the truth from 'Perkin', although his prisoner had confessed to Henry's version of it. It was all very laboured, and the long lists of various 'relatives' of 'Perkin' cannot be accepted as proof that they were in fact related to him. Nothing was said publicly about his designs or any of the 'practices that had been held with him; nor was a word said or written about the Duchess of Burgundy's part in it: he nobly refused to implicate anyone of noble blood who had supported him. So that many men lacking what they had looked for, looked about for they knew not what; and were more in doubt than before'.[8] Gainsford says that the King set two guards over him, but allowed him to sleep in the palace; 'Perkin', he alleges, became distressed and enraged by turns (again this mention of a forceful personality), so that his keepers were often afraid of him. He was separated from his wife; this last deprivation may have finally broken him, and made him resolve to escape.[9]

Sir George Buck maintains that 'Perkin' had relied on Henry's false promises of fair dealing should he give himself up, and that at first Henry 'used him very bountifully, but that soon his jealousy got the better of him and he abated his favour and bounty towards him, whereby he was restrained of much of that liberty which he had at his first coming'.[10] Perhaps the young man had genuinely believed that to confess himself an impostor would satisfy Henry, who was trying to safeguard his dynasty, and that perhaps he would not proceed any further against him now that he had him in his power. If so, he badly misjudged the King, and he may not have known (unless King James had told him) that Henry was then in the midst of his negotiations with the Spanish Sovereigns to marry his son Prince Arthur to the Infanta Catherine of Aragon: the principal condition of the Spanish King and Queen being that there should be no claimants to the English throne arising to threaten the marriage. Without Henry's promise, they refused to let their daughter travel to England.

At Christmas-time that year, when the royal family had removed to Shene Palace to celebrate Christmas, (the Pretender was presumably there too, since Henry kept him at court), on 21st December, there 'suddenly began a great fire which continued till midnight. Part of the old building was burnt, with hangings, beds, apparell, plate and many jewels'.[11] No indication is given of how the fire started, but if it was done deliberately and had got out of hand, the Pretender does not seem to have taken advantage of it to escape, as perhaps he was being given the chance to do by Henry.

That the King was growing increasingly irritated by the problem of what to do with 'Perkin' is obvious, and gives some ground for concluding that, if ever he had been in doubt, Henry now knew very well who he was. Apologists for Henry reject with horror the idea that he could have contemplated executing his own brother-in-law: they are either choosing to ignore, or do not fully appreciate the ruthlessness of the new Tudor dynasty — so much more apparent, admittedly, in Henry's despotic son, Henry VIII, of whose callousness Sir Thomas More, his Chancellor, was fully aware when he said of him 'Depend upon it, if my head could win him a castle in France, it should not fail to go'. Most historians agree that Henry was looking for a means to bring the whole sorry story to a conclusion, and it was his devious nature to contrive that his victims should encompass their own destruction by planning escape, or in engaging in any other form of plotting which would justify Henry in exacting the ultimate penalty. Possibly the fire at Shene was the first attempt to involve the Pretender in his own downfall, but it miscarried.

Next year, however, on 9th June 1498, while at Shene Palace, the Pretender did escape, probably with Henry's connivance. He fled by night, apparently hoping to make for the coast, but did not realise that Henry was hoping for just such an escapade. He wandered about for three days and then asked the Prior at Shene Priory near Richmond in Surrey, to give him sanctuary, reminding him of that Abbot of Westminster and the Bishop of Carlisle who, in spite of King Henry IV's usurpation, had given sanctuary to Richard II, also a royal refugee. But the Prior immediately informed Henry, though the Pretender implored his intercession with the King.

He was brought to London and put in the stocks at Westminster. . . 'then carried through the streets of London and put to the rack, and made to confess his "true birth" again, and to write it out in his own hand. Lastly, mounted on divers scaffolds, he read it out in public'. His 'confession' which he was now forced to read out was very much what he had 'confessed' before, reiterating that when he returned to Ireland from

Flanders, those who helped him were John O'Water, Steven Poytron, John Tiler, Robert de Burgh and the Earls of Desmond and Kildare. But he added that, after leaving France he attempted to sail to England from Flanders, but was driven back to Flanders, before going to Scotland, thence to Ireland, and so into England. The 'confession' stops abruptly there.[12]

Sir George Buck, continuing his story of the last months of Prince Richard's life, writes: '. . . Whereupon he grew malcontent and despairing of his safety. And thereupon soon after, he passing by the monastery at Sheen, he entered it suddenly and gave his guard the slip, claiming the privilege of that holy house, and the which was granted to him. And so he was rid of his keeper and of his fears. When the King heard this, he sent again messengers and mediators to go and persuade him to return to the court, and with great and large promises of honours and of advancement, as before. But Perkin durst not trust the King, because he had broken such promises before.

'And then the King dealt with the Prior to deliver Perkin to him. But he was a good and pitiful man and would not yield to deliver his prisoner or guest unless the King would promise to use him favourably. And the King made faithful promise to do this, and Perkin was again delivered to him. But as soon as he had him in his hands, he sent him to the Tower, and where he was hardly used, and much lamented with the care and misery of his imprisonment and grief, and insomuch as he would curse his princely state with groans and oftentimes deep sighs, and would desire and wish that he had rather been the son of a peasant than of a king or of any Plantagenet. And indeed everyone could tell he fared the worse for his name, for it was observed that there were three men who were most feared of the king, therefore most hated by him: Edward Plantagenet, Earl of Warwick, Perkin Warbeck (alias Richard Plantagenet), and Edmund de la Pole, son of King Richard's sister, all of the family of York. But the king feared Perkin much more than the other twain, being of a more ambitious and active spirit and more sensible of his wrongs than they. Therefore he took much more care and employed more counsel and treasure in the seeking and suppressing him, and answerably aggravated his miseries and disgraces, which now began to exceed. For now he was not only taken forth of the Tower and carried in the most ignominious manner abroad and set in a pillory, otherwhile in the stocks. But he was not yet arrived at the worst of his entertainment in the Tower, for anon some wise and eloquent and treacherous orators were sent to persuade him to submit himself to the king and to crave his pardon and to confess his fault and to renounce his blood and his birth and his title and to take the name of Perkin Warbeck, that of a poor Dutchman, upon him, and they might the more colourably do it, because he was brought up in the Lower Germany. But he utterly refused to slander or to belie himself, and in no case to abuse and to deface his lineage.

'But when the King saw that he could not be wrought to this recantation by fair means nor by any cunning persuasion or any flattering devices, then his durance was made much more hard, and now he was lodged and more hardly and poorly fed and worse clad, until at length he by miseries and by torments and other extremities was forced to say anything and content to unsay what the king would have him. And then after that he was taken from the Tower and by these cruel methods tortured, he made a recantation and a renunciation and of his princely name of Plantagenet, and of his parentage, and of his title to the crown, and he confessed and professed to be but a mean and base son of Warbeck and some lowborn woman. And he confessed himself to be very base and mean, as you may see at large in the chronicles of Grafton and of Edward Hall etc.

'And he was constrained to sign this confession, and this being done, he was brought by the officers unto the more public places of London and Westminster, and as before related, there he was used like a base malefactor, and he was sent to the pillory; and now he was prepared and accommodated to speak anything basely. And then he was commanded to read and to pronounce with a loud voice the writing containing the foresaid recantation and renunciation. And he obeyed and read it, as that he persuaded the multitude to think he was so mean and so base a man as he professed.

'And it sounded so basely and so vilely in the ears of the people standing about him and giving credence to that vile and base matter which was delivered by him and of himself, as it had been current. And immediately the fickle common people changed their opinion of Perkin and of his princely birth and quality and said that now he was ignoble in that he was but a counterfeit and an impostor and a base and ignoble fellow and a foreigner and a poor Fleming. Nor was it suspected, or at the least at that time or a good while after, that this was a forced and counterfeit confession drawn from him by threats and by terrors and torture; for that many of them which had heard thereof had not the wit and reason to conceive and consider that racks and torments will make a man say anything, and belie himself, and falsely accuse any other man (although he be a good and just man). And in testimony hereof there be many examples of men who in torture have not only been brought to accuse their fellow thieves, but other, and falsely.'[13] Sir George Buck goes on to describe 'Gehenne' or 'Arcanum (secret) Gehenne' as a torture 'whereby the prisoner's body by extreme torture is brought into any mortal state or symptom of death, or made incurable and deadly. Then to avoid the imputation of murder, the prisoner by a short and private process is condemned of some capital crime and presently executed whilst there is yet some life in him. And to that censure Perkin at last came.'[14]

It seems generally agreed by the chroniclers that 'Perkin' was again brought to London and made to undergo yet another public confession and a more rigorous confinement afterwards. On 15th June, the Friday after his recapture, a scaffolding was erected on barrels in Westminster, on which he was put in the stocks for a 'good part of the forenoon' (Hall says 'before the door of Westminster Hall and there stood an whole day'). On Monday next he was exhibited on another scaffold in Cheapside from ten in the morning till three in the afternoon, after which he was taken to the Tower and imprisoned in a place where he could see 'neither sun nor moon'.[15]

Stow bears this out: 'Perken Werbecke endeavouring to steale secretly out of the land was taken again by his keepers and by the kings commandment cast into the Tower of London, and afterwards hee was showed in Westminster, and Cheape, stocked on scaffolds, to the great wonderment of many people: where he read his confession written with his owne hand'.[16]

There is also general agreement among chroniclers that the Prince's 'escape' was an affair arranged or at least connived at by Henry (as Buck has hinted that it was the custom of torturers to encourage their victim in some indictable offence, in order to condemn them to death).

In the Sanuto Diaries of 30th July 1498, there is a note of the receipt by the Western merchants of advice from England 'that King Henry, apprehensive of some insurrection, had placed Perkin, who called himself Duke of York, under arrest, and this because the King arranged with some of Perkin's attendants that they should suggest to Perkin to escape out of his Majesty's hands; and thus did the youth do; so the King had him put in prison, where he will end his days.'[17]

Bacon's version is that 'Perkin' 'took to his heels and made speed to the sea-coast', but that 'all corners were laid for him, in such sort that he was fain to turn back, and take refuge in the House of Bethlehem, the Priory of Shene, which had the privilege of sanctuary.' The Prior, a much revered man, apparently came to Henry and petitioned for Perkin's life, but the King replied 'Take him and set him in the stocks'. And so, 'promising the Prior his (Perkin's) life, Henry caused him to be brought forth. . .and fettered and set in the stocks, and the next day after the like.' It was generally believed that the Pretender had been betrayed, and that this escape was not without the King's knowledge, and that the King 'all the time of his flight had him on a line: and that the King did this to pick a quarrel with him to put him to death and be rid of him at once.'[18]

Remembering the clause which James IV insisted on inserting into the peace treaty which his envoys concluded with those of Henry, it is possible that the Pretender was trying to get to the coast in order to take ship to Scotland: perhaps the Scottish King had assured him that there would always be a home for him and the Lady Catherine there. But without advisors to help him, and in the pitiful state to which he was now reduced, he could see nothing clearly, and he certainly did not know how Henry's mind was working to encompass his final destruction.

In Bergenroth's introduction to his translation of the Spanish State Papers, he reveals that Henry was in a state of indecision as to what to do with 'Perkin': perhaps his reluctance can be construed as a realisation that the young man was in fact his brother-in-law, and an unwillingness to hurt his gentle Queen, as much as to his characteristic wish to throw the onus of the execution of his victims on to some other person or circumstance than himself. Bergenroth says Henry instructed de Puebla to write and ask King Ferdinand what he should do with 'Perkin', but he received no reply and, after waiting some months, decided to set in motion the last acts in the tragedy.

For the most extraordinary discovery made by Bergenroth after long and tenacious toil in the most primitive conditions in the Castle of Simancas in Spain, was the key to the private and most secret ciphers used by King Ferdinand and Queen Isabella in their correspondence with their Ambassadors abroad, with particular reference to de Puebla in London. Each Latin number referred to persons of royal blood in Europe, and the relevant chapter is headed 'The Pope, the Emperor, Kings and other persons of blood royal. . .' and contains the direction that persons who do not belong to royal families must be looked for in other places. 'Perkin's' name is listed in this chapter under the Latin cipher number DCCCCVII as 'The Duke of York', appearing between the Duchess Margaret of Burgundy and King Alphonso of Naples.[19] As Bergenroth points out, much greater reliance can surely be placed on documents which were never intended to be divulged, than on statements made by Ambassadors with political objectives to pursue. He had worked out the key to the cipher with great strain on his eyes, and the original official key to it was discovered later, and completely bore out his deciphering.

INTRODUCTION

'Even the single exception which Henry made with regard to Ferdinand and Isabella will not bear investigation. For, if documents which are destined to remain in the hands of the most confidential servants, and which have no political object in view, deserve greater reliance than declarations of ambassadors made for certain purposes, Ferdinand and Isabella also considered Perkin Warbeck to be the Duke of York. The document to which I refer is *the original of a key to the cipher in Latin numbers, used by De Puebla and preserved at Simancas.* One chapter of it is headed 'The Pope, the Emperor, Kings, and other persons of the Blood Royal.'

There is even the direction added, that *persons who do not belong to royal families must be looked for in other places.* Perkin Warbeck, not under this name, but under that of the Duke of York, is to be found in the chapter of royal personages; his cipher is DCCCCVII, and his neighbours on either side are the Duchess Margaret and King Alfonso of Naples. Even to those who firmly believe that Perkin Warbeck was an impostor, it must at least be clear that he was treated by the continental princes just as the real Duke of York would have been treated.'

Extract from the introduction to the calendar of Spanish state papers, 1485–1509, translated by G.A. Bergenroth. Photocopied by kind permission of the Round Room, public record office.

Although it did not suit the Spanish King and Queen to acknowledge 'Perkin' as the Duke of York at that time, they must have been sufficiently convinced by secret reports from their Ambassadors, as well as by the support of the Emperor Maximilian, the Duchess of Burgundy and the King of Scotland, that he was who he claimed to be, to include him in their most secret codes under his real name. Why indeed, if that list of royalty was never to be divulged, did they bother? It will be remembered that the Duchess Margaret wrote to them describing the rigorous examination to which she had subjected the Pretender when he first came to her court. Politically they hoped to gain Henry's aid in thwarting the French King's invasion of Italy, and they believed, not unreasonably, that any change of monarchy in England would certainly cause delay to their plans in this respect. Diplomatically, they were still negotiating with Henry for the marriage of his elder son Prince Arthur to their daughter Catherine, but were insisting on Henry's fulfilment of their condition that no claimant to the throne of England should be left alive at the time of the marriage. Principally, of course, this applied to the young Edward, Earl of Warwick, whom Henry had kept in prison in the Tower for the last thirteen years, just because he was a Plantagenet prince. But, since the Spanish Sovereigns named 'Perkin' as the Duke of York, he must be included in the conditions for what has rightly been called by the Infanta Catherine herself 'The marriage made in blood.'[20]

CHAPTER TWENTY

The Real Murder of the Princes

The Archduke Philip's Ambassador, Henry de Berghes, Bishop of Cambrai, was in London on a visit. King Henry gave out that the Bishop had expressed a desire to see the Pretender, with whom he had done business in the Low Countries. We are indebted to the Spanish Ambassador in London, Dr. de Puebla, for a description of the scene, in a long letter which he wrote on 25th August 1498 to his Sovereigns King Ferdinand and Queen Isabella:-

'. . . the King therefore sent a few days ago for Perkin and asked him why he had deceived the Archduke and the whole country: [a note by Bergenroth says it is not clear in the original despatch, whether Henry or the Bishop of Cambrai asked 'Perkin' the reasons for his imposture; Bergenroth points out de Puebla's somewhat equivocal style of writing, in which he uses 'he said' or 'he told me' where it is not clear who the 'he' in question is]; '"Perkin" answered as he had done before, and solemnly swore to God that the Duchess Madame Margaret knew as well as himself that he was not the son of King Edward. The King then said to the Bishop of Cambrai and to me that "Perkin" had deceived the Pope, the King of the Romans, the King of Scotland and almost all the Princes of Christendom, except your Highnesses. I saw how much altered "Perkin" was. He is so much changed that I, and all other persons here, believe his life will be very short. He must pay for what he had done.'[1] Only in that last sentence does de Puebla seem to recognise that the ageing of 'Perkin' was not altogether due to the passage of time: what 'payment' had been exacted from 'Perkin' he wisely does not say.

But in his introduction to his translation of these Spanish State Papers Bergenroth, after emphasing de Puebla's ambiguous method of describing a scene, suggests that he was a somewhat unreliable witness because of his almost slavish devotion to King Henry, and his desire to represent all King Henry did in the most favourable light, even to his own

Sovereigns. De Puebla had been sent to London early in 1488 to negotiate the marriage of the Infanta Catalina to Prince Arthur: he returned to Spain in 1489 and Sasiola was chosen to replace him, but as Sasiola did not wish to go, de Puebla was sent again. Bergenroth says that even Henry disliked him, and considered that Ferdinand and Isabella were mistaken about his qualities. He was dependent on Henry, but could be spiteful even to him if he thought that he was not being properly remunerated. He was the most unpopular man in London owing to his choice of living in the poorest quarters and begging for food for himself and his servant, rather than spending his own money. Bergenroth tells the story of de Puebla's arrival at Westminster when the royal family were at dinner and says that, when his name was announced to Henry, he asked 'What does the old Doctor want now?' to which one of his courtiers replied 'Food', and the King laughed. Even the Spanish merchants in London disliked him for his toadying to King Henry; they nicknamed him the agent of King Henry's Exchequer and asked if he was sent to superintend the affairs of Spain, or to do the business of the King of England. The Knight Commander Londono and the Sub-Prior of Santa Cruz wrote to Ferdinand and Isabella on 18th July 1498 'all the paper in England would not suffice to describe the character of that man' [de Puebla].

With regard to the interview between King Henry, the Bishop of Cambrai and 'Perkin', Bergenroth suggests that what actually happened was that Henry or the Bishop asked 'Perkin' the reasons for his imposture and, obtaining no reply, the King said angrily that he had deceived the Pope, the King of France, the Archduke, the King of the Romans, the King of Scotland and almost all the Princes of Christendom, except the King and Queen of Spain, and that Henry 'made him confess that he was an impostor and that the Duchess Margaret knew it.' In view of the great physical change in 'Perkin's' appearance noted by de Puebla, it is most likely that the young man was in no fit state to refuse to say what Henry dictated, and that de Puebla was merely recounting the scene in terms which were the most favourable to Henry. And we certainly know now, thanks to Bergenroth's deciphering of the Spanish royal secret codes, that the Spanish Sovereigns accepted that 'Perkin' was the real Duke of York, whether or not they conveyed their secret to Henry. Bergenroth comments: 'When we hear the name "Perkin Warbeck", we think of a poor impostor and nothing else, but in the days of Henry VII the person now designated by that appellation was generally believed to be the son of King Edward IV'. He goes on to say that Henry probably neither knew nor cared who he was, and only insisted that he was a native of the Low Countries because 'it is much more difficult to pass off an Englishman as a Spaniard, Portuguese or a Frenchman, than as a native of the Low Countries.' I cannot agree that Henry neither knew nor cared who he was, because all his actions gave away the fact of 'Perkin's' importance to him, but it is interesting if he really acknowledged that 'Perkin' was an Englishman.

As a further sidelight on de Puebla's devious character, Bergenroth cites an instance when he was at one time the Spanish Ambassador also in Scotland; he saw, or thought he saw, an opportunity to bring off what he considered to be a diplomatic 'coup' of his own: he suggested to King James IV that he should marry Doña Juana, who was a daughter of King Ferdinand's 'by a former marriage'. But in reality she was an illegitimate daughter of the Spanish King, as de Puebla well knew. When Ferdinand found out what de Puebla had tried to do, he angrily recalled him to Spain, saying that the truth would have come out. As a result, de Puebla was delighted to come to London and wished to remain there and not to have to return to Spain. Hence his slavish dependence on Henry, whose every wish he sought not only to fulfil but to anticipate: his meanness, frequent lies and habitual servility earned him the dislike of most of Henry's court, and of Henry himself.[2] But his servility also had its uses.

After the execution of the Pretender, Ferdinand and Isabella took the line that they had always doubted him, but we now know that this was not so. Being right after the event is a natural human failing, but it is worth asking oneself if Isabella's public attitude to the Pretender, if not that of her husband, was coloured by her strong sense of having been slighted by Edward IV who, when he won the throne by conquest, was offered the hand of several Continental princesses, among them Bona of Savoy, Louis XI's sister-in-law, and Isabella herself, sister of King Henry IV of Castile, but chose instead to marry Elizabeth Woodville, a commoner and a widow. She wrote to Richard III to this effect twenty years afterwards, telling him of her hostility to his brother and detailing the cause of it.[3]

It certainly appears that not a great deal of credence was given to the 'confession', and that there were forces on the Continent who still believed in the Pretender's true birth. Maximilian, negotiating a treaty with King Ferdinand, by which both sovereigns were to agree not to give aid to Henry's enemies, tried to insert a clause expressly exempting the Duke of York, and was only persuaded to desist from his efforts after long negotiations. In spite of what historians have concluded about 'Perkin' being discarded once he had 'confessed' to imposture, it will be seen that both Maximilian and James IV went to some trouble to safeguard his position, and the following extract from de Fuensalida seems to be a warning to Ferdinand and Isabella that 'Perequin' might still succeed, and that the marriage between Prince Arthur and the Infanta Catalina [or Catherine, as she would be called in England] was very inadvisable in the circumstances. De Fuensalida returned to the theme of rival powers intending 'to liberate Perequin and cause disturbance in that kingdom in spite of the marriage which your Highnesses have arranged with England.'[4] It is of the utmost significance that, even at this late stage in the marriage negotiations of the young Prince Arthur and the Infanta, the Spanish King and Queen made one excuse after another to delay sending her to England. Perhaps even de Fuensalida did not fully appreciate that this marriage, diplomatically desirable to both England and Spain, was the reason why the Spanish monarchs would not support the Pretender. The fact that 'Perkin' was executed at the same time as the Earl of Warwick surely has a deeper significance than the official view that Henry found 'Perkin' a convenient instrument with which to bring down the true heir. Had Henry really believed 'Perkin' to be an impostor, he could surely have now treated him with the ridicule which he had reserved for Lambert Simnel, who had also taken up arms against Henry, and who was still happily serving Henry as a falconer. But Henry's fear of, and hatred for, the Yorkists even extended to King Richard's illegitimate son, John of Gloucester, who had been arrested, imprisoned and finally executed because he had received an invitation to go to Ireland: and to the Earl of Suffolk, younger brother of the Earl of Lincoln who had died at Stoke.

It was at this late juncture that an Augustinian friar called Patrick, living on the borders of Suffolk, put up a young man named Ralph Wilford to pretend that he was the Earl of Warwick. The absurdity of the claim gave rise to the general feeling that it was all a trick of Henry's to have the excuse to make an end of both the young Yorkists; making it appear that he had no alternative but to be rid of them. Both Patrick and Wilford were quickly apprehended; Wilford was hanged on Shrove Tuesday at St. Thomas Watring's and the friar was condemned to perpetual imprisonment. Many other priests and friars were next accused of aiding 'Warbeck' (no longer 'Osbeck', apparently) in his 'treasonable purposes, intending to make him King'.[5]

The stage was now set for Henry to put in motion the final despicable act. It is an indication of his guilty conscience that he always needed some kind of 'justification', even if he had to set it up himself, for his despotic actions. The long-drawn-out negotiations with Spain were concluded; the contrived affair of Wilford and Patrick had satisfactorily angered the people and induced them to believe that treason was rife: the full tragedy could now begin.

Henry's simple and effective plan was to involve both his prisoners in a 'treasonable enterprise' to suborn their guards (though by what means, since they are unlikely to have possessed any money to do so, it was not made clear), and to escape from the Tower. The plot was supposed to have involved the murder of the Lieutenant of the Tower, Sir John Digby, and the 'corruption' of his servants and the guards Strangway, Blewet, Astwood and Roger (the very servants who had already been paid by Henry to trap and betray the prisoners). It was brought to the Pretender's notice that his cousin, the Earl of Warwick, was being held in the cell immediately above his own, and he was 'allowed' by his jailers, who he believed were on his side, to communicate with Warwick and to suggest an escape. Where it was proposed that the young men could go, even if they managed to escape, is not divulged. Historians are generally agreed that the young Warwick was feeble-minded, whether from birth or by reason of his long incarceration in the Tower is not known, but as Stow noted 'as all natural creatures love liberty' Warwick asserted his willingness and 'thereunto to his destruction assented'.[6] One assumes that the Pretender was allowed to believe that a ship would be secretly chartered for them and that his jailers would turn a blind eye while they escaped. It must be a measure of the Pretender's broken state that he apparently had no plan to rescue his wife. Thomas Astwood, Walter Bluet or Blewet and John Fynche were the jailers directly concerned, whom 'Perkin' is supposed to have bribed. The pathetic attempt at escape was duly made by the young men, who were immediately arrested by the same jailers, and their fate was sealed.

On 16th November 1499 the Pretender was, with John Watre or Awater, arraigned for high treason. This John Watre or Awater was one of the first promoters of the Pretender's enterprise at the time of his first landing in Ireland, when John Lavallen was Mayor of Cork: both of them are mentioned in the 'confession'. (Madden says that 'Perkin' had been an apprentice to John Watre. In 1493 the same Watre with his son Philip, Dean of Limerick, were cited to appear before Parliament in Dublin, and in the general pardon to the rebel Irish, Lord Barry and John Watre are expressly excepted.[7]

There is an account of the Pretender's trial in the Plumpton Correspondence: 'A.D. 1499 the xvi day of Novembre was areyned in the Whyte Hall at Westmynster the forenamed Parkyn and iii other (Fabyan).' Hall says: 'He being repulsed and put backe from all hope. . .and John Awater. . .arreyned and condemyned at Westmynster. The trial was before Sir John Sely Knight Marshal and Sir John Turberville Marshal of the Marshalsea (Rot.Parl.VI.367). . .the offences charged must have been the attempt to break out of the King's ward, and treasonable practises committed out of the realm. . .'

There follows a letter from John Pullan to his 'especyall good master, Sir Robart Plumpton, Knight', describing the trial: '. . .and ther they all wer attended and judgment given that they should be drawn on hirdills from the Tower throwout London to the Tyburne and ther to be hanged and cutt down quicke [alive] and ther bowells to be taken out and burned: ther heads to be stricke of and quartered, ther heads and quarters to be disposed at the King's pleasure. On 18th November Monday next Astwood and Bluet and others wer charged, judgment to be given next Friday. Thursday 21st November in Westmynster Hall was brought therle [the Earl] of Warwick and arrened [here follows a list of peers before whom he was arraigned] And ther therle of Warweke confessed thenditments that wer layd to his charge and like Judgment was given of him as is afore rehersed.' The Pretender was charged in the name of Warbeck or Warbek, (and it would be interesting to know how Henry explained the reversion to 'Warbeck' when the Pretender had been reading his confession all over London in the name of Osbeck). In the 53rd Report of the deputy keeper of the Public Records, Appendix II, there is reference to the alleged conspiracy against Henry VII, and the trial of Edward of Warwick, from the Baga de Secretis K.B. [8]: '. . .that William Barry, called the Lord Barry of Munster, who together with Water received instructions from 'Perkin Woseback' and kept them secret from the king. . .that therefore they be atteyned and convyct of high treason'.[9] Bacon, who was an acknowledged admirer of the Tudors, deeply deplored the death of the 'poor Prince, the Earl of Warwick, [arraigned] not for the attempt to escape. . .the imprisonment not being for treason, the escape by law could not be treason — but for conspiring with Perkin to raise sedition and to destroy the King. The Earl, confessing the indictment, had judgment, and was shortly after beheaded on Tower Hill'.

The fact that Thomas Astwood, Walter Bluet and John Fynche were hanged has been used by some historians to argue that Henry would not have hanged men who had helped him to achieve his ends, but Henry was a law unto himself, and he is unlikely to have felt unduly squeamish about the deaths of three men who could have in any case destroyed his accusation against the Princes by revealing that it was the King for whom they had all along been working.

On 23rd November 1499 the Pretender and John Awater were drawn to Tyburn on hurdles and there '"Perkin". . .standing on a lytle skaffolde, redde his Confession which before you have heard, and toke it on hys death to be true, and so he and John Awater asked the King forgeveness, and dyed paciently'.[10] Some accounts say that the Pretender was spared the horrible death of being drawn and quartered, but since Henry was anxious to prove that he was of humble birth, he did not accord him the death reserved for the nobility. All accounts register surprise at the humility with which the Pretender met his death. and the Milanese Ambassador noted that he remained 'dignified, even in adversity'[11]

Bacon's comment on 'Perkin' is: 'Thus did this winding ivy of a Plantagenet kill the true tree itself, for on 21st November the wretched young Earl of Warwick, who was said innocently to have given away the whole of their plans to the King and his Council, was arraigned at Westminster before that same Earl of Oxford who had fought for Henry at Bosworth, and who was now High Constable of England and Hereditary Grand Chamberlain. 'Bacon goes on: 'The peers summoned to give judgment according to the laws and customs of England were: Edward, Duke of Buckingham [son of the traitor Duke]; Thomas, Earl of Surrey; Henry, Earl of Essex; Lords Ormond, Latimer, De la Warr, Clinton, Mountjoy, Hastings, Berners, Lincoln, Willoughby, Wilton, Dacre, Daubeney, De Brook and Sir John Kendal, Prior of the Order of St. John of Jerusalem [no less a person than he who had been conspiring for so long for the Pretender, but who was now presumably trying to cover his tracks by demonstrating his loyalty to Henry]; and several lesser persons. Not one showed compassion for the young man who, if his father the Duke of Clarence had not been attainted, might well have been their King. This was the end, not only of this noble and commiserable person Edward, the Earl of Warwick, eldest son to the Duke of Clarence, but likewise of the line male of the Plantagenets, which had flourished in great royalty and renown from the time of the famous King of England, King Henry the Second.'[12]

Undoubtedly Henry, whose Plantagenet blood was both illegitimate and remote, had set himself to reduce the power and wealth of the old aristocracy. (It may be remembered that one of the Pretender's points in his 'Proclamation' was that Henry Tudor 'depressed and deprived the great and sent them to undeserved deaths, to make way for mean and worthless persons; especially that he had unjustly executed Sir William Stanley, to whose aid he chiefly owed his victory at Bosworth'.)

The young Warwick was supposed to have made a hole in the vault of a certain chamber in which he resided. . . 'that he might converse with the traitor Warbeck, who was lodged below the Earl, who many times spoke to the said Peter [Perkin]. . .comforting him, saying "How goes it with you? Be of good cheer", and so forth. The Earl, being arraigned, pleaded guilty, quietly confessing the Indictment concerning his consent and willingness to obtain his Liberty.'[13], and the usual hideous sentence for high treason was commuted to execution on Tower Hill on 28th November.

The corpses of the two young Princes were taken to the cemetery of the Augustines, and the severed heads adorned London Bridge. The Earl of Warwick was later interred with his ancestors at Bisham Abbey in Berkshire, and the Pretender, Richard, Duke of York, lies in the Church of Austin Friars in Old Broad Street in the City of London, under his alias of 'Perkin Warbeck'. Curiously, in the same Church lie also William Colyngbourne, traitor to Richard III, and Sir James Tyrell, the supposed murderer of the Princes in the Tower.

It is reliably recorded that, after the deaths of these two young men, King Henry aged twenty years in a few weeks. Naturally, historians ascribe this sudden deterioration in Henry's health solely to the effect his execution of the young Earl of Warwick had on his mind knowing, as Henry did, that he was innocent of any crime except that of being a Plantagenet. But bearing in our minds the doubts and uncertainties which Henry's actions and confused accusations in regard to 'Perkin Warbeck' reveal, added to his anxiety to know King Ferdinand's view on the subject, is it not possible that, after 'Perkin's' death, Henry's inmost heart told him that he had executed, by the most horrible means, his wife's own brother? And what of that tragic young woman, his wife, Queen Elizabeth? Did she and the Lady Catherine never refer to it in private? Did the horror and tragedy of it lead to her own decline in health, so that she died in childbirth only three and a half years later, bowed down also by the death of her eldest son Arthur? Did both Henry and his wife believe, with the superstitions of the time, that Providence had exacted the death of their son Prince Arthur at the age of fifteen, so soon after his wedding to Catherine of Aragon, as a punishment for the deaths of not one Plantagenet Prince, but two?

Bergenroth records the decline in Henry's physical condition; in his introduction to his translation of the Spanish State Papers he comments: '. . .according to de Puebla. . .Henry aged twenty years in a few weeks. Ill-omened prophecies were rife. In secret, Henry ordered a Welsh priest to tell his fortune, but when that priest hinted that hidden dangers were still threatening, Henry ordered him to keep silent. The King became very devout, hearing a sermon every morning, and for a long period he continued his devotions during the day. By degrees he regained his mental health, but he never regained full physical fitness, suffering many illnesses of the body'.[14]

On 11th January 1500, de Puebla wrote to the 'Very High and Mighty Princes the King and Queen of Aragon and Castile: This Kingdom is at present so situated as has not been seen for the last five hundred years till now, as those say who know best, and as appears by the Chronicles; because there were always brambles and thorns of such a kind that the English had not occasion to remain peacefully in obedience to their King; there being divers heirs of the kingdom, and of such a quality that the matter could be disputed between the two sides. But now all has been thoroughly cleansed and purged, so that not a doubtful drop of royal blood remains in this kingdom except the true blood of the King and Queen, and above all that of the Lord Prince Arthur.'[15]

De Puebla was too diplomatic to say, of course, or perhaps he did not know, that Henry's own blood was marred by two illegitimacies in his line, and that his Queen, Elizabeth of York, had been declared a bastard by the Act of Titulus Regius; that Act which Henry thought he had destroyed, but of which the original survives.

The passion of the Tudor monarchs for executing all and sundry who defied or opposed them, is reflected in the letter of a French visitor to London in 1558 (the last year of the reign of Mary Tudor and Philip of Spain). He wrote: 'In this country you will scarcely find any noblemen some of whose relations have not been beheaded. For my part, with reverence to my readers, I had rather be a hog-driver and keep my head on. For this disorder falls furiously on the heads of great Lords. For a while they appear in vast pomp and magnificence; in a trice you behold them under the hands of the executioner.'[16]

By way of an epitaph on the Pretender, a playwright named John Ford registered his play 'The Chronicle History of Perkin Warbeck: A Strange Truth' in the Stationers Register on 24th February 1634. Although John Ford drew his material entirely from Tudor sources, mainly Shakespeare and Bacon, it is interesting that throughout his play, he invests 'Perkin' with a royal dignity of manner and appearance which induces all who meet him to believe his claim. This, as we have seen, is at least part of the truth. Taking poetic licence, Ford brings the impostor Lambert Simnel to mock 'Perkin' in the stocks: Simnel calls him the Jew's, Osbeck's, son, of Tournay, and a loose runagate. 'Perkin' replies by calling Henry 'Duke of Richmond', whereupon Simnel advises him to confess and ask Henry for mercy, pointing out the comfort of his own situation in contrast to the mounting ignominy and danger of 'Perkin's' lot. In reply, John Ford puts the following words into the mouth of 'Perkin':-

'But sirrah, ran there in thy veins one drop
'Of such a royal blood as flows in mine,
'Thou would'st not change condition to be second
'In England's state, without the crown itself.
'Coarse creatures are incapable of excellence:
'But let the world, as all to whom I am
'This day a spectacle, to time deliver,
'And by tradition fix posterity
'Without another chronicle than truth,
'How constantly my resolution suffered
'A martyrdom of majesty.'

The Lady Catherine never uttered one word of blame or censure of the husband whom Bacon says 'she entirely loved'. She continued to be in favour at Henry's court; perhaps because he genuinely admired her, but he was adamant in refusing her permission to return to Scotland. Bacon admits that Henry had been most anxious to ascertain whether she had any child by 'Perkin', and was relieved to find that there was 'no such thing' — an anxiety which seems somewhat odd, since Henry insisted that 'Perkin' was the son of a Flemish boatman, and remembering that Henry would in any case have had the 'boatman's grandchild' in his power — hardly a threat to his throne.

If, as seems likely, the Lady Catherine's mother was indeed Annabella, younger daughter of James I of Scotland by his Queen, Jane Beaufort, Catherine would have been related to Henry through her Beaufort grandmother; Henry's own mother being Lady Margaret Beaufort. At the ceremony at Shene Palace to celebrate the betrothal of Henry's daughter Margaret to James IV of Scotland, the Lady Catherine was not only present but took precedence next after the Royal family.

She waited eleven years before remarrying — perhaps carrying all those years her silent grief for her handsome Richard: perhaps out of deference to Henry's wishes. On 2nd August 1510 the new King, Henry VIII, granted her estates in Berkshire on her marriage to James Strangways, Usher of the Bedchamber, on condition that she did not leave the country, even to return to Scotland, without the King's permission.

In February 1512, Henry VIII granted further estates to Catherine and her husband. He died five years later, and in July 1517 Catherine married Sir Matthew Cradock and had by him an only daughter who became the founder of the house of the Earls of Pembroke. She lived with Sir Matthew for fourteen years at Plas House, Swansea. He died in 1531, and his tomb in the chapel of St. Hubert in the parish church at Swansea bears her name on it as well as his; but she lived on to marry again when she was about sixty. Her last husband was Christopher Assheton, with whom she lived at Fyfield Manor, Berkshire, and she is buried with him in Fyfield Church, having made her Will shortly before her death in 1537. There is of course no reference in it to her first husband.

The Duchess Margaret of Burgundy, who has been vilified by Tudor historians as 'Henry's Juno, being activated by nothing but remorseless hatred for him', nevertheless wrote to him after her nephew's death, asking for his pardon and assuring him of her obedience.[17] Henry called his Council together to decide how he should reply, and it is pleasant to record that it was decided to send her a courteous answer.[18] She herself died at Malines in 1503 and is buried in the Church of the Cordeliers.

Since Sir Thomas More has been to a very great degree responsible for the widespread acceptance of the legend of the murder of the sons of Edward IV, although he said some took leave to doubt 'whether they were destroyed in his [Richard III's] days or no . . .', it seems fitting to quote Sir Thomas More's further words on the subject:-

'Not only for that Perkin Warbeck, by many folks' malice and more folks' folly so long space deceiving the world, was as well by princes as the poorer people reputed and taken for the younger of those two; but *also for that all things were in late days so covertly managed, one thing pretended and another meant, that there was nothing so plain and openly proved but that yet for the common custom of close and covert dealing men had it ever inwardly suspect,** as many well-counterfeited jewels make the true mistrusted. Howbeit, concerning that opinion, with the occasions moving either party, we shall have place more at large to treat if we hereafter happen to write the time of the late noble Prince of famous memory, King Henry the Seventh, or perchance that history of Perkin in a compendious account by itself.'

Such a 'compendious account' not being forthcoming from Saint Thomas More, I have ventured to supply it myself.

*My italics.

'The Princes in the Tower': The Official Version

Not until he had been on the throne for nearly seventeen years, did Henry VII find his own means of writing what he considered to be the final chapter on the deaths of the young Princes in the Tower. His reign had been troubled throughout by insurrections, impostors and pretenders arising from the Yorkists' dreams of revival. Two historians, writing in the sixteenth and seventeenth centuries, pay tribute to the resilience and fortitude of King Henry's character, particularly with regard to 'Warbeck's' insurrection: John Speed, writing in the late sixteenth century, commented 'the push it gave to his [King Henry's] soveraignty did thoroughly try his sitting, being of force enough to have cast an ordinarie rider out of sadle'[1], while Bacon considered it 'might have had another end, if hee [Warbeck] had not met with a King both wise, stout, [bold] and fortunate'.[2]

In 1502 there were still five sons of the family of Richard III's sister Elizabeth and her husband John de la Pole, Duke of Suffolk, and three sons of Margaret, sister of the executed Earl of Warwick, left as possible Plantagenet heirs. It was most unlikely that any of them would now lay claim to the throne, but King Henry had to secure that throne for his only surviving son Henry. It is of the utmost significance that it was only after the deaths of the Earl of Warwick and 'Perkin Warbeck' that Henry began to see in the de la Pole family a potential danger. Almost up to that time Edmund de la Pole, Earl of Suffolk and his brothers William and Richard had remained in Henry's good graces, but Edmund and Richard suddenly fled to Maximilian's court in July or August 1501, where they attempted to get aid for a new conspiracy. William de la Pole remained behind in England, and Henry imprisoned him without charge in the Tower, where he remained for thirty-eight years. Henry had had to promise the Archduke Philip, who pleaded for the life of Edmund Earl of Suffolk, that he would not execute him: he therefore extracted a promise from his far from unwilling son, later Henry VIII, that he would execute Suffolk when he came to the throne.

It was now vital to prove, not only that the young sons of Edward IV were dead, but also that they had left no heirs who could lay claim to the crown in future. With so many executions having been necessary to protect his own throne, there were now few men left who could supply the information he needed.

One man who had survived from Richard III's days was Sir James Tyrell, who presumably knew the truth, if he could be persuaded to divulge it. At first Henry had been ready to favour Tyrell, granting him two general pardons in 1486, and in December that year sending him on an embassy to Maximilian, and granting him the Stewardship of Ogmore. Tyrell had apparently remained loyal to King Henry at the time of the Battle of Stoke in 1487, but since then he had been made Governor of Guisnes Castle in Picardy, and had had his estates in Wales exchanged for lands in France. Perhaps his safety in being so far removed from the King made him a little bold, for he was said to have been entertaining the Earl of Suffolk at Guisnes, and Henry attempted to inveigle him out. First, he sent an order for Tyrell's arrest on a charge of being in correspondence with the Earl of Suffolk, but Tyrell ignored the order. Next, Henry sent Richard Fox, Bishop of Winchester and Keeper of the Privy Seal, with the promise of a safe-conduct if Tyrell would come aboard the ship sent by Henry for the discussion of the matter; the Bishop adding his own personal assurance. Tyrell allowed himself to believe it, but once aboard the royal ship he was arrested with his son Thomas and brought to England for trial at the Tower of London. He was tried on 'matters of treason' though the charge was not specified, and he was executed in May 1502.

After Tyrell's death, King Henry felt able to give out a story of how the Princes had perished in the Tower on Richard III's orders. He did not make it official, but gave it out in such a way that it has gone down to history as the implication of Tyrell in the murder, although no confession has ever been seen. Henry was fortunate in having at his elbow Cardinal John Morton who, in Bacon's words, was 'not without an inveterate malice against the House of York'. Morton died in 1500, but he left behind him notes on events which included items on the reign of Richard III, and which are generally accepted as being the foundation for Sir Thomas More's 'History of King Richard III'[3],

More was a brilliant boy and was sent as a twelve-year-old to live in the household of Morton, who became his patron, More naturally absorbed much of Morton's sagacious advice, and probably all his knowledge of the reigns of Edward IV and Richard III, More being only seven years old at the time of Bosworth. Even though More besprinkles his 'History of King Richard III' liberally with 'some wise men think', 'I by credible information have learned', and 'after that way that I have so heard by such men and by such means as methinks it were hard but it should be true', nevertheless it is More's account which is taken as the factual one. Briefly, it runs as follows:-

Immediately after King Richard's coronation, he and Queen Anne set off on a Royal Progress to the Midlands and the North. The Princes were left in the Tower of London. But when the royal party reached Gloucester, Richard decided that the boys must die. He therefore sent a messenger, John Green, to the Constable of the Tower of London, Sir Robert Brackenbury, with a letter instructing him to put the two children to death. But apparently Brackenbury refused to carry out these horrifying orders, and John Green returned to King Richard, who had by now reached Warwick, to tell him so. To give the tale a suitable touch of verisimilitude, we are told that, while sitting on the privy, Richard complained to one of his henchmen (pages) that no-one would do his bidding; whereupon the page had the brilliant idea of suggesting Sir James Tyrell, who was resting on a pallet in the antechamber. Accordingly, on his page's recommendation, Richard sent the compliant Sir James to London with another letter authorising him to take over the Tower for one night from Sir Robert Brackenbury, so that he and his groom, John Dighton, together with a professional murderer named Miles Forrest and another individual named Will Slaughter, known as Black Will, could carry out the murder:-

'Then all the others being removed from them, this Miles Forrest and John Dighton about midnight (the innocent children lying in their beds) came into the chamber, and suddenly lapped them up among the bedclothes, so bewrapped and entangled them, keeping down by force the featherbed and pillows hard into their mouths, that within a while, smothered and stifled, they gave up to God their innocent souls into the joys of heaven, leaving to the tormentors their bodies dead in the bed. After the wretches perceived them, first by the struggling with the pains of death and after, long lying still, to be thoroughly dead, they laid their bodies naked out upon the bed and fetched Sir James to see them. Who, upon the sight of them, caused those murderers to bury them at the stair-foot, meetly deep in the ground under a great heap of stones.'

Two paragraphs later, More goes on:- 'Whereupon they say that a priest of Sir Robert Brackenbury took up the bodies again and secretly interred them in such place as, by the occasion of his death, for he alone knew it, could never since come to light'. In his very next sentence he tells us that, when Sir James Tyrell and Dighton were in the Tower 'for treason committed against the most famous Prince King Henry the Seventh, both Dighton and he were examined and confessed the murder in manner above written, but whither the bodies were removed thay could nothing tell.'

King Richard was reported to have been so delighted with the news of his nephews' deaths that he knighted Sir James Tyrell on the spot.

There are so many glaring improbabilities and contradictions in this story that one can certainly believe that More was repeating, perhaps at second or third hand, what Dighton gave out after Tyrell's execution. It is hardly worth commenting on the likelihood of Richard taking the advice of a nameless page as to whom to employ to arrange the murder of his nephews, or of sending a letter half across England with this dangerous order to Brackenbury, who is said to have refused to do the deed. This reported refusal earned him the name of 'gentle' Brackenbury, but nevertheless two years later he must have overcome his revulsion for his sovereign, for he fought and died with him at Bosworth.

Of the murderers, the name of Will Slaughter is not traceable, neither is that of John Dighton, but a John Dighton was awarded the 'Baillieship of Aytone in the county of Stafford during his life with the wages accustomed'.[4] A man of the name of Miles Forrest was Keeper of the Wardrobe at Barnard Castle and died in 1484; his widow Joan and their son Edward received an annuity of 5 marks from King Richard. There was also a Miles Forrest (possibly the same one) attendant on Richard's mother Cecily Duchess of York, and a footman by the name of Henry Forrest at Middleham Castle. As for Sir James Tyrell himself, he was not only already a knight, but had been made a knight banneret by Richard on his Scottish campaign.

Bacon's comment on More's story is that Dighton was 'forthwith set at liberty and was the principal means of divulging this tradition', and

'Tyrell and Dighton agreed in a tale, as the King gave out'[5] — a very useful bonus for Henry, and one for which he had no doubt paid. More himself says 'Dighton indeed yet walks alive, in good possibility to be hanged ere he die', but he wrote at least thirty years after the events, so Dighton must have been by then a very old man for those times, and if he was a known murderer, why did Henry allow him to go about freely? Because 'he spake best for the king'[6] — in other words, he repeated whatever Henry told him to say, and earned his freedom by doing so.

The story of the priest having re-buried the bodies was of course intended as a cover for the fact that 'diligent search' had been made for them, but nothing had been found. No wonder that More appended to his story of the murder the qualification (so often overlooked) that some were yet in doubt whether they had been murdered in King Richard's days at all.

And it is on More's story, half-refuted by More who had it as hearsay; seized on by Shakespeare as a horror story to please the best of the Tudors, Elizabeth I, that the ever-popular legend of the deaths of the 'Princes in the Tower' has prospered and become so much a part of what we believe is history that apparently not even the truth can dislodge it. But if truth is really, as the old proverb says, the daughter of time, one day history will accept the true identity of Richard of England.

References

Chapter One

1 Tanner, L.E., & Wright, W., 'Recent Investigations regarding the Fate of the Princes in the Tower', from Archaeologia, Vol. lxxxiv, pp. 4–5 (1934).
2 Illustrations of Ancient State and Chivalry: Roxburghe Club, 1840, pp. 27–40.
3 Calendar of Patent Rolls, 1476–1485, p. 75.

Chapter Two

1 Molinet, Jean, Chroniques, Vol. I. Chapter XCIX, p. 431.
2 York Civic Records: Davies, pp. 148–150, Vol. I. ed. Angelo Raine (YAS), 1938.
3 More, Sir Thomas, 'History of King Richard III', p. 99.
4 The Great Chronicle of London, p. 234.
5 Christ Church Letters, ed. J.B. Sheppard, Camden Society, 1877, p. 64.
6 Vergil, Polydore, 'History of the Reigns of Henry VI, Edward IV and Richard III', Camden Edition, 1844, p. 68

Chapter Three

1 More, p. 53.
2 Harleian MSS 433, Vol. I. p. 145.
3 Public Record Office: Warrants for Issues E404/78/3/47, 22nd March, 1485.

4 Roth, Dr. Cecil, 'Sir Edward Brampton, an Anglo-Jewish Adventurer during the Wars of the Roses', from Transactions of the Jewish Historical Society of England, 1952, Vol. 16, p. 166.

Chapter Four

1 Harleian MSS 433, Vol. III, p. 114.
2 Buck, Sir George, 'The History of King Richard the Third', ed. Dr. A.N.Kincaid, 1979, pp. 142–3.
3 Vergil, 'Historia Anglica' 1485–1537, p. 13 n.
4 Bacon, Francis, 'The Reign of King Henry VII', Folio Soc. edition, p. 40.
5 Halsted, Caroline, 'Richard the Third', 1844, Vol. II. p. 181.
6 Divisie Chronicle (Die xxxi Divisie, folio ccccxcii, kat.x)
7 Buck, p. 138.
8 Ellis, Sir Henry, 'Original Letters' 2nd Series I. pp. 159–60.
9 Harleian MSS 433, Vol. II. p. 114.
10 Ibid, p. 129.
11 Ibid, p. 178.

Chapter Five

1 Halsted, Vol II pp. 439–475.
2 Kendall, Paul Murray, 'Richard III', 1955, p. 369.
3 Halsted, Vol II pp. 474–5.
4 Ibid, p. 466.
5 'Letters and Papers of Henry VIII', ed. by Brewer, Vol. VI: No. 1528 and Vol. VII No. 1368.
6 Molinet, Jean, 'Chroniques', 1476–1506, ed. J.A. Buchon, Paris 1827–8. p. 436.
7 Markham, Sir Clements, 'Richard III: His Life and Character' pp. 274–276, London, 1906.
8 Bacon, p. 56.

Chapter Six

1 Morgan, John, 'Have the Princes' Bones Been Found in the Tower?' Paper in Richard III Society Library, 1934.

2 More, p. 106 and p. 102.

3 Ibid, p. 106.

4 Buck, Book III, p. 139.

5 Archaeologia, 1934, p. 26.

6 Molinet, pp. 431–2.

7 Tanner, pp. 6–7.

8 Ibid, p. 7.

9 Lulofs, Maaike, Divisie Chronicle, from The Ricardian, Vol. 3. (1974) No. 46, p. 13.

Chapter Seven

1 Egerton MS 616.3. British Library.

2 Bacon, p. 162–3.

3 Walpole, Horace, 'Supplement to the Historic Doubts', 1798, Vol. II. p. 216.

4 Gainsford, Thomas, 'The True and Wonderful History of Perkin Warbeck', from Harleian Miscellany, Vol. 6. p. 559.

Chapter Eight

1 Archives de la Ville de Tournai, 1513.

2 Ibid. Fonds des Actes divers. 1498.

3 Ibid. Testaments. 1513.

4 MS Vitellus, folio 168 R to 170 Vo etc.

5 Gairdner, James, 'The Story of Perkin Warbeck', p. 267.

6 Desmons, Dr. 'A Tournaisian pretender to the throne of England', article in the Revue Tournaisienne, (c.1901), p. 57.

7 Chastelain, Jean-Didier, 'L'Imposture de Perkin Warbeck', Chapter X, p. 102 note (1), also Accounts of the Lord High Treasurer of Scotland in Register House, Edinburgh, Appendix B, pp. 326–7.

8 Desmons, p. 97.

9 Chastelain, Chapter II, p. 18.

10 Roth, p. 166.

11 Ibid, p. 167.

12 Ibid, p. 168.

13 Ibid, p. 170.

14 Desmons, p. 97.
15 Chastelain, Chapter II, p. 19.

Chapter Nine

1 Chastelain, Chapter II, p. 20.
2 Gairdner, p. 274.
3 Ibid, p. 273.
4 Bacon, p. 131.
5 André, Bernard, 'Memorials of Henry VII', p. 72.
6 Gairdner, (Story of Perkin Warbeck), pp. 268–9.
7 Treasurer's Accounts of Scotland, 1491–1492 (Letters & Papers etc.) ii. 326–7.
8 Gainsford, (Harlean Miscellany), Vol. 6, 1745, p. 537.
9 Vergil, (Historia Anglica), p. 159.

Chapter Ten

1 Dictionary of National Biography, Vol. XII, p. 1034.
2 Buck, Appendix C, Perkin Warbeck, p. 329.
3 Gairdner, p. 275.
4 Hall, p. 463.
5 Bacon, p. 134–5.
6 Gairdner, p. 275.
7 Chastelain, Chapter III, p. 31.
8 Gainsford, p. 557.
9 Bacon, p. 137.
10 Buck, Book III, p. 144.
11 Ulmann, Dr. Heinrich, 'Kaiser Maximilian I.' 2 Vols. Stuttgart 1884–1891 (Archives of Vienna).

Chapter Eleven

1 Deposition of Bernard de Vignolles, a Frenchman, dated 14th March, 1496, at Rouen. Given in full by Sir Frederic Madden in Archaeologia (Documents relating to Perkin Warbeck) in French, pp. 205–209, and quoting also Rymer's transcript in MS Add. 5485, fol. 230.

2 Ibid.

3 Ibid.

4 Gairdner, pp. 276–7.

5 Vergil, p. 571. (Note: Vergil is alone in using the word 'atteyntatus' in connection with Henry VII's punishment of Elizabeth Woodville, but she was not attainted by him.)

6 Bacon, pp. 142–3.

7 Gainsford, p. 562.

8 Calendar of Spanish State Papers, 1485–1509, translated by G.A. Bergenroth, pp. 185–6.

Chapter Twelve

1 Rymer, T., Foedera, xii. 635.

2 Egerton MS. 616. 3. British Library.

3 Molinet, Vol. II, p. 396.

4 Deposition of de Vignolles.

5 Molinet, Vol. II, p. 396.

6 Seton Watson, R.W., 'Maximilian I, Holy Roman Emperor', 1902, pp. 1–8, p. 78.

7 Waas, Glenn Elwood, 'The Legendary Character of Kaiser Maximilian', New York, 1941, pp. 5–22.

8 Ibid, p. 68, (note 292). Story put into Latin verse by historian Hutten.

9 Ulmann, Vol. I, p. 263.

10 Molinet, Vol. II, p. 398.

11 Ulmann, Vol. I.p.263, (translated from a Latin poem into German, undated copy in Archives of Vienna.)

12 Vergil, p. 73.

13 City Chronicle MS. Cotton Vitellus, A.xvi.152.

14 Gainsford, p. 563.

15 André, p. 69.

16 Bacon, p. 148.

17 Buck, p. 161.

18 Ibid, p. 161.

19 More, pp. 102–3.

20 Chastelain, p. 38, note (2).

21 Letters and Papers of Henry VII, ed. Brewer, vol. iii. Preface, p. cxiii.

22 Chastelain, p. 37.
23 Ulmann, Vol. I. pp. 188–90.
24 Bacon, p. 149.
25 Hampton, W.E. Article in The Ricardian, No. 63, p. 9.
26 Deposition of de Vignolles.
27 Ibid.
28 Chastelain, p. 43.
29 Buck, p. 161.
30 Gairdner, p. 289.
31 See Appendix III. (Archives of Antwerp. Chastelain alone gives text in full, pp. 45–7.)
32 André, ed Gairdner, full text in Appendix A, p. 393.
33 Archaeologia, p. 168.

Chapter Thirteen

1 Chastelain, p. 50.
2 Calendar of Venetian State Papers, ed. Brown, p. 649.
3 Hall, p. 472.
4 Calendar of Spanish State Papers, p. 67.
5 Calendar of Venetian State Papers, Vol. IV., No. 1042.
6 Ryland's History of Waterford, 8 Vols., 1834, pp. 30–31.
7 Madden, Sir Frederic, 'Documents relating to Perkin Warbeck, with Remarks on his History', in Archaeologia, 1837, p. 159.
8 Chastelain, p. 50.
9 Madden, p. 171.

Chapter Fourteen

1 Calendar of Spanish State Papers. Letters from de Ayala, Spanish Ambassador to Scotland, to the Spanish King and Queen, 1490.
2 Letters & Papers etc. of Richard III and Henry VII, ed. by Gairdner, Accounts of the Lord High Treasurer of Scotland, Rolls Series, Vol. II., pp. 327–329.
3 Bacon, pp. 159–161.
4 Tytler, P.F., 'History of Scotland', Vol. IV., pp. 375–385 and 423–426. (1831).
5 Accounts of the Lord High Treasurer of Scotland, for 1495–6.

6 Gainsford, p. 572.

7 Dickson, Thomas, Accounts of Lord High Treasurer of Scotland, 1496, Vol. I., p. cxxx.

Chapter Fifteen

1 Madden, p. 181.

2 Chastelain, pp. 59–60, note (i).

3 Ibid, p. 61 note (1).

4 Letters and Papers of Richard III and Henry VII, ed. Gairdner, Vol. II., pp. 329–30.

5 Sanuto Diaries, 1496. (Letter from Piero Contarini, Venetian Ambassador in London, to the Signory).

6 Sanuto Diaries, 1496.

7 Calendar of Venetian State Papers, 1495–1498.

8 Bacon, p. 182; also Gainsford, p. 580.

9 Ellis, Sir Henry, Original Letters, ed. by Gairdner; also Gairdner, 'The Story of Perkin Warbeck', p. 303. (Bothwell's letter to Henry VII).

10 Ellis, (Bothwell's letter to Henry VII) also Gairdner, p. 305.

11 Ellis (Bothwell's letter to Henry VII) also Gairdner p. 304.

12 Pinkerton, B.M., History of Scotland, Contemporary Letters, Vol. II. pp. 438, 443.

13 Accounts of the Lord High Treasurer of Scotland, 1496.

14 Calendar of Spanish State Papers, I., pp. 85, 88, 91, 96, 97 and 115.

15 Gairdner, 'Story of Perkin Warbeck', p. 311.

16 Ellis, Original Letters (Bothwell); also Gairdner, p. 311.

17 Calendar of Venetian State Papers, I. No. 707; also Bacon, pp. 182–3.

18 Proclamation of Prince Richard from Scotland, given in full by Chastelain in Chapter VII, and by Bacon, pp. 162–165.

19 Ellis, Original Letters, I. 26., and Gairdner, p. 309.

20 Tytler, p. 428, and Bacon p. 186.

21 Gainsford, p. 559.

22 Ibid, pp. 580–8.

Chapter Sixteen

1 Accounts of the Lord High Treasurer of Scotland, Vol. I. p. cxlii note i.
2 Calendar of Spanish State Papers, p. 141.
3 Rymer, Foedera Vol. XII., p. 647.
4 Gairdner, pp. 306–7 and 310.
5 Gainsford, p. 580.
6 Ibid, p. 578.
7 Sanuto Diaries: July 14th 1497.
8 Gainsford, p. 580.
9 Bacon, p. 182.
10 Cotton MS: Vesp. C.XXVI.f.2., and Gairdner, p. 316.
11 Accounts of the Lord High Treasurer of Scotland, Vol. I. p. 343.
12 Bodleian: Wood, 401:55 and 407:37.
13 Accounts of the Lord High Treasurer of Scotland, Vol. I. p. 344.
14 Letters & Papers of Richard III and Henry VII, Vol. 2. 185–6, and Gairdner (Story of Perkin Warbeck), p. 319.
15 André, p. 70, and Venetian Calendar No. 755.
16 Gairdner, pp. 320–1.
17 Madden, p. 187, note n, and Gairdner, pp. 324–6.
18 Calendar of Spanish State Papers, I. p. 186 and p. lxxxii.
19 Madden, p. 188.

Chapter Seventeen

1 Sforza Archives: Milanese envoy to Ludovico Sforza, Sept. 8th 1497.
2 Sanuto Diaries, June 15th 1496.
3 Ibid, November 13th 1496.
4 Letters of Gutierre Gomez de Fuensalida, Spanish Ambassador in Germany, Flanders and England, 1490–1507, to King Ferdinand of Spain, Vol. I.
5 Chastelain, p. 86.
6 Sanuto Diaries, 17th Sept. 1497, p. 265.
7 Ibid, p. 265.
8 Hall, p. 480.
9 Ellis, Original Letters, p. 36.

10 Gainsford, p. 586.

11 Ellis, Original Letters, p. 34.

12 Holinshed's Chronicle, p. 784.

13 Chastelain, p. 91.

14 MS City Chronicle Vitellus A. xvi. (f. 166b).

15 Sanuto Diaries, p. 265.

16 Rymer, Feodera, XIII, p. 696.

17 Cotton MS. Calig. D. VI. f. 22.

18 Toulmin, Joshua, D.D., 'The History of Taunton in the County of Somerset', 1822, pp. 401–406, and Granger's 'Biographical History', Vol. I. p. 24.

19 Ellis: Henry VII's Letter to the Mayor of Waterford, (History of Waterford), p. 35.

20 Bacon, p. 188.

21 Taylor, the Rev. T., 'St. Michael's Mount', 1932, pp. 76–196.

22 Hardy, W.J., 'The Handwriting of the Kings and Queens of England', 1893, pp. 48–50.

23 Chastelain, p. 98.

24 Holinshed, p. 790, also Bacon, p. 186.

25 Bacon, p. 186.

26 Gainsford, p. 591, and Hall, p. 485.

27 Ellis: Henry VII's Letter to the Mayor of Waterford, p. 36.

28 Letters and Papers of Richard III and Henry VII, Vol. 2., pp. 73–4: (Henry VII's letter to Thomas Stokes).

29 Calendar of Spanish State Papers, I. p. 145. (Henry VII's Letter to de Puebla).

30 Holinshed, (Reprint, 1808, Vol. V., p. 464, also quoted by Gainsford.

31 Ibid, p. 464.

32 Ellis: Henry VII's Letter to the Mayor of Waterford, p. 36.

33 Hall, p. 482.

34 Calendar of Spanish State Papers (de Fuensalida to King Ferdinand of Spain), Vol. I. 1485–1509.

Chapter Eighteen

1 Carew Calendar, Miscell. 469, also Gairdner (Perkin Warbeck) pp. 328–9.

2 André, p. 73.

3 Chastelain, p. 102. (note from p. 101).

4 Desmons, p. 98, gives English version from MS Vitellus A. xvi 1497.

5 MS Vitellus A. xvi f. 168.

6 Hall, p. 485.

7 Desmons, p. 189, quoting Hall, p. 485.

8 Ibid, p. 99, note (2).

9 Ibid, p. 100.

Chapter Nineteen

1 Madden, p. 189.

2 Gainsford, p. 590.

3 MS Vitellus, A. xvi f. 170.

4 Excerpta Historica, (compiled by Samuel Bentley 1831) p. 117.

5 Calendar of Milanese State Papers, p. 335.

6 Chastelain, p. 95.

7 Bacon, p. 188.

8 Ibid, p. 189.

9 Gainsford, p. 590.

10 Buck, p. 150.

11 Stow, John: Annales, or a General History of England, 1631, pp. 476–488.

12 Gainsford, p. 590.

13 Buck, pp. 150–2.

14 Ibid, p. 153.

15 Hall, p. 487.

16 Stow, p. 488.

17 Sanuto Diaries, 30th July, 1498.

18 Bacon, p. 194.

19 Calendar of Spanish State Papers, p. lxxxv.

20 Bacon, p. 197.

Chapter Twenty

1 Calendar of Spanish State Papers, (Letter from de Puebla to King Ferdinand of Spain), 25th August 1498.

2 Calendar of Spanish State Papers, (Introduction), p. lxxxv.
3 Harl MSS 433 Vol. III pp. 24–25.
4 Calendar of Spanish State Papers, (de Fuensalida to King Ferdinand of Spain), August 1498.
5 Vergil, p. 69.
6 Stow, 53rd Report, Public Records, Appendix II, pp. 30–36, and pp. 216–18.
7 Rymer MS Add. 4618, No. 2.
8 Stow, 53rd Report, Public Records, Appendix II, pp. 30–36, and pp. 216–18.
9 Rymer, Add. 4618, No. 2.
10 Madden, p. 190.
11 Calendar of Milanese State Papers, p. 335.
12 Bacon, p. 197.
13 Stow, 53rd Report, Public Records, Appendix II, pp. 30–36, and pp. 216–18.
14 Calendar of Spanish State Papers, (Introduction), p. lxxxv.
15 Calendar of Spanish State Papers, (Letter from de Puebla to King Ferdinand of Spain), 11th January, 1500.
16 Letters and Papers of Henry VIII (ed. Brewer), Vol. VI, No. 1528 and Vol. VII No. 1368.
17 Calendar of Spanish State Papers (Letters etc. between England and Spain, trans. by Bergenroth), Vol. I 1485–1509, p. 196. letter from Margaret Duchess of Burgundy to Henry VII after 7th Sept 1498.
18 Letters and Papers of Richard III and Henry VII (ed. Gairdner) Vol. II., p. 198.

Epilogue

1 Speed, John, 'The History of Great Britain from Julius Caesar to James I', ed. 1611, p. 738.
2 Bacon, p. 196.
3 Kincaid, Dr. A.N., 'Notes and Queries', Vol. 28, No. 2., April 1981, from Article on Sir Edward Hoby: 'King Richard; Shakespeare Play or Morton Tract?'
4 Harl. MSS 433, Vol. I. p. 162.
5 Bacon, p. 139.
6 Ibid, p. 138.

Bibliography.

ANDRÉ, Bernard: Memorials of Henry VII. (b.1450, died about 1521).

ARCHAEOLOGIA: Vol. XXVII. (Sir Frederic Madden's quotations from, and Contributions to:) 1838.

BACON, Francis, The History of the Reign of King Henry VII. Folio Society Edition, 1881. (b.1561, died 1626.)

BRIGHT, The Rev. J.F.: The History of England, Parts I and II, 1449–1485 and 1485–1688. pub. 1896.

BUCK, Sir George: King Richard the Third: edit. by Dr. A.N. Kinaid, 1979. (Buck b. 1560, died 1623).

CALENDAR of SPANISH STATE PAPERS, trans. by G.A. Bergenroth, 1862.

CALENDAR of VENETIAN STATE PAPERS, ed. by Rawdon Brown, 1864.

CALMETTE, J., and PÉRINELLE, G.,: Louis XI et L'Angleterre, edit. Auguste Picard, Paris, 1930.

CHAMBERS, R.W.,: Thomas More; London 1935.

CHASTELAIN, Jean-Didier, L'Imposture de Perkin Warbeck: Brussels, 1952.

CHRIMES, S.B., Henry VII, London, 1972.

CHRIST CHURCH LETTERS, ed. J.B. Sheppard, Camden Society, 2nd Series, London 1877.

CHRONICLES of LONDON, ed. Kingsford 1905. Facsimile ed. Alan Sutton, 1977.

COMMYNES, Philippe de, Mémoires, trans. by Michael Jones: Penguin Classics 1972. (de Commynes b. 1447, died 1511.)

COSTAIN, Thomas B., The Last Plantagenets, (from The Pageant of England, 1377–1485; Tandem, 1973.)

COTTON MSS, (British Library). (Sir Robert Cotton, Elizabethan historian and collector of MSS).

CROYLAND CHRONICLE, (Third and Fourth Continuator: Ingulph's

History of the Abbey of Croyland; trans, by and ed. Henry T. Riley 1854.)

DAVIES, Robert,: Extracts from the Municipal Records of the City of York during the Reigns of Edward IV, Edward V and Richard III. London 1843.

DICKSON, Thomas,: History of Scotland and Accounts of the Lord High Treasurer of Scotland Vol. I 1473–1498 (ed. T. Dickson 1877.)

DIVISIE CHRONICLE: (Holland): c.1500.

ELLIS, Sir Henry, Original Letters, ed. by J. Gairdner, The Camden Society, 1839.

EXCERPTA HISTORICA,: Collection made by Samuel Bentley, 1831.

FOWLER, Kenneth,: The Age of Plantagenet and Valois, London, 1980.

GAINSFORD, Thomas, (Harlean Miscellany Vol. 6,1745: The True and Wonderful History of Perkin Warbeck), taken from Hall, Holinshed and More, Grafton, etc.) died 1624. London, 1618.

GAIRDNER, James,: History of the Life and Reign of Richard III, including the Story of Perkin Warbeck. (19th Century historian). Folio Society, 1898.

GAIRDNER, J.,: ed. LETTERS AND PAPERS of Richard III and Henry VII Vols. 1 and 2. (19th Century historian) Camden Society, 1861–3.

GRAFTON, Richard,: Chronicle (Henry the Seventh). 2 Vols. (16th Century historian): London 1809.

GRANGER,: Biographical History, Vol. I: 1790.

GREAT CHRONICLE of LONDON (c.1498) ed. A.H. Thomas and I.D. Thornley,: London, 1938.

HALL, Edward,: Chronicle; ed. Henry Ellis: (16th Century historian): London 1809.

HALSTED, Caroline,: Richard III: (19th Century historian): Longmans, Brown, Green and Longmans, pub. 1844.)

HAMMOND, P.W.: and SUTTON, A.F., The Road to Bosworth:, Guild Publishing, London 1985.

HAMMOND, P.W.,: and WHITE, W.,: Richard III: Loyalty Lordship, and Law: Article entitled 'The Sons of Edward IV: a re-examination of the evidence on their deaths and on the Bones in Westminster Abbey': Richard III and Yorkist History Trust 1986.

HARDY, W.J.,: The Handwriting of the Kings and Queens of England., 1893.

HARVEY, John,: The Plantagenets. Collins: Fontana Library, 1948.

HORROX, Rosemary, and HAMMOND, P.W., editors of HARLEIAN MSS 433, Vols. I, II, III and IV. Alan Sutton for Richard III Society. 1979.

KENDALL, Paul Murray,: Richard III (b.1911, died 1973) London 1955.

KENDALL, Paul Murray,: Louis XI. London 1960.

KINGSFORD, C.L.,: English Historical Literature in the 15th Century. Oxford 1913.

LAMB, V.B.,: The Betrayal of Richard III: London 1959.

LETTERS & PAPERS, Foreign and Domestic of the Reign of Henry VIII, ed. J.S. Brewer: London 1862–1932.

LYNE-PIRKIS, Dr. Richard,: Lecture on 'The Princes' given to the Richard III Society. 1963.

MACKIE, R.L.,: King James IV of Scotland. Edinburgh 1958.

MADDEN, Sir Frederic,: Documents relating to Perkin Warbeck with Remarks on his History. ARCHAEOLOGIA XXVII. (19th Century historian). 1838.

MANCINI, Dominic.: The Usurpation of Richard III. (ed. trans. & Introduction by C.A.J. Armstrong, 2nd ed. 1969. (Italian priest who came to England in 1482 and left after Richard III's coronation in 1483.)

MARKHAM, Sir Clements,: Richard III: His Life and Character. London 1906.

MOLINET, Jean,: Chronicles 1476–1506; ed. J.A. Buchon, Paris, 1827–8. (Molinet b. 1435, died 1507.)

MORE, Sir Thomas, History of King Richard III, from The Great Debate, ed. by Paul Kendal, The Folio Society, London, 1965. (More b. 1478; died 1535.)

MORE, Sir Thomas, 'The Historie of the Pitifull Life and Unfortunate Death of Edward the Fifth and the then Duke of York his brother'.

O'CONNELL, The Rev. Sir John,: Saint Thomas More. London 1935.

PASTON LETTERS, 1422–1509 (4 Vols); ed. James Gairdner, Edinburgh, 1910.

PINKERTON, B.M.,: History of Scotland; Contemporary Letters, and Medallic History of England,; 1790 and 1797.

ROSS, Dr. Charles,: Edward IV. Methuen, 1974. (20th century historian.)

RYMER, Thomas,: Foedera: (compiled in 1709–11. London 1709–11.)

SETON WATSON, R.W.: Maximilian I, Holy Roman Emperor, Westminster 1902.

SPEED, John,: The Historie of Great Britaine, London 1623. (17th century historian).

STOW, John,: The Annales of England. London 1601. (Stow b. c.1525, died 1605).

TANNER, L.E., & WRIGHT, W.,: 'Recent Investigations Regarding the Fate of the Princes in the Tower'. ARCHAEOLOGIA LXXXIV,: 1935.

TAYLOR, The Rev.T.,: St. Michael's Mount; Cambridge, 1932.

TOULMIN, Joshua,: History of Taunton in the County of Somerset; (18th century).

TREVELYAN, G.M.,: English Social History; Pelican Books; Penguin. 1942.

TYTLER, P.F.,.: History of Scotland (including the Lord High Treasurer's Accounts 1480–1499). 1831.

ULMANN, Heinrich,: Kaiser Maximilian I (2 Vols). Stuttgart 1884–1891.

VERGIL, Polydore,: Historia Anglica, 1485–1537. Camden Society, 1844. (Vergil came to England in 1500 or soon after, died 1555)

WAAS, Glenn Elwood,: The Legendary Character of Kaiser Maximilian, New York 1941.

WALPOLE, Horace,: Historic Doubts on the Life and Reign of King Richard III, from The Great Debate, ed. by Paul Kendal, The Folio Society, London 1965.

WILLIAMSON, Audrey,: 'The Mystery of the Princes: An Investigation into a Supposed Murder': Alan Sutton 1978.

Articles

ARCHIVES de la ville de TOURNAI: Notes sur la famille de l'aventurier Perkin Warbeck. Actes divers layette de 1517.

BARR, Kenneth,:   Richard III — Foreign Policy/Spain. The Ricardian No.35, pp 4–8.

BUNNETT, R.J.A.,:   Did the Princes leave the Tower? The Ricardian No.17, Jan. 1967, pp.3–6.

BUNNETT, R.J.A.,:   The 1933 Examination of the Alleged Bones of the Princes. The Ricardian No.28, March 1970. pp.13–14.

CARTER, Barry,:   The Marriage of Margaret of York. The Ricardian, No.24., March 1969, pp.9–10.

COATES, Dr.J.I.,:   Pretenders to the English Crown during the Reign of King Henry VII (1485–1509). The Ricardian No. 16, Oct. 1966, pp.2–5.

COATES, Dr.J.I.,:   'Perkin Warbeck' and the Werbecque Family. The Ricardian No.21., May 1968, pp.2–6.

COMPILATION: Of replies to the Article: Did the Sons of Edward IV outlive Henry VII? The Ricardian, Vol.V, No.64, March 1979, pp.24–26.

CRAWFORD, Anne,:   John Howard, Duke of Norfolk: A Possible Murderer of the Princes? The Ricardian, Vol.V., No.70., Sept. 1980, pp.230–234.

CUSSANS, J.E.,:   Notes on the Perkin Warbeck Insurrection. Article written by Dr.Cussans, a Fellow of the Royal Historical Society.

DESMONS, Dr.,:   Un tournaisien prétendant au trône d'Angleterre, Revue Tournaisienne, Nos.4–5, 1901.

HALL, Douglas.,:   Richard III — The Great Debate. The Ricardian No.12., May 1965, pp.14–15.

HALL, Douglas,:   The Princes in the Tower — A Hypothesis. The Ricardian No.17., Jan.1967, pp.3–6.

HALL, Douglas,:   The Princes in the Tower — A Challenge. The Ricardian, No.33. June 1971, pp.9–12.

HAMMOND, Peter,:   Was Perkin Warbeck the Duke of York? The Ricardian No.17, Jan.1967, pp.2–3.

HAMMOND, Peter,:   The Bones of the 'Princes' in Westminster Abbey,. The Ricardian, Vol.IV, No.52, March 1976, pp.22–5.

HAMMOND, Peter,:   Research Notes and Queries: Sir Robert Brackenbury. The Ricardian No.43, Dec. 1973, pp.15–16.

HAMPTON, W.E.,:   Sir James Tyrell: with some Notes on the Austin Friars. The Ricardian, Vol.IV, No. 63, Dec. 1978, pp.9–22.

HAMPTON, W.E.,:   Witchcraft and the Sons of York. The Ricardian, Vol.V., No.68., March 1980, pp.170–178.

HARMON, Julius Frasch,: The Mystery of Perkin Warbeck's Wife Reveals the Innocence of King Richard the Third. The Ricardian, No.14, Jan.1966, pp.2–5.

HENES, Edwin, Jr.,:   Direct Copy of a 'Historical Sketch of Perkin Warbeck, Pretender to the Crown of England', Geo.Chauncy Briner, The Knickerbocker Press, N.Y. 1902.

HICKS, Michael,:   The Middle Brother: 'False, Fleeting, Perjur'd Clarence'. The Ricardian, Vol.V., No.72, March 1981, pp.302–310.

HUTCHINS, John,   b.1698, Rector of Holy Trinity in Wareham and of Swyre, in the County of Dorset,: John Morton, Archbishop of Canterbury. Extract from the History of Antiquities

	of Dorset, under the title 'Eminent Persons.'
JACKSON, Edwin C.,:	Seminar on Richard: An Eternal Mystery. The Ricardian No.24, March 1969, pp.11–14.
JARMAN, Rosemary,:	Some More 'Secret Bones'. The Ricardian No.25, p.10.
JONES, Philomena,:	Anne Mowbray. The Ricardian, Vol.IV., No.61, June 1978, pp.17–20.
KINCAID, A.N.,:	George Buck Senior and George Buck Junior. The Ricardian, Vol.IV., No.60, March 1978, pp.2–8.
LESLAU, Jack,:	Did the Sons of Edward IV outlive Henry VII? The Ricardian, Vol.IV., No.62, Sept. 1978, pp.2–14.
LYNE-PIRKIS, Dr.,:	The Bones Found in the Tower. A talk given by a noted anatomist, Dr. Lyne-Pirkis, questioning the findings of the Tanner and Wright Investigation of 1933. (1963.)
MIDDLETON, Anne,:	'Historic Doubts' on Mancini. The Ricardian No.23, Dec.1968, pp.11–15.
MORGAN, John,:	Have the Princes' Bones been found in the Tower? Article on the discoveries and the Tanner-Wright report. 1934. (Richard III Society Library).
MORGAN, John,:	Did Norfolk dispose of the Princes in the Tower? The Ricardian, No.16, Oct.1966, pp.7–8.
MOWAT, A.J.,:	Have we cause to praise Thomas More? The Ricardian No.43, Dec. 1973, pp.13–14.
MOZLEY, T., M.A.,	Rector of Plymtree in Dorset c.1610.: Article on Henry VII, Prince Arthur and Cardinal Morton, including a Biographical Sketch of Cardinal Morton by John Budden, a relative? of the Morton family.
NEWMAN, Peter R.,:	Political Expediency. The Ricardian No.25, June 1969, pp.15–17.

NOKES, Elizabeth,:   Back to the 'Bones'. The Ricardian No.30,
                       Sept.1970, p.18.

NOKES, E.M.,:   The Princes in the Tower — who was really
                       guilty? The Ricardian, No.31, Dec. 1970,
                       pp.18–20.

PETRE, J.O.,:   Bastardy and the Princes: A further Note.
                       The Ricardian, Vol.V., No.64, March
                       1979, pp.27–29.

RAMSDEN, John A.,:   Corpus Christi College, Oxford: A Tudor
                       Defence of Richard III. The Ricardian,
                       No.20, Jan.1968, p.12.

RAMSDEN, John A.,:   The Enconium of Richard III, Part II. The
                       Ricardian No.23., Dec. 1968, pp.2–7.

RIJK, J.W.F.X. de,:   The Case against Richard III. The Ricardian
                       No.16, Oct. 1966, p.6.

ROTH, Dr. Cecil,;   D.Phil., F.R.Hist.Soc.,: Sir Edward
M.A.,:   Brampton: An Anglo-Jewish Adventurer
                       during the Wars of the Roses. (Richard
                       III Society Library).

ROTH, Dr.Cecil, M.A., Ph.D., F.R.Hist.S.: Sir Edward Brampton,
                       Governor of Guernsey, and the Mystery
                       of Richard, Duke of York. Lecture given
                       at Caxton Hall on Feb.11th 1959. (Richard
                       III Society Library.)

SHULMAN, D.,   Did the Sons of Edward IV outlive Henry
and Leslau, J.,:   VII?. The Ricardian, Vol.V., No. 65,
                       June 1979, pp.55–63.

SMITHIES, Alan,:   Where could the Princes be sent?.
                       The Ricardian No.28, March 1970,
                       pp.6–7.

SMITHIES, Alan,:   Margaret of York. Lecture given to the
                       Richard III Society at Leicester University
                       on 21st August 1976.

SMITHIES, Alan,:   The Identity of Richard III's first Apologist.
                       The Ricardian No.21., May 1968,
                       p.17.

SNYDER, William H.,.   The History of the Life and Reign of
                       King Richard the Third, (Sir George

	Buck). The Ricardian, No.25, June 1969, pp.3–6.
SPEARES, J.A., O.B.E.,:	Secret Diplomacy between the Plantagenets and the French Courts of Louis XI/Charles VIII. Lecture given to the Richard III Society at Leicester University on 21st August 1976.
WIGRAM, Isolde,:	Sir Thomas More's 'Historie'. The Ricardian, No.12., May 1965, pp.7–9.
WIGRAM, Isolde,:	The Princes: An Attempted Synthesis. The Ricardian No.18, May 1967, pp.5–8.
WIGRAM, Isolde,:	Mancini — Doubts — Refutations. The Ricardian, No.25, June 1969, pp.11–12.
WIGRAM, Isolde,:	Clarence still Perjur'd. The Ricardian, Vol.V, No.73, June 1981, pp.352–355.
WIGRAM, Isolde,:	Some Reasons why Perkin Warbeck was likely to have been who he claimed to be: Richard, second son of King Edward IV. (Richard III Society Library).
WILLIAMS, Barrie,:	Ruy de Sousa's Embassy and the Fate of Richard Duke of York. The Ricardian Vol.V. No.73, June 1981. 341–345.
WILLIAMS, Barrie,:	The Portuguese Connection and the Significance of the 'holy Princess'. The Ricardian, Vol.VI, No.80, March 1983. pp.138–145.
WILLIAMS, Barrie,:	The Portuguese Marriage Negotiations: A Reply. The Ricardian, Vol.VI, No.82, Sept.1983, pp.235–6.
WILLIAMS, Barrie,:	Sir Edward Brampton: The Portuguese Years. The Ricardian, Vol.VI., No.84, March 1984, pp.294–8.
WYLIE, John A.,:	The Princes in the Tower 1483: Death from Natural Causes? The Ricardian, Vol.VII, No.91, Dec. 1985, pp.178–182.

BOOKS OF FACT/FICTION.

TEY, Josephine,	'The Daughter of Time', pub.1951.
WILLIAMSON, Hugh Ross,	'The Identity of Perkin Warbeck', from 'Historical Enigmas', pub.1950.

PLAY.

FORD, John,:	The Chronicle History of Perkin Warbeck: A Strange Truth. Written in 1634. (Richard III Society Library)

APPENDIX 1

The Archives of Tournai. 1893

The Family of de Werbecque.

1. DIERIC (THIERY) de WERBECQUE, carpenter (boat-builder), native of Berne-les-Audenarde, bought the right of burghership of Tournai for 8 sous, four pence (tournaisian), on 22nd June 1429. He is mentioned in an Act passed at the Aldermanry of St. Brice in 1442, and lived on the bank of the Scheldt in the parish of St. John des Cauffours. He died before May 1474, leaving one legitimate son, as follows:-

2. JEHAN de WERBECQUE, later JEHAN WERBECQUE, pilot, took up his right of burghership at Tournai as the son of a native burgher, during the year of his marriage, 11th May, 1474. He is mentioned in an Act dated 1489. He died before Dec. 1498, having married in 1473 NICAISE (or CAISINE) FAROUL or FARO, of a family long established in Tournai. By an Act passed before the Mayor and Aldermen of St. Brice on 20th Dec. 1498, Delle NICAISE FAROUL, widow of JEHAN WERBECQUE, accompanied by PIERRE FLAN and by ADRIEN CARLIER, tutors and guardians of her children PIERRECHON and JEHANNE WERBECQUE, sold to JEHAN VALLOIS, son of the late HAYNNE VALLOIS, merchant, a house situated on the Scheldt at Cauffours.

Shortly after, NICAISE remarried, with JEHAN DE LA CROIX, who died before November 1509, because it is attested to this lady being a widow on 20th of this month and year. By her last wish, she left a legacy to her parish church of St. John des Cauffours, where she wished to be buried in the chapel of St. Julien: then to the poor of the Hospice of St. Jehan le Plancque (NICAISINE FAROU left a legacy for perpetual Mass to be said for her soul in the chapel of this house): to the Hospice of Marvis, and to the two

natural sons of her first husband. Her sole heiress was JEHENNE
WERBECQUE, then her only child, married to Master JEHAN
CAMBIER. Executors of the Will were LOY DE LA RUE,
procurator-general of Tournai; JEHAN CAMBIER, son-in-law
of the testatrix; ADRIEN CARLIER, her godson, and GERARD
WATELIER. The day of probate, which was Wednesday, 13th
April 1513, after Easter, the day after the death of the testatrix,
this Act was deposited in the hands of the Mayor and Aldermen
of St. Brice by Seigneur FIRMIN MACQUE, vice-curé of St.
Jehan. JEHAN WERBECQUE was the father of four children,
two legitimate and two natural. Legitimate:-

1. PIERRECHON or PIERRE WERBECQUE, called Perkin
   Warbeck, born in 1474, known to the world for his having
   represented the late Richard of York, younger son of Edward
   IV, King of England, and in this role carried the title of
   Richard IV, King of France and England, Lord of Ireland.
   He was instructed and politically educated by travels at the
   expense of the Dowager Duchess of Burgundy, Margaret of
   York of the House of Plantagenet, who wished to bring about
   a revolt in England against the dynasty of the Welsh Tudor.
   In 1495 at the Court of James IV of Scotland, he married Lady
   Catherine Seton or Gordon, daughter of the Earl of Huntly,
   and great-granddaughter of James I Stuart, King of Scotland,
   and Queen Jane, born of England Beaufort-Somerset. Being
   taken prisoner by the troops of Henry VII in the county
   of Kent, WERBECQUE was imprisoned in the Tower of
   London. His life was saved, but not the liberty which he
   wished to recover. A plan of escape concocted with Edward
   Plantagenet, Earl of Warwick, his companion in captivity,
   was discovered. The two fugitives were arrested, and the
   real heir to the English throne, Edward VI, king without a
   crown, lost his head on the scaffold, while our compatriot
   WERBECQUE (end of November–December 1499) was
   hanged at Tyburn aged 25 years. The historian Lingard
   reports that according to a document — imperfect and
   unsatisfactory — 'Perkin Warbeck' acknowledged that he was
   born in Tournai, that he was the son of JEHAN OSBECK and

of CATHERINE DE FARO, names by which it is easy to see and recognise the father and mother given above.

As to the Queen Catherine, called the White Rose of Scotland and Mistress Warbeck, née GORDON, after having been lady-in-waiting to the Queen of England, she remarried with Sir MATTHEW CRADOCK, gentleman of Scottish origin, near whom she lies in the church at Swansea in Wales.

2. JEHANNE WERBECQUE, married before 1509, to Master JEHAN CAMBIER, with whom she was still living in 1517.

Natural children:-

3. COLIN or NICOLAS WERBECQUE, brought up at Pipais in the house of MATHIEU BALGUIEM, as testified by Delle NICAISE FAROU in her Will; received a legacy from this lady of 12 Flemish pounds.

4. INNOCENT WERBECQUE, received from his father the sum of ten pounds, and as legacy from Delle NICAISE FAROU, five pounds and other monies advanced by her.

N.B.   The above extracts from the Archives of Tournai, are embellished by the historian Chastel de la Howarderie, with many mistakes. I have given them in their entirety, since the information on the WERBECQUE family is all we have.

The description 'Delle' applied to NICAISE FAROUL above, is explained in a note superscribed on the letter which 'Perkin' is supposed to have written to his 'mother': 'À Mademoiselle ma mère . . .': In those days only ladies of exalted position were addressed in French as 'Madame'; in the lesser ranks even married women were called 'Mademoiselle' of which 'Delle' is a diminution.

APPENDIX II

Translation of Latin original letter written by the Pretender to the Queen of Spain. (Egerton MS 616.3 British Library)

'My most honoured Lady and Cousin,

. . . Whereas the Prince of Wales, eldest son of Edward formerly King of England, of pious memory, my dearest lord and father, was miserably put to death and I myself, then about nine years old, was also delivered to a certain lord to be killed, it pleased the Divine Clemency that that lord, having compassion on my innocence, preserved me alive and in safety, first, however, causing me to swear on the Holy Sacrament, that to no-one should I disclose my name, origin or family, until a certain number of years had passed. He sent me therefore abroad, with two persons who should watch over and take charge of me; and thus I, an orphan, bereaved of my royal father and brother, an exile from my kingdom and deprived of country, inheritance and fortune, a fugitive in the midst of extreme perils, led my miserable life, in fear, and weeping and grief, and for the space of nearly eight years lay hid in divers provinces. At length, one of those who had charge of me being dead, and the other returned to his country and never afterwards seen, scarcely had I emerged from childhood, alone and without means, I remained for a time in the Kingdom of Portugal, and thence sailed to Ireland, where being recognised by the illustrious lords, the Earls of Desmond and Kildare, my cousins, as also by other noblemen of the island, I was received with great joy and honour. Thence being invited by the King of France, with many ships and attendants, and having been promised aid and assistance against Henry of Richmond, the wicked usurper of the Kingdom of England, I came to the aforesaid King of France, who received me honourably as a kinsman and friend. But on his failing to afford me the promised assistance, I betook myself to the illustrious Princess, the Lady Duchess of Burgundy, sister of my father, my dearest aunt who, with her known humanity and virtue, welcomed me with all piety and honour; out of regard also to her, the most serene King of the Romans (Maximilian) and his son, the Archduke of Austria, and the Duke of Saxony, my dearest cousins, as likewise the Kings of Denmark and Scotland, who sent to me their envoys, for the purpose of friendship and alliance. The great nobles of the Kingdom of England did the same, who execrate the proud and wicked tyranny of this Henry of Richmond.

'But, (most Serene Princess, Lady and Cousin) since, on account of our relationship and your renowned virtues, by which you surpass all other princes of the world, in justice, actions and prosperity, you ought no less than other princes to compassionate our condition, and succour us with pious love, I pray and implore your Majesty will use your influence with your Serene Spouse that, together with your Clemency, he may be induced to pity the numerous calamities of our family, and in my right, which is also yours, to further me and mine with his favour, aid and assistance. For I promise, if the Divine Grace should restore to me my hereditary kingdome, that I will continue with both your Majesties in closer alliance and friendship than ever King Edward was, and that I and my Kingdom will be ever ready to fulfill your pleasure, no less than your own realms.

Farewell to your noble Majesty!

Written from the town od Dendermonde, the 8th calends of September (25th August) 1493.

> Of your Excellent Majesty
> the cousin, Richard Plantagenet, second son
> of Edward, formerly King, Duke of York, etc.
> Richard.'

Addressed 'To the most Serene and Excellent Princess, the Lady Isabel, Queen of Castile, Arragon, Sicily, Granada etc., and my most honoured Lady and Cousin'.

APPENDIX III

*Full text of the document (original in Latin) signed by Richard Duke of York, at Malines on 24th January, 1495

'We, Richard, by the grace of God, King of England and France, Duke of York, Lord of Ireland and Prince of Wales, only son of the King Edward IV, and legitimate heir of the Kingdoms, duchies, Lordships and Principalities mentioned; to all who will see or hear these letters, greeting.

'Given that human conditions — governed by the instability of fortune and exposed to her blows — whether it be a poor man or a King, as an ordinary mortal the butt of a blind hostility, one must retain confidence in Divine Clemency, which Providence has always known how to extend to all things, which will end in removing errors of every kind and in giving merit to those to whom honour belongs.

'It is incontestable that the States of our late Lord and Father Edward, King of England and France, Duke of York, Lord of Ireland and Prince of Wales, devolve on Us by virtue of the right of legitimacy. But adverse Fortune decreed that these States were occupied by others, and that they are still so to-day to Our great hurt and prejudice. The goodness and munificence of the Serene Prince and Lord Maximilian, King of the Romans, Our well-loved Lord, gives Us nevertheless the firm hope that We will recover Our heritage.

'However, given the uncertainty of human destiny, it could be that Our fatal day arrives for Us before We are re-established in Our before-mentioned heritage. Also, so that the usurpers on the one hand cannot find in it a stimulant, or gain the conviction that one condones their iniquity, and considering on the other hand the immense benefits received from Our Serene Highness Lord Maximilian, King of the Romans, We have, after hard deliberation, We being assured of the width and size of the gift which follows, and envisaging the case of Our not having legitimate successors, given, ceded and transferred by the present act and by the conditions described below, all Our possessions of the Kingdoms of England and France, of the Duchy of York, the Lordship of Ireland and of the Principality of Wales, with all the rights accruing thereto to whatever title at present or in the future, into the hands of his Serene Highness Lord Maximilian, King of the Romans, for himself and after his decease, for his son the pious and illustrious Prince and Lord Archduke Philip, and for the male legitimate children of the latter, that is to say the male children of a legitimate marriage of the said Lord King, in the event that We die without legitimate male-descendants or that, having legitimate male descendants, they may die without issue, in the which We leave Ourselves to the judgment of the Divine Clemency. In the case of this eventuality Our most Serene Lord Maximilian, King of the Romans or his successors will be immediately enabled to reclaim, acquire and possess the Kingdoms of England and France, the Duchy of York, the Lordship of Ireland and the Principality of Wales, with all the titles, dignities, rights and goods pertaining thereto. This cession and transfer, or other appellation with which one may designate it, We have by a definite deposition incapable of any doubt whatever, promised it in perpetuity to Our Serene Lord Maximilian King of the Romans, that he accepts for himself and for his children, stipulating that he will never renounce the said gift, nor violate nor contravene, but will guarantee the perpetual validity of it. We solemnly swear on the Holy Scriptures never to go back on the foregoing, but to observe it on the contrary in general as in particular, and above all never to ask Our most Holy Lord the Pope or his successors to be excused from Our oath, no matter for what reason, never to dispose of Our own will of these concessions, renouncing all rights, judicial on any pretext such as being a minor in age, constraint, respect or error.

'Given at Malines, under Our signature and Our personal seal.'

For more ample verification and attestation, the act of this spontaneous gift was established in the presence of the subscribed donor, the Most Reverend Father and Most Illustrious Prince and Lord Bartholdi, Archbishop of Mayence, Elector of the Holy Roman Empire, and of the not less Illustrious Lady Margaret of England, Duchess of Burgundy, of Brabant etc, widow of Duke Charles of noble memory, also of the Lords Chevaliers Ladron de Guevara and Thomas de Plaines, Councillors of Our most Excellent Prince and Lord Archduke Philip, called as witnesses.

'The 24th day of January in the year of Our Lord one thousand, four hundred and ninety-five,

Signed, Richard of England.'

'I, Francois de Busleiden, doctor and Canon Provost of Liege, notary by imperial favour, being present with the Princes and witnesses above-mentioned, and having seen and heard all things accomplished as they were enacted, the most Illustrious Prince and Lord Richard required me as witness to their truthfulness, and I have endorsed the declarations faithfully reproduced above and edited this note with my own hand, the day and year as above.'

*Archives de la Chambre des Comptes in Brussels, now in the Archives of Vienna.
So far as I know, Jean-Didier Chastelain is the only historian who gives the above document in full (translated by him into French from the original Latin) in his book 'L'Imposture de Perkin Warbeck', 1952. He does not give his source.

APPENDIX IV

*From the Spanish State Papers in Simancas: Original in
Latin*

'1495: Richard Duke of York to Lady Katherine Gordon.

'Most noble lady, it is not without reason that all turn their eyes to you;
that all admire, love and obey you. For they see your twofold virtues by
which you are so much distinguished above all other mortals. Whilst,
on the one hand, they admire your riches and immutable prosperity,
which secure to you the nobility of your lineage and the loftiness of
your rank, they are, on the other hand, struck by your rather divine
than human beauty, and believe that you are not born in our days, but
descended from Heaven.

'All look at your face, so bright and serene that it gives splendour to
the cloudy sky; all look at your eyes as brilliant as stars, which make all
pain to be forgotten, and turn despair into delight; all look at your neck,
which outshines pearls; all look at your fine forehead, your purple light
of youth, your fair hair; in one word at the splendid perfection of your
person; — and looking at, they cannot choose but admire you; admiring,
they cannot choose but love you; loving, they cannot choose but obey
you.

'I shall, perhaps, be the happiest of all your admirers, and the happiest
man on earth, since I have reason to hope you will think me worthy of
your love. If I represent to my mind all your perfections, I am not only
compelled to love, to adore and to worship you, but love makes me your
slave. Whether waking or sleeping, I cannot find rest or happiness except
in your affection. All my hopes rest in you, and in you alone.

'Most noble lady, my soul, look mercifully down upon me your slave,
who has ever been devoted to you from the first hour he saw you. Love
is not an earthly thing, it is heaven born. Do not think it below yourself
to obey love's dictates. Not only kings but also gods and goddesses have
bent their necks beneath its yoke,

'I beseech you, most noble lady, to accept for ever one who in all things will cheerfully do your will as long as his days shall last. Farewell, my soul and my consolation. You, the brightest ornament of Scotland, farewell, farewell.'

Indorsed in Spanish: 'From the Prince of Wales to the Princess of Wales'. Latin. Copy.

A footnote by Bergenroth says: 'The Princess of Wales (the Infanta Catherine of Aragon, who was contracted to marry Prince Arthur at this time) could never have been called the brightest ornament of Scotland. It is unlikely to have been written by James IV to one of his lady loves and sent by Henry VII to Ferdinand, as Henry wanted James IV to marry Ferdinand's daughter Mary. But James would certainly have seen Richard's proposal to Lady Catherine Gordon and probably given a copy of it to the Spanish Ambassador for its political importance. Moreover the Princess of Wales had the same name, Catherine, and hence the confusion may have arisen.' It must also be noted that the Spanish Infanta Catherine did not actually become Princess of Wales until her marriage to Prince Arthur on the 14th November, 1501; nor did the Prince Arthur, Prince of Wales, have the choice of bride as mentioned by the writer, although he must have written her many letters during the time they were contracted to marry. It must also be noted that the writer says he loved her 'from the first hour he saw her': Prince Arthur did not see his bride until she arrived in England to marry him. One can only conclude, therefore, that the Spaniard who endorsed the letter 'From the Prince of Wales to the Princess of Wales' was attempting, probably on his Sovereigns' orders, to deny authorship of this tender and loving missive to the real writer, Prince Richard of York, because it would have revealed him in his true colours.

Bergenroth also notes that, while the Pretender was still an honoured guest at the court of King James, Maximilian's only son the Archduke Philip had married the Spanish Infanta Juana, heiress of Castile and Aragon, and that King Ferdinand and Queen Isabella would not consent to their other daughter Catherine marrying Henry's elder son Prince Arthur, while any Pretender to the throne of England remained alive. This condition has always been interpreted by historians as referring exclusively to the young Earl of Warwick, son of the Duke of Clarence, whom Henry was still holding prisoner in the Tower for no other reason than that he was a Yorkist heir. In fact, the more Henry and the Spanish monarchs affected to despise and denigrate Prince Richard of York, the more important they thereby acknowledge him to be. From now on Henry, the Spanish sovereigns and Charles VIII of France, would all have liked to get the Pretender into their hands for their own political purposes.

APPENDIX V.

The Proclamation

The proclamation made from Scotland before the raid into England of 1496. Taken from Chastelain 'L'imposture de Perkin Warbeck' 1952.

'Richard, by the Grace of God, King of England, Lord of Ireland, Prince of Wales: To all those who will hear, see or read our present letters, greeting.

'It hath pleased God, who putteth down the mighty from their seat and exalteth the humble and suffereth not the hopes of the just to perish in the end, to give us means at the length to shew ourselves armed unto our lieges and people of England. But far be it from us to intend their hurt or damage, or to make war upon them, otherwise than to deliver ourself and them from tyranny and oppression. For our mortal enemy, Henry Tudor, a false usurper of the crown of England, which to us by natural and lineal right appertaineth, knowing in his own heart our undoubted right — we being the very Richard, Duke of York, younger son and now surviving heir male of the noble and victorious Edward the Fourth, late King of England — hath not only deprived us of our kingdom, but likewise by all foul and wicked means sought to betray us and bereave us of our life. Yet if his tyranny only extended itself to our person, although our royal blood teaches us to be sensible of injuries, it should be less to our grief. But this Tudor, who boasteth himself to have overthrown a tyrant, hath, ever since his first entrance into his usurped reign, put little in practice but tyranny and the feats thereof.

'For King Richard, our unnatural uncle, although desire of rule did blind him, yet in his other actions, like a true Plantagenet, was noble, and loved the honour of the realm and the contentment and comfort of his nobles and people. But this our mortal enemy, agreeable to the meanness of his birth, hath trodden under foot the honour of this nation, selling our best confederates for money, and making merchandise of the blood, estates, and fortunes of our peers and subjects by feigned wars and dishonourable peace, only to enrich his coffers. Nor unlike hath been his hateful misgovernment and evil deportments at home. First he hath, to fortify his false quarrel, caused divers nobles of this our realm, whom he held suspect and stood in dread of, to be cruelly murdered; as our cousin, Sir William Stanley, Lord Chamberlain; Sir Simon Mountfort; Sir Robert Ratcliffe; William Daubeney; Humphrey Stafford, and many others; besides such as have dearly bought their lives with intolerable ransoms — some of which nobles are now in the sanctuary. Also he hath long kept, and yet keepeth in prison, our right entirely well-beloved cousin, Edward, son and heir to our uncle, Duke of Clarence, and others, withholding from them their rightful inheritance, to the intent they should never be of might and power to aid and assist us at our need, after the duty of their legiances. He also married by compulsion certain of our sisters, and also the sister of our said cousin, the Earl of Warwick, and divers other ladies of the royal blood, unto certain of his kinsmen and friends of simple and low degree, and putting apart all well-disposed nobles, he hath none in favour and trust about his person but Bishop Fox, Smith, Bray, Lovel, Oliver King, David Owen, Riseley, Turberville, Tiler, Chomley, Empson, James Hobart, John Cut, Garth, Henry Wyat, and such other caitiffs and villians by birth, which, by subtile inventions and pilling [robbing] of the people, have been the principal finders, occasioners, and counsellors of the misrule and mischief now reigning in England.

'We remembering these premises, with the great and execrable offences daily committed and done by our foresaid great enemy and his adherents, in breaking the liberties and franchises of our mother the holy church* upon pretences of wicked and heathenish policy, to the high displeasure of Almighty God, besides the manifold treasons, abominable murders, manslaughters, robberies, extortions, the daily pilling of the people by dismes [tenths], taxes, tallages, benevolences, and other unlawful impositions and grievous exactions, with many other heinous effects, to the likely destruction and desolation of the whole realm: shall by God's grace, and the help and assistance of the great lords of our blood, with the counsel of other sad [grave] persons, see that the commodities of our realm be employed to the most advantage of the same; the intercourse of merchandise betwixt realm and realm to be ministered and handled as shall more be to the common weal and prosperity of our subjects; and all such dismes, taxes, tallages, benevolences, unlawful impositions and grievous exactions, as be above rehearsed, to be fordone and laid apart, and never from henceforth to be called upon, but in such cases as our noble progenitors, Kings of England, have of old time been accustomed to have the aid, succour, and help of their subjects and true liege-men.

'And farther, we do, out of our grace and clemency, hereby as well publish and promise to all our subjects remission and free pardon of all by-past offences whatsoever against our person or estate, in adhering to our said enemy — by whom, we know well, they have been misled — if they shall within time convenient submit themselves unto us. And for such as shall come with the foremost to assist our righteous quarrel, we shall make them so far partakers of our princely favour and bounty as shall be highly for the comfort of them and theirs, both during their life and after their death. As also we shall, by all means which God shall put into our hands, demean ourselves to give royal contentment to all degrees and estates of our people, maintaining the liberties of holy church in their entire, preserving the honours, privileges and preeminences of our nobles from contempt of disparagement, according to the dignity of their blood. We shall also unyoke our people from all heavy burdens and endurances, and confirm our cities, boroughs and towns in their charters and freedoms, with enlargement where it shall be deserved; and in all points give our subjects cause to think that the blessed and debonair government of our noble father King Edward, in his last times, is in us revived.

'And forasmuch as the putting to death or taking alive of our said mortal enemy may be a means to stay much effusion of blood, which otherwise may ensue if by compulsion or fair promises he shall draw after him any number of our subjects to resist us, which we desire to avoid — though we be certainly informed that our said enemy is purposed and prepared to fly the land, having already made over great masses of the treasure of our crown, the better to support him in foreign parts — we do hereby declare that whosoever shall take or distress our said enemy, though the party be of never so mean a condition, he shall be by us rewarded with a thousand pound in money, forthwith to be laid down to him, and an hundred marks by the year inheritance — besides what he may otherwise merit, both toward God and all good people, for the destruction of such a tyrant.

'Lastly, we do all men to wit [know], and herein we take also God to witness, that whereas God hath moved the heart of our dearest cousin, the King of Scotland, to aid us in person in this our righteous quarrel, it is altogether without any pact or promise, or so much as demand of any thing that may prejudice our crown or subjects: but contrariwise, with promise on our said cousin's part that whensoever he shall find us in sufficient strength to get the upper hand of our enemy — which we hope will be very suddenly — he will forthwith peaceably return into his own kingdom; contenting himself only with the glory of so honourable an enterprise, and our true and faithful love and amity: which we shall ever, by the grace of Almighty God, so order as shall be to the great comfort of both kingdoms.'

*i.e. By common law, the crown could not begin an action (by indictment) in a murder case until after a year and a day had elapsed, during which time the relatives of the murdered person were entitled to initiate their own action ('by way of appeal'). Experience showed that in fact the relatives ('the party') were often bought off, or simply lost interest, and so their suit was discontinued.

APPENDIX VI

Letter written in his own hand by the Duke of York to Sir Bernard de la Forsse at Fuentarabia, Spain, in October 1496. Spanish State Papers.

'Right trusty and our right entirely welbeloved, We grete you hartely wele / Signifying unto you that we be credibly enformed of the grete love, favour and kyndenes that ye in tyme passed shewed unto our most drad lord and Fadyr Kyng Edward the fourth, whos soule god rest, with the sage and pollitique counselles that ye in sundry wises ful lovingly gave unto him: wherby he opteyned the avauncement and promotyng of his maters and causes: wherfore ye stode right moche in the favour of his grace. Desire and hartely pray you to be from hensforth unto us as lovyng faithfull and kynde Counseillour and Frende as ye were unto our said Fader in shewing your gode and discrete myndes for us in such maters and causes as by your grete wisdom ye shal seme best to be moved for our wele comforte and relief and that it wol please you to exorte move and stir your lovers and frendes to do the same and that we may understond the gode hert and mynde that our most dere Cosyn the Kynge of Spayne bereth towards us. And in your doyng ye may be sure to have us as lovyng a gode lord unto you or better than evir was our said lord and Fader. And eny thinge that ye shal of reson desire of us that may concern the wele of you and of our right trusty and welbeloved [here there is a word 'unt' half obliterated] your son Anthony de la Force: which hath full lovingly geven his longe attendaunce upon us in sundry Countreys, we shal wt [with] gode herte be redy to accomplissh, and parfourme the same, when it shal plese almighty god to sende us unto our right in England, and that it may plese you to geve credence unto your said Son of suche thinges as he shal shewe unto you. And our Lord Jhu presue [preserve] you in alle honour ioy and felicite, and send you the accomplisshement of your noble hartes desir. From Edinburgh in Scotland, the xviij day of Octobre.'

It is signed with a bold flourish in the thoroughly English style of that time 'Richard off England' and addressed: 'To our right trusty and right entierly welbeloved Bernard de la Forse knyght at Fount Raby in Spayne.'

Underneath is the word 'indorsed' in a Spanish hand, with a cross, under which are the words 'a su al*', and again under that, the words 'del duĝ de Yorĝ'. The seal is gone, and only the mark of the wax remains. It is written on half a sheet of paper, on which there is no paper mark, and the letter is fastened by a band of ribbon. Madden suggests that the endorsement 'To Their Highnesses from the Duke of York' (which he presumably reads into the few words in Spanish quoted above) was made by the then Spanish Secretary of State, Almazan. As it was not addressed to their Highnesses Ferdinand and Isabella, but to Sir Bernard de la Forsse, it is probable that it was intercepted by Almazan and never reached Sir Bernard, because he does not appear to have replied. It is of interest that the endorser, if it was Almazan, refers to the writer as the Duke of York.

* a su Altesse?

APPENDIX VII

The Confession

The original of this confession is to date undiscovered. This copy is taken from the Library of Burgundy, Brussels and dated 1497.

'Ffirst it is to be knowen that I was born in the Towne of Turney (in Fflaunders) and my ffaders name is called John Osbeck: which said John Osbeck was Controller of the Towne of Turney. And my moders name is Kateryn de ffaro.* And one of my grauntsires upon my ffaders side was called Deryck Osbeck; which died; after whose deth my grauntmother was married unto the win [?] [an abbreviation of 'w' in the next: could this be 'widower'?] named Petir fflamme; and that other of my grauntsires was called Petir flan [Hall omits exactly ten words preceding this] which was Receyvour of the foresaid Towne of Turney and Deane of the Botemen that be [Rowe: Hall] upon the watir or Ryver of Leystave [Scheldt]. And my grauntsire upon my moders side was Petir ffaro, the which had in his kepyng the keys of the Gate of Seynt Johns win [within] the abovenamed Towne of Turney. Also I had an Uncle named Maister John Stalyn dwelling in the parisshe of Saynt Pyas win the same Towne, which had maried my ffaders sister, whose name was Johane or Jane w [with?] whom I dwelled a certyn season; and afterward I was led by my moder to Andwarp for to lerne flemmysshe in an house of a Cosyn of myne, officer of the said Towne, called John Stienbek, w whom I was the space of half a yere. And after that I retourned agayn unto Turney by reason of the warres that wer in fflaunders. And win a yere following I was sent w a Merchant of thesaid Towne of Turney named Berlo, and his maister's name, Alex, to the Marte of Andwarp, where as I fill syke, which sykenesse continued upon me v [five] monethes; and the said Berlo set me to boorde in a Skynners hous that dwelled beside the hous of the Englessh nacion. And by hym I was brought from thens to the Barowe Marte and loged at the Signe of thold man where I abode the space of ij [two] monethes. And after this the said Berlo set me w a merchaunt in Middelburgh to service w whome I dwelled from Cristmas unto Easter; and than I went into Portyngale in the company of Sir Edward Bramptons wif in a ship which was called the Quenes ship. And whan I was comen thider I was put in service to a Knyght that dwelled in Lusshebourne [Lisbon] which was called Petir Vacz de Cogna, w whome I dwelled an hole yere, which said Knyght had but one Iye; and than because I desired to se other Countrees I toke licence of hym. And than I put my silf in service w a Breton called Pregent Meno, the which brought me w hym into Ireland. And whan we wer there aryved in the Towne of Corke, they of the Towne, because I was arayed w some clothes of silk of my said Maisters, came unto me and threped** upon me that I shuld be the Duke of Clarence sone, that was before tyme at Develyn [Dublin]. And for as moche as I denyed it there was brought unto me the Holy Euaungelist and the Crosse by the Mayre of the Towne, which was called John Lewelyn [Le Wellen: Hall]; and there in the presence of hym and other I toke my Othe as trouth was that I was not the forsaid Dukes Son, nother of none of his blood. And after this came unto me an Englisshman, whose name was Steffe Poytron w one John Water, and said to me insweryng grete Othis, that they knew wele I was Kyng Richardes Bastarde Son; to whom I answered w hie Othis that I were not. And than they advised me not to be afferd but that I shuld take it upon me Boldly, and iff I wold so do they wold ayde and assiste me w all theyr powr agayn the Kyng of Englond: And not only they, but they were well assured that therles of Desmond and Kildare shuld do the same, ffor they forsid not what party [forced not what parte they tooke: Hall] so that they myght be revenged upon the Kyng of Englond; and so agaynst my will made me to lerne Inglisshe, and taught me what I shuld doo and say. And after this they called me Duke of York, the second son of Kyng Edward the Ffourth, because Kyng Richardes Bastarde Son was in the handes of the Kyng of Englond. And upon this the said John Water, Steffe Poytron, John Tiler (Taylor) Huberd Bourgh w many other, as the forsaid Erles, entred into this fals Quarell. And win short tyme after this the frensshe Kyng sent unto me an Embasset into Irelond, whose names was Loyte Lucas and Maister Steffe ffrion to advertise me to come into ffraunce;

and thens I went into ffraunce, and from thens into fflaunders, and from fflaunders into Irelond. And from Irelond into Scotland and so into Englond'.

*There is a place called Faro on the South Coast of the Algarve in Portugal.
**Threap, threep (Scot. & Northern) = to insist, to press eagerly.

Index